Alchemists of the Stage

Martial Ros
Tel: 01962

MIRELLA SCHINO

Alchemists of the Stage
Theatre Laboratories
in Europe

Translated from Italian and French by
PAUL WARRINGTON
(AlfaBeta)

Routledge
Taylor & Francis Group

Holstebro – Malta – Wrocław
London – New York

ICARUS Publishing Enterprise is a joint initiative
of Odin Teatret (Denmark), The Grotowski Institute (Poland)
and Theatre Arts Researching the Foundations (Malta)

First published in Italy as
Alchimisti della scena. Teatri laboratori del Novecento europeo,
Roma and Bari: Laterza, 2009

Cover design and layout Barbara Kaczmarek
Typesetting Stanisław Rękar
Index Agata Kaczmarek
Production editor Adela Karsznia

Published by
Icarus Publishing Enterprise and Routledge
www.icaruspublishing.com
www.routledge.com

The Grotowski Institute
Rynek-Ratusz 27, 50-101 Wrocław, Poland

Routledge
2 Park Square, Milton Park, Abingdon, OX14 4RN, UK
711 Third Avenue, New York, NY 10017, USA
Routledge is an imprint of Taylor and Francis Group, an informa business

ISBN 978-0-415-72296-4

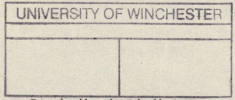
Printed and bound in Poland by JAKS

Contents

IV

The relationship between Studios in the first half
of the twentieth century and theatre laboratories in the second.
The appearance of the Red Queen and her race.

· 191 ·

V

Five pieces from different mosaics with
views of vanished landscapes.

· 223 ·

PREFACE

The Laboratory Dimension

Theatre laboratories were a significant innovation of twentieth century European theatre. This innovation was however merely a new face of the much older and more remote zone of theatrical creation: the space that exists between art and life, between the craft and the person. Right from the start, theatre laboratories were something of a paradox.

The aim of this book is not to recount their history but to reconstruct a discussion which began like all apparently futile discussions: by pondering over the meaning of certain words. The discussion evolved around a landscape that theatre maps are still unable to represent, and attempted to throw light on its main problems and issues: the *laboratory dimension.*

Theatre laboratory, workshop, *atelier, taller*: these are not exactly different translations or versions of the same term. Rather they indicate a mobile concept, one that spins around and off the road, even the alternative road. Consequently (and not only for this reason) it is not easy to sum up what is *usually meant* by theatre laboratory in twentieth century Europe. In many countries the expression does not even exist.

Theatre laboratories are undoubtedly not a genre or a uniform category. They may include theatres that focus on political struggles or social issues; others intent on researching the actor's art; still others seeking primarily inner values or different forms of artistic creation.

The term theatre laboratory does not designate an external point of reference or a model to be followed. Rather it points to an interiorised radar, a mental orientation, a propensity or a signal, important in equal measure for oneself and for others, but which may indicate very different paths.

In Europe the concept of theatre laboratory belongs to the history of the theatre. It is automatically associated with a few names, in particular that of Stanislavski. It is in Stanislavski's work, performed in his Studios, that the question of the theatre laboratory appears to materialise. It was not in his Art Theatre, an institution which produced performances, but rather in the Studios, the places where Stanislavski concentrated on pedagogical and pure research, often not directly aimed at creating performances.

Paradoxically, the term theatre laboratory came to be used as the opposite of performance. In any case, it indicates all those theatres in which the preparation of performances is not the only activity that goes on. But creating a performance can also be an intricate, organic and labyrinthine job, usually the opposite of a linear process. Therefore the term theatre laboratory is sometimes used as a signal representing the existence of a complex, or at any rate different, creative path.

There are other historical personalities who immediately spring to mind when talking about laboratories. First of all, Evgeni Vakhtangov and Vsevolod Meyerhold. Then, further in the background, Copeau, who put up his theatre's shutters and went off with some of his actors to Burgundy. Then Decroux, who was famed for his painstaking, tireless work not always aiming at a final performance. Other protagonists of the Great Theatre Reform – Appia, for instance, Craig, and the directors of the French *Cartel* – stand even further back and are probably not really part of the laboratory scene at all. From this point of view, the 'laboratory question' has its roots in what the Poles call *Wielka Reforma*, the Great Reform, or what others call the 'birth of the director', 'modern theatrical art' or 'new theatre'. All these terms seek to express the radical changes going on in the theatre in the first three decades of the twentieth century.

It is noteworthy that interest in the laboratory question was revived by the innovative theatres of the 1960s, like a spring-replenished river, or rather like an offshoot, only partly conscious, of the Studios of the beginning of the century. Yet the 1960s phase may be seen as a new movement, its followers subsequently viewing the major directors of the turn of the century as their precursors.

In the innovative theatres of the 1960s, the beacons of light for theatre laboratories were Jerzy Grotowski, Peter Brook and Eugenio Barba, to name just three. And in the background, Joan Littlewood's Theatre Workshop and Ariane Mnouchkine's Théâtre du Soleil were also active in this breakthrough. Our discussion focuses on Europe, but we must nevertheless mention here the theatres of Enrique Buenaventura, Santiago García and Patricia Ariza in Colombia or that of Antunes Filho in Brazil. And over in Asia, that of Tadashi Suzuki in Japan. But that is going beyond the limits we have set ourselves. As we shall see, the discussion that this book centres on does not even seek to identify all the historical instances that may be defined as theatre laboratories. In any case we shall refer chiefly to twentieth century Europe.

Some keywords need to be explained for the unusual compound 'theatre laboratory' to take on real meaning (albeit a different meaning from case to case). The first is *training*: a permanent activity performed by the actor independently of periods spent rehearsing a performance. Another keyword is *body*, taken to mean physical expression. It is usually combined with the importance of a symbolic language.

In the English-speaking world, where the laboratory is linked to alternative performances, laboratory basically appears to mean a protected, separate place where it is possible to continuously explore in order to perfect one's art or craft, without having to make compromises. Its status as a place protected against any kind of business or commercial logic allows it to be a social meeting place: theatre and the handicapped, theatre and prison inmates, theatre and schoolchildren, and so on.

In a European context, this quality is supplemented by another which derives from the experiences of Jerzy

Grotowski: a meeting with oneself, ethics, spiritual dimension and value.

Pedagogy is also a word that is often used in every geographic or cultural area, when discussing the laboratory question. It should be viewed as an autonomous process of basic training for the actor and also – for more mature theatres – a desire to transmit knowledge.

It would surely be wrong to argue that a theatre cannot be called a laboratory unless it has a given attitude towards the body, pedagogy and training. Yet these words must always be considered, as they constantly crop up.

Another keyword is *science* and more specifically, theatre science. We will talk about that further on.

Placed in the middle of the book, like a long interlude in the discussion, are five monographs: on Stanislavski's Opera Studio, Meyerhold's Studios, two essays on Grotowski, including a summary of his activity, as well as a study of Odin Teatret. We felt it important to explore in depth the main points of reference of the theatre laboratory question. This has also been a way of giving out basic information. It is indeed a book of the new millennium, attempting to communicate with those who, due to their age, may have been left out of a very intense experience. This experience is in no way concluded or buried but is less familiar than what happened in the theatre in the 1960s, 70s and 80s.

There are facts, stories and meetings that happen without leaving a visible trace. Often they are not spoken or written about, yet it would be wrong to say that they make no difference to future events, as if those things had never happened. Indeed such stories, meetings and events often end up being the mysterious heart of a bigger picture, of history.

When asking from country to country what a theatre laboratory is, one may be given an example of one or two experiences going by such a name: some theatres born in the 1960s in New York, for instance, Stanislavski's Studios, and of course Grotowski and his Teatr Laboratorium. Yet I feel that no one can deny that the *hidden centre* of the history of the theatre in the twentieth century lies in a desire and a longing for what should be called the *laboratory dimension*: that sphere of the theatre seemingly unconnected with performance, yet actually closely related to it.

And so too the discussion I am about to recount, be it fundamental, petty, muddled or engaging, has a place in the mysterious heart of history. Only in this way can it be understood: as one of the many secret centres of history and not just as a plain though interesting academic discussion.

As I said at the beginning, this is not a book about the history of theatre laboratories. Rather it talks about the questions that arose, in a given milieu, from practice and from the study of theatre laboratories. It describes the resulting stimuli, suggestions, illusions and tendencies, which are not homogeneous, but may be complementary or even opposing. It depicts the laboratory dimension: a mental horizon that for some people, in given historical contexts, is or has been fundamental.

The word laboratory stirs up associations with scientific research. But during the course of our discussion, Polish scholar Leszek Kolankiewicz, speaking about Jerzy Grotowski's laboratory vocation, suggested that we consider this in terms of the laboratory of an alchemist, since this, unlike a scientific lab, firstly implies an inner transmutation of the researcher himself. This is an essential point to remember when considering the peculiar nature of the laboratory dimension in twentieth century European theatre.

I

Recalling a strange discussion:
the first questions and the first definitions.
Leszek Kolankiewicz introduces the themes
of Grotowski and alchemy.

During the course of celebrations in Holstebro to mark the fortieth anniversary of Odin Teatret in the autumn of 2004, during a long festive dinner, one of Odin's 'children', Alice Pardeihlan, got up to sing. Her mother is Roberta Carreri – an Italian and an actor at Odin Teatret since 1974. Alice, twenty-three years old, slim, shining eyes, charming and brimming with enthusiasm, sang with a firm voice that appeared well-trained and accustomed to the microphone.

Sitting at a table a short distance away was perhaps the oldest person in the room: Clive Barker, many years previously an actor in one of the first theatre laboratories, Joan Littlewood's Theatre Workshop, and now a university professor. Gazing at the girl who was singing, he began humming the same tune to himself, a little hoarsely. At the same table, two other scholars, Nicola Savarese and myself, watched him with interest as he echoed the song of the young girl, so joyful and full of life. His head was rocking slightly and his eyes were moist, as happens sometimes to people who are close to the end, or at least think they are. He died a few months later.

After Alice's song, two of Odin's oldest actors stood up: Torgeir Wethal, a Norwegian, and Iben Nagel Rasmussen, a Dane. They spoke about the foundation of their theatre, their early years in Norway and in Denmark, Grotowski's very tough summer seminars for Scandinavian actors and the unrealised project to create a 'commune', where the actors could work at the theatre and earn money through farming, especially pig breeding. It was getting late, and we had been toasting all evening.

Clive Barker still seemed to be thinking about something in the past. Savarese turned to me and whispered: 'Why hasn't Clive been invited to the conference on theatre laboratories? You remember, in Bologna, when he spoke about laboratories and rubbish?' I was dumbstruck. It was October 2004, and a couple of days prior to the conference *Why a Theatre Laboratory?*, organised by Odin Teatret and the University of Aarhus, to which we had both been invited. Clive Barker had not been included in the conference schedule, perhaps because he was too old or too busy, even though he'd been an actor and had trained actors with Joan Littlewood, before becoming a professor at the University of Warwick and co-editor of *New Theatre Quarterly*.

Nicola Savarese and I both thought we could remember what he had said during a session of the ISTA,[1] many years earlier in Bologna, in 1990, when he had been asked to talk about his work with Joan Littlewood. The only thing is we remembered different things.

'I remember that very well', Savarese murmured, 'he began to talk about a pile of rubbish'. The very image continued to make him laugh. I couldn't remember anything about rubbish.

In the meantime Iben Nagel Rasmussen was recounting the celebration of Odin's second anniversary with a cake and two candles, in Holstebro, in 1966. Barba had invited Torgeir Wethal to blow them out, and Torgeir, whose level-headed-ness appears to prevent him from showing any excesses, blew just one of the candles out.

I whispered to Nicola that I didn't recall anything about rubbish. And there was no laboratory: that time, in Bologna, Clive Barker had spoken about *Oh, What a Lovely War*. I remembered very well that he had talked about the rehearsals for the performance, about censorship problems and audience reactions.

But Savarese insisted on the islands of rubbish: about laboratories and trash.

I didn't give in: Clive had described the way in which the Theatre Workshop would prepare its productions and use improvisation on stage to get around the British censorship of the early 1960s.

Clive had talked about an island of rubbish, Savarese replied patiently: a pile of garbage floating around in the middle of the ocean and pulling along with it one or two wretched survi-

[1] ISTA is the International School of Theatre Anthropology, founded and directed by Eugenio Barba, more of which further on.

vors from a shipwreck. Clive had added that this was a suitable image for appreciating what a theatre laboratory is like.

Savarese was right, as I ascertained a few weeks later reading my notes on Clive Barker's talk in Bologna. He had ex-
pounded about theatre laboratories and called them 'islands
of rubbish'.

With this image this book begins.

Clive's dream

Clive Barker had said: 'Doing theatre research is just like
floating in the middle of the ocean, hanging on to an island
of smelly, shitty rubbish. You wonder where you are going.
Then you wonder whether or not the work will be present-
able. Then you present it. Sometimes the audience will tell
you the performance works. That means something has been
transformed. But we don't know how or why. At other times,
all that is left is the rubbish. And that is the real difference between a theatre laboratory and a scientific laboratory, where
right until the end you don't know whether what is in the test
tube will be the proof of a *successful* experiment. At least in
a science lab you know that the test tube contains a chemical
compound, not just some dirty water'.

He then spoke about Joan Littlewood and the Theatre
Workshop in London in the early 1960s. 'Working with Joan
was a really bad experience. Yet it formed the foundation for
my work in the profession. I couldn't get my head around
anything. The work was approximate, chaotic and tiresome.
All the time we were whinging, wondering in which direction we were headed. Joan herself did not know, and yet we
were following her. It was like the blind leading the blind.
We were wandering about without a destination and without
a method. Then, at the end, we came up with a play that had
a start, a middle and an end: *Oh, What a Lovely War* – a production that marked an era. They said it was both tragic and
comical, that it was an event. But none of us knew what we

had done to achieve such a result, and what we needed to do to attain another, equally valid one. Nothing at all might have happened. Then we would have simply stayed hanging on to our island of rubbish '.

He said that his stint with Joan Littlewood had been the most important thing he had been lucky enough to participate in. It was such a tough job that he had had to stop. And he had imagined another way of experiencing the theatre, inventing a method to introduce youngsters to the stage, based on play and improvisation (*Theatre Games*).[2] He then became a university lecturer and in 1985 had reinvented the journal *Theatre Quarterly*, changing its name to *New Theatre Quarterly*, one of the most important theatrical journals in the English-speaking world.

Clive Barker concluded: 'Sometimes, even now, after so many years and in my old age, I have a recurring nightmare. I dream that while I am at home, in peace, or in my office at the university, Joan calls me, tells me to leave everything and go and see her, because she wants to start a new production. But I think about my work, my things, my family, my journal. And I think about the island of rubbish, and how hard it was to hang on to it. No more Joan!

But that is not the appalling part of the dream. The nightmare is that while I am angrily mumbling all this, and many other things, I am busy packing my case.

That's the terrifying part: not even in my dreams can I, or do I want to, say no to her'.

A discussion and its context

In this book I will narrate a discussion that began in what I can only describe as a state of bewilderment.

This discussion – which was variously dialogue, confrontation, controversy, dispute – started with an unexpected

[2] Cf. Clive Barker, *Theatre Games* (London: Methuen, 1977).

question. Imagine a bishop who assembles together clergy and worshippers to examine what the church is. Or imagine an old guerrilla fighter who chairs a round table in order to understand what is meant by guerrilla warfare. Imagine him with a kalashnikov resting on the chair next to him, carefully questioning bystanders about possible models and origins of guerrilla fighting which has been his life – its meaning, its legitimacy and status in history.

This was what happened when Eugenio Barba, founder and protagonist of one of the most enduring theatre laboratories in history, decided that the time had come to discuss the meaning, usefulness and historical truth of theatre laboratories. His questions seemed futile, turning facts and circumstances that, in a particular milieu at least, had always been a common territory of understanding and dialogue – or a well-thought-out metaphor – into a problem.

Barba's was not a one-off reflection, a way of making it clear to himself the paths he had followed. He wanted to debate his questions and analyse them as if they were an objective problem. But he wanted to discuss this within his milieu.

The discussion commenced as we moved into the twenty-first century. Both theatre and book people close to Barba expressed their opinions. Examples and ideas were presented, models and beliefs were cast into doubt. This lively exchange of ideas lasted a long time – almost four years – and culminated in the international conference *Why a Theatre Laboratory?* in Aarhus, Denmark, in October 2004.[3] But it was a dis-

---

[3] The conference, entitled *Why a Theatre Laboratory? Risks and Innovations in Europe 1898–1999*, an international symposium marking the fortieth anniversary of Odin Teatret, was held in Aarhus from 4–6 October 2004. The speakers were: Janne Risum ('Introduction'), Mirella Schino ('Theatre Laboratory as Blasphemy'), Erik Exe Christoffersen ('In Search of the Essence') Franco Ruffini ('K. S. Stanislavski: why a theatre laboratory?'), Béatrice Picon-Vallin ('Vsevolod Meyerhold: why a theatre laboratory?'), Patrice Pavis ('Jacques Copeau: why a theatre laboratory?'), Marco De Marinis, ('Étienne Decroux: why a theatre laboratory?'), Zbigniew Osiński and Leszek Kolankiewicz ('Grotowski–Flaszen: why a theatre laboratory?'), Georges Banu ('Peter Brook: why a theatre laboratory?'), Georges Banu and Béatrice Picon-Vallin ('Le Théâtre du Soleil: why a theatre laboratory?'), Ferdinando Taviani ('Odin Teatret: why a theatre

cussion rooted in a common knowledge of the practices of the theatre laboratory. It was not a round table among experts. It was an argument that seemed to be never-ending, emerging at every meeting, both private and public, and pouring out into books and articles. It was, above all, a research process within a precise milieu, namely ISTA, which in turn was the place where those with an interest in the theatre as a laboratory were concentrated.

ISTA, International School of Theatre Anthropology, was founded by Eugenio Barba in 1979. It is a mental rather than a physical place. It is a complicated structure, comprising a staff of about fifty teachers from all over the world, and with thirty to eighty participants. It generally involves the whole of Odin Teatret, with all its efficient organisational machine.

In a certain sense ISTA is a laboratory that has grown up beside a theatre laboratory.

It is a place for dialogue and comparative research, for posing questions, for raising and testing doubts. It is not a school. But one of its aims is to transmit knowledge and experiences, and this is probably the facet that has been most prominent in recent years. Its purpose is not to produce a performance, although it has created several productions under the name of *Theatrum Mundi*. It is not of course a theatre group, but generates constant yet intermittent working relations.

ISTA is generally known for its studies into the principles of actors' and dancers' technique, of their scenic presence. This embodied knowledge underlies the acting forms of performers from different genres and traditions. ISTA organises working sessions lasting from two weeks to two months, held when and where it is possible or requested. The first was staged in Bonn, Germany, in 1980 and the most recent in Wrocław, Poland, in 2005: fourteen international sessions altogether, twenty-five years of meetings, research and debate.

---

laboratory?'), Nicola Savarese ('Irradiations in Asia'), Raquel Carrió ('Irradiations in Latin America'), Richard Schechner ('Irradiations in the USA: why a theatre laboratory in the third millennium?') and Eugenio Barba ('Final Reflections').

Twenty-five years is a long time.

The teachers of the various sessions come from many theatre and dance genres: Indian Orissi dance and Kathakali, Japanese Nihon Buyo, Noh and Butoh, Balinese Gambuh, Topeng
and Legong, Peking Opera and Afro-Brasilian candomblé,
Decroux's corporeal mime and Meyerhold's biomechanics,
Odin Teatret's actors, opera singers, improvisation experts
like Dario Fo, Keith Johnstone and Clive Barker. Grotowski,
when present, used to be available to participants for personal dialogue. To all these practitioners must be added the
scholars. This is the 'artistic and scientific staff' of ISTA.

Changes do occur. Only one or two people – in addition to
Barba – have been present at all ISTA sessions. But there is a
core of people who tend to return and resume the discussion
where they left off: Odin actors, several artists from Asia, the
USA and Latin America, a few scholars. This is the 'milieu'.

Then there are participants whose selection is decided by
Barba according to two visible criteria: variety and no more
than two per country. Depending on the sessions, they may
be between thirty and eighty in all, and may usually attend
only once. They are actors, dancers, directors, choreographers, theatre school teachers, critics and scholars of all ages.
In the first seven ISTA sessions, participation was free. Since
the ISTA in Brecon, Wales, in 1992, a fee has been demanded
by local organisers, but it is always low, considering the duration and the number of teaching staff.

From a mental viewpoint, ISTA is very close to the thinking of the theatre laboratories. It reflects in a practical way on
the problems that every theatre laboratory has to tackle. It is
a place devised for studying the actor. It concentrates on the
enigma of the actor's apprenticeship and on the adventure
which theatrical research entails. Which, as Clive Barker argued, is a real roller-coaster. It raises questions about the human being in an organised performance situation and about
the physical and mental state before and after the performance. ISTA focuses on all problems relating to scenic repre-

sentation, as long as the human being / actor is at the centre of the study.

Like slides placed under the microscope, ISTA's participants learn, and above all analyse, the first steps in the apprenticeship of Asian performers, of Odin Teatret's and other Western actors, of Decroux's corporeal mime or Meyerhold's biomechanics. They study assiduously their postures, habits and beliefs. And their study, for once, occurs *together with* the subjects being studied. But each ISTA could be a surprise. A session was once devoted to the creation of a performance, a new *Theatrum Mundi* production, involving both Asian and Western actors. Often there are barters and exchanges with the local community.

During an ISTA session study and research are solitary enterprises, but are also conducted in small groups. It is not easy, due to the limited space, the presence of other researchers, the hours spent fervidly discussing or silently and patiently observing actors working or demonstrating, always with the tacit assumption that this is a place of absolute passion. Then there are the limits and the obstacles that everyone has to face and the difficulty of dialogue between people who view the theatre as their own field of research, but from very different viewpoints.

This is the place where Barba developed his reflections on theatre anthropology. It has been a space for practical work and for raising deliberately naive questions, focusing directly, with apparent ease, on the most profound structures of theatre craft, on the most deeply-rooted and shared beliefs, on the most secret zones. The questions served to scrutinise well-known phenomena with new eyes, or to estrange them. ISTA was the place for questions that no one had ever asked, and that probably no one will ask for decades to come.

Usually, in theatre circles, few questions are asked, and they are always the same: about dramaturgy, the relationship between the actor and the character, identification or *verfremdung* and a few technical questions on the voice.

The questions raised by the ISTA on the human being on stage were new and surprising. They ranged from the most concrete and apparently insignificant of issues (the way in which an actor plants his feet on the ground) to the most obscure, such as the possible existence of mental 'pre-expressive' principles. These questions have favoured a great deal of exploration, and understanding them enables one to become familiar with the type of mentality, problems and issues that may exist in a theatre laboratory.

Questions posed by ISTA

There was a session that focused on the question of the actor's 'organicity' and his 'organic effect' on the spectator. One was held on improvisation, another on the modes of representing and embodying on stage 'male and female' roles. Yet another on how the experience of the actor's presence can be transformed into concepts and historiography. We discussed theatrical traditions, the old Asian and the new Western traditions of the twentieth century and their founders. We asked ourselves questions about the exercises invented by the founding fathers of the new theatre in the twentieth century, and about the 'recurring principles' in the actor's techniques from various cultures. They were all questions relating to the theatre's deepest structures, the invisible ones. Many questions led nowhere. Others seemed to make the darkness cloaking the art of the actor recede by a few meters.

We discussed the nature of tensions in the actor's performing body, the principles of their oppositions and their 'dance'; coherence and incoherence in the physical score; the subscore as another concrete reality equivalent to Stanislavski's subtext; what energy is; the definition of dramaturgy, and whether it consists of just the text or also includes the narrative devices of the performance. We spoke about the effect of a 'different life' that a performance may generate in the spectator, and we asked ourselves whether one can talk of an

organic effect only for the actor or also for the whole performance. We also dealt with simpler topics, such as the 'subterranean history of the theatre', the role of music, silence, rhythm
and flow, and we sought to establish whether or not there is a
dramaturgy of the actor and a dramaturgy of the spectator.

We reflected on balance and imbalance in the actor's physical postures and, at the same time, on the *value* of the theatre.
We investigated the role of the various 'memories': physical,
mental, sensorial, historical memories. We observed the different ways actors place their feet on the ground in order to de-
form their 'natural' way of walking. We compared various forms
of learning and specific teaching methods, imprinting, verbal
transmission and incorporated professional know-how, the actor's tacit knowledge and the ways in which all this happens,
knowingly or unwittingly. We looked at dilated actions and min-
iaturised actions. We discussed male and female energy, the
connection between the actor's and the character's gender, or
between energy type – soft or vigorous – and sexual gender.

We analysed the difference between daily and extra-daily
movements. And we raised the problem (passionately, yet vain-
ly) of whether the actor's mind can be moulded in an extra-daily
manner. A time will come when the 'buzz' filling the ISTA will
end and a deep silence will fall over the land of the theatre.

Of course I am using an inaccurate term here: discussing.
This term evokes words alone. ISTA research has been physical rather than verbal: the assimilation of the 'first day's' practical steps in the apprenticeship of many performing genres,
the deconstruction of scores and whole performances, the as-
siduous scrutiny of a movement, a posture, a gait repeated
time and time again, the detailed analysis of performers' demonstrations, as well as lectures and round tables. Observation,
talks, training, demonstrations, discussions: in reality all forms
of research, where we debated and agreed to disagree.

Only rarely did the intense ISTA timetable enable real discussions to develop. Yet ISTA's research activity and discoveries would blossom later through individual work and often

gave rise to a sort of long-distance discussion. A milieu had been created, a network of questions, frames of reference, dialogues and debates. It was a paradoxical, in a sense virtual, milieu but one that was very much alive.

The question of 'theatre laboratories' was raised and discussed within a particular milieu which was so cohesive that we might even talk about a 'collective mind'. But only within ISTA. It was a small world of people who, over a twenty-five-year period, had got into the habit of discussing fiercely together: directors and scholars, who were perhaps more into theoretical discussion, and actors who had been imbued with a 'laboratory' attitude and at times believed it was futile to talk about it. What was unique in this small world was the presence of scholars and practitioners, of experts in the different branches and genres of theatre and dance, of venerable traditions and contemporary expressions, elderly persons and youngsters. Sometimes there were misunderstandings, moments of tedium and non-participation. Yet, for some of us, the shared experience, the curiosity and the mutual respect outweighed in the end any differences there may have been.

A problem of choosing sides

The question of 'why' was perhaps too obvious: we all had shared interests and needs. It was in the theatre laboratories that the art of the actor had been rediscovered, acquiring its fundamental significance. During the various ISTA sessions, this art was studied in its manifold aspects and from different points of view. For many of us, moreover, it was in ISTA that we became acquainted with and accustomed to key figures of laboratoriality of the second half of the twentieth century, such as Grotowski and Barba, as well as masterly performers from other traditions.

I use the term *laboratoriality* to indicate everything going on in theatre laboratories, as well as the propensity to create new laboratories recognising their value and importance. This newly-coined term is undoubtedly an ugly one, but it has the advantage of suggesting an immediate association with the Russian term *studinnost*, the strong interest, even fervour, in theatre-making shown by the younger generation in Russia at the beginning of the twentieth century. We might translate this word as 'studiosity', indicating a place, the Studio, and what happens there: pure research on the art of the actor without necessarily aiming at performance. The predilection for creating Studios and the acknowledgement of their value characterised the work of many protagonists of the Great Theatre Reform of the theatre in the early twentieth century, great directors and theoreticians such as Stanislavski, Meyerhold and Appia and many of the actors collaborating with them. But more on this later.

Starting in the year 2000, as I have already said, Barba would ask us about theatre laboratories whenever we met. They were simple questions, and for this very reason we were taken by surprise. Their purpose was to start from scratch. He would ask: what is a theatre laboratory? In what way is it different from an experimental theatre? Or from what he himself had previously called the Third Theatre? He also asked why one theatre could be defined as a laboratory while another could not, and if the theatres usually considered as laboratories really were such. Theatres like his, or Grotowski's and Ludwik Flaszen's Teatr Laboratorium, or Peter Brook's CIRT (Centre International de Recherche Théâtrale): why could they legitimately be considered laboratories? And could they still be designated thus despite their changes over the years? And if these changes made no difference, *what* was it that defined the degree of laboratoriality of a theatre group?

The discussion quickly grew to cover the history of the theatre of the late nineteenth and early twentieth centuries. It has often been said that the Studios, the schools, the separate zones devoted to pure research, typical of the new theatres of the early twentieth century, were similar to, indeed the same as, the theatre laboratories of the 1960s. It was a general assumption that there was a thread connecting the Studios of Stanislavski, Meyerhold, Copeau's group Les Copiaus, the schools of Decroux and Piscator, Jerzy Grotowski's Teatr Laboratorium or Barba's Odin Teatret, or Brook's or Mnouchkine's theatres. Now Barba was asking: why do we have theatre laboratories? Can Meyerhold's and Stanislavski's Studios be so called? And if they can, why? He thought so, but he wanted to find out from us. He asked why Stanislavski had opened one Studio after another right inside his theatre. Why Meyerhold had intertwined his activity in workshops and Studios with that of his theatre. Why they appeared to want to separate the two activities? Why this division between theatres and Studios, and not simply a theatre laboratory?

Barba said: 'Despite the radical differences – historical, morphological and contextual – I have always thought there has been a continuum, an essential similarity, between the theatres of the Great Reform of the early twentieth century and the experience of the theatre laboratories of the second half of the century'.

He added that for him a laboratory had always represented a well-defined milieu with a specific working culture, know-how and professional ethos, characterised by the multifaceted differences of its individual members. He had thought of this kind of theatrical milieu as an example of a laboratory. But now he was no longer able to explain what united them, apart from the fact of going against the main current of practices and ideas of their time, and their desperate search for something essential in the theatre: namely another reality. A different reality that can be attained only through the actor's craft.

And he concluded: 'I suggest you keep this question in mind: is there really something uniting those theatres that called themselves, and that we call, "laboratories"? Or is it just a recurring name, a symptom of our intellectual idleness?'[4]

---

[4] For the most part, the questions derive from circulars sent by Barba over the four years of discussions. In a few cases they come from notes I have taken at the various meetings.

What we knew

Answers to this stream of questions were not easy. Especially since we didn't really know what a theatre laboratory actually was. It wasn't a problem for us, and never really had been. 'We', that is a small, varied group of scholars who had close ties with ISTA but did not fully represent it, and were only a few of the speakers at the future Aarhus conference *Why a Theatre Laboratory?* It is this small group that I insist on indicating, improperly no doubt, as 'us': these few scholars, mainly Italian, who used to meet Barba regularly and expound on theatre-related problems in public. For four years we discussed with him what a theatre laboratory was and the problems relating to it.

These meetings continued in a host of different places and situations.

As previously mentioned, our group kept our debate going. This created a middle zone between public discussion and private reflection. These were certainly the most fruitful moments, yielding the most unexpected results. We usually came together under the name University of Eurasian Theatre. This anomalous University met first at Scilla, then at Caulonia, two tiny villages in the extreme south of Italy, where the small experimental Teatro Proskenion had managed to create around Barba and 'us' (a few scholars and his accompanying actors) the setting for a group of youngsters interested in practical work and discussing our questions. This led to a permanent get-together, one week every year. In addition to the meeting at Teatro Proskenion, this University met elsewhere: at Teatro Potlach in Fara Sabina, Teatro Ridotto in Bologna and Teatro delle Albe in Ravenna.

As the years passed (almost fifteen since the first session), discussions continued with an ever smaller group, which in the end was reduced to six, Barba included. A number that allowed those who took part to jump from one topic to another, the real purpose of which was to take us further and deeper into labyrinths and tunnels, the mines of theatre science.

Attempts at making a definition

Those of us discussing what a theatre laboratory actually was knew the answers from direct experience, study or practice. We could see the difference between theatre laboratories and other theatres, perceive it with our skin and our brain. Of course a laboratory theatre is different from a simple experimental theatre, and all of 'us' had had direct experience of it, both as practitioners and as theatre scholars. The fact that it was not *easy* to define the difference did not mean that it did not exist. We also shared a network of precise mental and historical references, which came to our minds as soon as Barba called us to discuss theatre laboratories. What, or who, were the theatre laboratories? That was an easy answer for every one of us.

Someone thought of the young Russian actors in the 1920s, stirred into action by the Soviet revolution, who concentrated on the newly invented practice of theatre exercises, often without having a performance in mind.

Others thought of Vakhtangov and his very young aspiring actors as they rehearsed, in white tie and tails, Carlo Gozzi's *Turandot*, in the biting cold and the hunger of Moscow in 1921.

Some mentioned the young British actors of the 1950s when, in the name of Brecht, Joan Littlewood resorted to improvisation on stage, provoking the UK censors.

In a corner of our minds was the image of young naked bodies from *Dionysus in 69*, staged by Richard Schechner and his Performance Group in 1968, taken from *The Bacchae*. In the performance the modern bacchae asked the spectators to flee with them and break the spell of the ongoing tragedy. On one occasion the invitation was taken up.

Were the performances too a part of the problem?

Everybody of course came up with Jerzy Grotowski's and Ludwik Flaszen's Teatr Laboratorium as an example that was too obvious even to be discussed. Not to mention Odin Teatret, the Nordisk Teaterlaboratorium.

We also thought about all the actors, young and old alike, who at the turn of the new millennium were implementing laboratorial conditions. Many of them had been through ISTA.

Barba's questions were pushing us away from our safe territories and beliefs, in search of subtler and sharper definitions. But we had the impression that, along with the shell of our evident and perhaps facile convictions, the base on which our shared knowledge lay might begin to falter.

But we tried anyway. 'We', scholars and practitioners, brought together at ISTA and forced to confront these questions, put forward a first round of answers. Many clever, significant and revealing things were said. I shall list these initial answers and definitions.

The orbit of theatre laboratories

The laboratory, we said, is a *parallel dimension* of the theatre. It follows an orbit which, however, cannot be defined with any degree of accuracy. And we added that probably, in order to function, it had to escape any definition. Even the existence of important models, such as those of Stanislavski or Grotowski, may lead us astray, since a laboratory cannot be defined according to its intentions or the models it chooses for itself. The term laboratory does not define a concept or a methodological paradigm, but rather a space. This space has the same architectural layout as a normal theatre, from which the space reserved for the audience has been amputated. A laboratory is a theatre devised as a home for actors, where the spectators are no longer the bosses but guests.

We said: a theatre laboratory is a protected milieu where time is plentiful. Time is an essential factor: research depends not on performing a large number of experiments but on giving oneself enough time for specific experiments that seek something precise, and which are organically separate from those performed merely to experiment.

We said: a laboratory is a theatre that is searching for a *distillate* of life. Not 'life' in general, or life as it appears to us, but a distillate.

We said: a laboratory is a structure that develops a research, re-creating artificial conditions and contexts. Like when earthquakes are studied inside a room, artificially re-creating in miniature all the conditions. We also said that the laboratory is a place for constructing a body free of automatisms.

During one of the University of Eurasian Theatre discussions, Franco Ruffini, an Italian theatre scholar with the scientific background of the physicist, was asked for a non-theatrical definition of laboratory, so as to refocus our starting point. He tried to give a logical form to the confusion of our problems and replied that a possible definition could be as follows: a laboratory is a fully equipped place where experiments are performed based on precise hypotheses which are to be tested, the results of which can be used and displayed.

Then we said: a laboratory is a place of pure research, a utopia. But utopia (*u-topos*), as far as the theatre is concerned, is not a *non*-place. Rather it is the place of the *non*. Thus a laboratory is a theatre that says *no* to the performance.

We said: we mustn't lose our bearings, focusing solely on the individuals who have created Studios or theatre laboratories. There is something more important, a general revolution over and above the activities of individuals. Perhaps it cannot be recognised in any of them, but it certainly can in the whole orbit of theatre laboratories. It is a revolution of the human being, brought about through theatre. A way of passing from the external scene to the inner scene.

Someone added: a laboratory is a path through which one loses oneself and one's beliefs are called into question. It is a house where the living and the dead both live, the students and the elderly learn together, a library and a workshop, my dreams and your disappointments.

Another pointed out: theatre laboratories appear when there is no longer a distinction between the two different channels of professional and amateur theatres. Historically the latter had always considered the theatre from an artistic-spiritual point of view but without being able to devote their whole time to it.

Barba spoke about Stanislavski, Meyerhold, Vakhtangov, Copeau and Artaud. 'What sort of debris have they left us?' he asked. 'Why have I built my house on this debris? A laboratory is a place where relationships are built.' And he added a little obscurely: 'Relationships with one's present and one's past. A laboratory is first and foremost a mental place, a workshop inside us. But not individual or private: it is the voice of the "other" within us. A place where you can protect your origins.'

We – it is always a symbolic 'we', the people that had created a veritable collective mind – said: the laboratory is the place where bombs are patiently tested; this is especially true for a theatre laboratory. Because the theatre is not at all distilled life, it is inverted life: above all, a fruitful destruction. Fire is indeed a symbol for the theatre.[5]

Barba, probably because the image of fire evokes by contrast that of water, narrated the story of a girl who, a few years previously, during a meeting of theatre groups in Argentina, presented her 'group', consisting of one person only: herself. She was the expression of the culture of the shipwreck. She had started acting in the provinces with other youngsters and managed to stay afloat for five years: a long time for a group. For five years they had worked, dreamed and seen their dreams come true: the illusions of a generation in an Argentina that had just come out of the dictatorship. Then the group suddenly broke up. She explained how awful it had

---

[5] Almost all of these statements mirror the views of those who took part in the discussion, as they appear from my notes on the various meetings or, more rarely, from their writings. To retain the effect of the discussion, I shall refer to the various books and essays only in cases of actual addresses. Nevertheless, I must at least highlight Franco Ruffini's book, *Il filo rosso: teatro e taccuini (1999–2006)* (The Red Line: Theatre and Notebooks – 1999–2006) (Rome: Officina edizioni, 2007), since it includes a chapter that recalls the discussion during the course of one of these meetings at the University of Eurasian Theatre in 2003, at Scilla, organised by Teatro Proskenion. Cf. 'Per linee trasversali' (By Transversal Lines), pp. 81–83.

been to meet solitude again: the only survivor of a shipwreck, of a capsized fragile craft.

However, all of these associations do not explain what a theatre laboratory is. Even Stanislavski or Grotowski would have been confused as the definitions piled up. Nevertheless, as I was writing them down, I realised how they described the force-field activated by theatre laboratories. Theatre laboratory, indeed, indicates not a way of theatre-making but rather a paradoxical way of looking at it. As if, instead of concentrating on the problems directly related to the performance, instead of observing modern-day theatre trends and the way performances are received and remembered, we inverted our gaze and observed not only the working process, but also the remoter zone, the boundary between the *normality* of daily life and the *diversity* of the human being while performing. A diversity that is not accepted as much as necessary in the theatre.

A paradoxical gaze

A paradoxical gaze sees outside and beyond the zone of theatrical tasks directly related to the performance. Such an approach does not only encompass the work involved in creation, but deems it legitimate and important to burrow and meander in less central areas[6]. In the second half of the twentieth century the theatre laboratory was the place for such paradoxical observation and practice.

A theatre laboratory is a theatre that *also* raises theatrical problems not directly-related to actual performance. It fo-

[6] However, this area does not coincide with the external activity of a theatre, but includes the field of technique. Grotowski has often mentioned that a certain type of rehearsal, which does not aim at a quick and efficient performance, belongs to this area. What Peter Brook says on this subject is also of interest: 'In the domain of ritual, in the domain of storytelling, in the domain of play [...] everything which is defined as research and everything that is technique all revolves around the same mystery, which is at each point an attempt to understand. The work of rehearsals is truly laboratory work...' Peter Brook, *With Grotowski. Theatre is Just a Form* (Wrocław: The Grotowski Institute, 2009), pp. 94–95.

cuses on a border zone where theatrical work takes root in daily routines and where the daily and extra-daily dimension in the lives of theatre people blend together. In turning one's gaze towards the *border zone that exists between work and everyday life*, the activity of theatre laboratories illuminates the extent of this zone and its potential as regards the work, the richness and variety of experiences that may occur there. Laboratoriality is thus the work that, in addition to an artistic process, also emphasises a cognitive process.

Grotowski

Historically, many of us naturally felt that Grotowski and the foundation, along with Flaszen, of his Teatr Laboratorium lay at the heart of the 'theatre laboratories' problem. Others put forward antecedents. But for everybody Grotowski was an essential point of reference, a case that we absolutely had to reflect upon.

For the formation and experience of all of 'us', Grotowski's example, his theatre, his words and his teaching were not so much a starting point as an imprinting:

Each of us is to some extent a mystery. Something creative may happen in theatre – between the director and the actor – exactly when a contact between two mysteries takes place.

By coming to know the mystery of another, one comes to know his own. And vice versa: by coming to know one's own, one comes to know the mystery of another. It is not possible with everyone. Speaking in this way, I do not intend to make a pronouncement on the worth of other people. Simply, life made us in such a way that we can meet: you and I. We can meet for life and death – carry out an act together. Create as if it were the last time, as if one was to die immediately after.

One might think that meeting is a creative feature exclusive to theatre, but after all if we analyze certain phenomena, for example in literature, we can find many analogies. In theatre, no doubt, meeting is essential. Perhaps it is not the only road to theatre, but I think it is only on this road that we are most devoured by what we do. It also seems to me that it is this search for going beyond that frees the fullness in the artist, the creative fullness in the director.

What do we look for in the actor? Without a doubt – himself. If we don't look for him, we cannot help him. If he doesn't interest us, if he isn't someone essential to us, we cannot help him. But we also look for ourselves in him, our deep 'I', our self. The word 'self', which is absolutely abstract when one refers it to oneself, when one immerses it in the world of introversion, makes sense when applied in reference to another. When one seeks 'self' in the other. However, not in a solemn, moral sense, referring to the whole species, so to speak. Rather, when one applies it with all its seriousness and yet at the same time excluding any noble hypocrisy. Even this phrasing is not very precise, because it presupposes something spiritual. Most likely the same mechanism is at work here as in private life, in relationships between people, where as a matter of fact everything too spiritual, too pure, is untrue. However we name it, there exists some kind of exchange: some kind of penetration in the actor and a return to oneself, and vice versa.[7]

During the conference in Aarhus in 2004 (the culmination and in a way the conclusion of this discussion), two Polish scholars, Zbigniew Osiński and Leszek Kolankiewicz, spoke about Grotowski. We will look at Osiński's talk in full in another chapter. But here, talking about the history of the discussion, we must begin to familiarise ourselves with the topics and the problems they raised.

Osiński, for instance, began his address as follows: 'In "Lettre à mes amis historiens", known in its English version as "Letter to the Speakers", Eugenio Barba wrote: "It is evident that my personal history and forty years with Odin Teatret determine my way of seeing. It is no accident. Each of us could say exactly the same thing. What we can do here is to try to give our own testimony – that's all"'. In this discussion all information regarding a witness was important.

[7] Jerzy Grotowski 'On the Genesis of Apocalypsis', trans. by Kris Salata, *TDR: The Drama Review*, 52. 2 (2008), 40–51 (p. 41). This is a text of Grotowski reconstructed from Leszek Kolankiewicz's transcriptions of a series of addresses given by the director between 1969 and 1970 to mark the tenth anniversary of the Teatr Laboratorium.

Kolankiewicz, a slender, smiling but bashful figure, stood up to reflect on the meaning of the concept of laboratory for Grotowski, on the reason for a term with scientific nuances, and on the profound implications of his laboratoriality. He presented to us an image of a theatre laboratory that was obscure yet glimmering with gold, a place where transmutations occurred, similar to the laboratory of an alchemist, full of surprises, a far cry from the slow, tortuous, fragile but progressive work performed in a scientist's lab. He told us that Grotowski's research was not random, yet it had no direct objective. He explained that an alchemist's laboratory implies – unlike a scientific lab – firstly a transmutation of the researcher. He said that the alchemist, in any country or context, always remains faithful to a mystical tradition, and that in his laboratory the first operation is conducted on himself, on his mental life, on his psychological entity and on his own experience. The alchemist does this with the rigour of scientific procedure but also in ways close to the problems inherent to the art. And his inner transmutation is always inseparable from the experiment.

Leszek Kolankiewicz, now a professor at Warsaw University, has not only studied Grotowski a great deal and seen many of his last productions but also collaborated closely with him in the paratheatre period and in the Theatre of Sources project. He is one of those scholars who deems field work to be an integral part of research, which I believe is true for all of 'us' at ISTA. He introduced the point of view of theatre anthropology in Polish studies, focusing in particular on what he called *performatyka*, the anthropology of performance. He took part for years in the work and the 'expeditions' of the Gardzienice theatre, and collaborates with the Grotowski Institute in Wrocław. Here follows his talk in Aarhus (translated by Grzegorz Ziółkowski with Paul Allain)[8]:

---

[8] The text of Kolankiewicz's speech will be published in a revised version in *Grotowski's Empty Room: A Challenge to the Theatre*, ed. by Paul Allain (Seagull Books, forthcoming 2009).

Many of the theatres discussed here – or maybe all of them – can be classified as laboratories, but only a few bore this title. Foremost among the latter was the Polish Teatr Laboratorium. I will therefore first provide some information about this institution's name.

Jerzy Grotowski and Ludwik Flaszen founded their theatre in the summer of 1959 in Opole, first taking over the name of the Teatr 13 Rzędów which existed previously. It was as late as 1 March 1962 when they changed it to Teatr Laboratorium Teatr 13 Rzędów. This date may be viewed as a key moment in history. The following premieres took place in Opole under the new name: *Akropolis*, by Stanisław Wyspiański (November 1962), *The Tragical History of Dr Faustus* by Christopher Marlowe (April 1963) and *Hamlet Study* based on texts by William Shakespeare and Stanisław Wyspiański (March 1964). Upon the transfer of Teatr Laboratorium Teatr 13 Rzędów from Opole to Wrocław – on 1 January 1965 – the name of the place was supplemented by the distinction: 'Institute of the Actor's Method'. *The Constant Prince* by Pedro Calderón de la Barca, in Juliusz Słowacki's translation, (April 1965) was presented in the theatre going by this name. In early 1967, when the company was working on *The Gospels*, which later evolved into *Apocalypsis cum figuris* (February 1969) – the last theatre piece directed by Grotowski – '13 Rzędów' disappeared from the name of the Teatr Laboratorium. From 1 January 1970 the name of the institution was shortened to 'The Institute of the Actor – Teatr Laboratorium'. The name survived without further changes until the end of its existence.

In a letter to the local authorities in Wrocław, Ludwik Flaszen, Rena Mirecka, Zygmunt Molik and Ryszard Cieślak, who were writing on behalf of the group, recalled all its historical names: 'As of 31 August 1984, the Theatre of 13 Rows, the Institute of the Actor's Method, Institute of the Actor – in other words the company of the Teatr Laboratorium, after exactly twenty-five years, has decided to dissolve'.[9]

It is worth adding that in the 1970s, when the team did not work on new theatre performances, but organized so-called paratheatre workshops (Grotowski retrospectively called this type of project a 'theatre of participation'), two words – 'institute' and 'laboratory', from the official name of the institution – were written on the posters in bold type. And a phrase was added to the name of the Teatr Labo-

---

[9] 'Teatr Laboratorium has decided to break up', in *The Grotowski Sourcebook*, ed. by Lisa Wolford and Richard Schechner (London and New York: Routledge, 1997), p. 169.

ratorium: 'a cultural research institute situating itself on the edge of art, especially theatre art', taken from an interview with Grotowski published in October 1976 by the official daily *Trybuna Ludu*.[10]

Grotowski eagerly resorted to scientific terminology at that time. Perhaps the most famous type of paratheatrical workshop, staged for the first time in October 1973 near Philadelphia in the United States, was called the Special Project – using a term derived from university terminology. Later, different types of paratheatrical workshops staged abroad – in France and Australia – were described with the term 'Complex Research Program'. In 1975 the Theatre of Nations season took place in Warsaw, Grotowski conducting the main part, called the 'University of Research of the Theatre of Nations' in Wrocław. In the mid-1970s, laboratories multiplied within the Teatr Laboratorium context. Documents report the creation of the Acting Therapy Laboratory, the Group Theory and Analysis Laboratory, the Laboratory of Event Methods, the Working Encounter Laboratory. Grotowski's most personal and secret research was called 'the Program of Prospective Research', whatever that might mean.

When in 1983 – after emigrating from Poland – Grotowski inaugurated the Objective Drama project in the United States, he described its institutional form in grant proposals, submitted first to New York University and finally to the University of California, Irvine, as laboratory. 'Grotowski's work codes may be religious by origin, but they are in the process of being isolated into technical codes by means of the work of the laboratory'.[11] So it was that in his later work as well, carried out with new teams outside the Polish Teatr Laboratorium, Grotowski sometimes used the title laboratory.

At the end of his life Grotowski combined research conducted at the Workcenter in Pontedera with academic work. He was appointed professor of the Collège de France in Paris and in 1997 took the Chair of Theatre Anthropology, which was created especially for him.

What made him use these names – 'laboratory', 'institute' – taken from institutional science? Why did he constantly place his artistic work in the context of scientific research?

Grotowski spoke about this in an interview 'Laboratorium w teatrze' (The Laboratory in the Theatre), given in April 1967, reprinted as a

---

[10] Cf. Jerzy Grotowski, 'Poszukiwania Teatru Laboratorium' (The Laboratory Theatre Explorations), interview with Tadeusz Burzyński, *Trybuna Ludu*, 252 (1976), p. 6.

[11] Richard Schechner, *Between Theater and Anthropology* (Philadelphia: University of Pennsylvania Press, 1985), p. 256.

separate text 'Methodical Exploration', and subsequently included in the book *Towards a Poor Theatre* edited by Eugenio Barba.[12] This text begins with Grotowski admitting his fascination for the Institute of Theoretical Physics in Copenhagen, founded in 1920 by Niels Bohr. Grotowski was obviously fascinated not by the subject of the research conducted there, but by the way it was organised: the physicists from different countries were allowed to carry out their boldest experiments in order to extract from findings the key directions in their research; research was conducted in the space of a no-man's-land, and was permanent in nature.

Grotowski emphasised that theatre and especially the art of the actor obviously do not fall within the domain of scientific research. But on the other hand he referred to Stanislavski and recalled the actor's need to master a method. He said: 'Taking into account the fact that the domain on which our attention is focused is not a scientific one, and not everything in it can be defined (indeed, many things must not be), we nevertheless try to determine our aims with all the precision and consequence typical of scientific research. The actor who works here is already a professional, and not only the creative act but also the laws governing it become the focus of his concerns.[13] In his text Grotowski called these general principles 'objective laws'.[14]

The Teatr Laboratorium was meant to resemble the Bohr Institute precisely because of the research-based nature of work on the actor's method and its operations on the borderline between art and other scientific disciplines (at that time Grotowski had already mentioned cultural anthropology, among others). Grotowski was fond of this comparison. In 1989 – when Zbigniew Osiński was negotiating with him the contents of the collection of his texts published in Poland – he stated that in this article (written more then twenty years earlier) the only accurate thing was the Laboratory's comparison with the Bohr Institute.

Jerzy Grotowski's brother Kazimierz, three years his senior, is a Professor of physics at the Jagellonian University in Kraków. He remembers that in the final years of World War II, which they spent in a village, their mother Emilia, who was a teacher, gave both her sons various books to read. Among these they both read Paul Brunton's

---

[12] Cf. Jerzy Grotowski, 'Methodical Exploration' in Grotowski, *Towards a Poor Theatre*, ed. by Eugenio Barba (New York: Routledge, 2002), pp. 127–132.
[13] Grotowski, 'Methodical Exploration', p. 129.
[14] *Ibid.*, p. 128.

A Search in Secret India about the Indian saint Śrī Ramana Maharishi and *New World of Physics* by Sir James Jeans, a British physicist and astronomer. Kazimierz Grotowski asserts that these books were decisive in shaping their paths in life. It is well known how much Jerzy Grotowski remembered his fascination as a ten-year-old boy: according to his will, his ashes were to be scattered on the slopes of Arunachala, the mountain where Śrī Ramana had his hermitage. But maybe Grotowski had also kept in his memory books about the latest scientific research on physics and astronomy.

His brother, in 'Portret rodzinny' (A Family Portrait) – an article written after Jerzy's death – recalls:

> We also spoke about physics and astrophysics. We communicated without any problem. In his entire involvement with theatre, philosophy, religion, science and anthropology, Jurek approached matters of the world from a position close to that of the naturalists. His theatre was to a great extent a place for experimentation.

And he added: 'In our conversations, we often argued about the meaning of terms that I considered to be strictly defined, like energy...'. In Kazimierz Grotowski's opinion, his brother was an experimenter, leading a 'search for the extraordinary in human experiences'. He confesses: 'We spoke about those very rare moments in life, for instance out in the wild, on high mountains, when a man feels the direct presence of God'.[15] (We should be aware that Kazimierz was also fascinated by India, undertook an expedition there, and went – unlike Jerzy who did not climb – high up in the Himalayas, where he visited Lamaist monasteries.)

Jerzy Grotowski approached the problems of his work from a position close to that of the scientist. Scientific research made an impression on him, and this is where his predilection for such names as laboratory, institute and so on comes from. But the domain which he cultivated – and he was perfectly aware of this – was neither scientific nor did it yield to scientific definitions. After all, Grotowski could have said the same as Jung: 'I find that all my thoughts circle around God'.[16] Yet Grotowski returned to the epithet 'objective' again and again. At first he was concerned with 'objective laws' which govern the actor's creative processes, and then with 'objec-

[15] Kazimierz Grotowski, 'Portret rodzinny', *Pamiętnik Teatralny*, special issue edited by Jarosław Fret, Grzegorz Janikowski and Grzegorz Ziółkowski, vol. XLIX, no. 1–4 (2000), 9–36 (p. 34). An English edition of this text will be published by Black Mountain Press in 2010.

[16] Carl Gustav Jung, *Memories, Dreams, Reflections*, recorded and edited by Aniela Jaffé, trans. by Richard and Clara Winston, (London: Fontana Press, 1995), p. 13.

tive drama' which can be distilled from the world's various liturgical performances.

In a well-known critique, Richard Schechner expressed his unease about this epithet in Grotowski's work, especially in Ritual Arts, when Grotowski kept employing the artistic-subjective method.[17] Schechner argues that Grotowski's investigations were not scientific – even when conducted at universities, for instance within the framework of the Objective Drama project at the University of California, Irvine. Neither in the course of the work, nor after its completion, were the hypothesis and findings subjected to open discussion. They were made known only to a small *coterie* or to individuals chosen from the circle of Grotowski's supporters. They were never verified in the way scientists – or, at the very least, serious scientists – verify the results published in, for instance, *Nature* or *Science*. These arguments are irrefutable.

However, Grotowski carried out his research within the framework of another paradigm. This paradigm differed from a scientific one in the same way that alchemical experiences were different from chemical experiments.

In October 1980, at a conference at York University in Toronto, he formulated the pragmatics of his Theatre of Sources project. This project was rolled out in Poland at a very particular moment in history. The first practical seminar took place in the summer of 1980, when Poland was hit by a wave of strikes, which resulted in the founding of Solidarity, the first independent workers' union in territories under the domain of Soviet Russia. The second practical seminar – planned for 1982 – was being prepared by an international team travelling around Poland in 1981, in a period of stormy civil conflict and the constant threat of invasion by the armies of the Warsaw Pact. A period that ended in December 1981 when martial law was imposed in Poland. At the conference in Toronto Grotowski determined the conditions under which the efficacy of the research should be tested – incidentally this fragment can be found in the Polish version of the text published in 1987, but was cut from the revised version published in *The Grotowski Sourcebook* ten years later (actually the text is wrongly dated): 'You should have a favourable place for [experiments], but then you must try [to carry them out] under another condition – under a bridge, in a hospital, in a prison.

---

[17] Cf. Richard Schechner, 'Exoduction: Shape-shifter, shaman, trickster, artist, adept, director, leader, Grotowski' in *The Grotowski Sourcebook*, pp. 458–92 (pp. 489–490).

If you manage in these three places, it means that you have really found what you have been looking for'.[18]

Of course he was not speaking about scientific experiments – but certainly what was at stake was an experiment carried out in a way that is not compromised and that demands the total involvement of the researcher. Grotowski put this instruction into practice when he left the forest base of the Teatr Laboratorium (a place favourable for work) with the second team of the Theatre of Sources and began travelling around a feverish Poland in order to conduct an investigation 'under a bridge', all the time taking into account that at some point it would have to be continued in a hospital or even in a prison.

I took part in these expeditions. In this period Grotowski read and eagerly commented on Martin Buber's books about the Hasidim. Needless to say, Grotowski was not a Jew and as such was not an inheritor of the Hasidic tradition. He was not from this ethnic background, but all the same he took up Afro-Haitian vodou traditions – just like Hasidism. And it is possible that when we were going across Poland in 1981 and visiting a few small towns and villages, being prepared for the worst, he looked like a *Zaddik* wandering around with his Hasidim. Hasidism was important for Grotowski because – according to an excellent hypothesis put forward by Buber – in Hasidism, the Kabbala as a system, which we know from *Sefer ha-Zohar*, was transformed into an ethos, a way of life.[19] In Hasidism the system is inseparable from the relationship between Hasidim ('the pious') and the *Zaddik* ('the just one') as an embodiment of knowledge, a personal example, a living legendary character. The system resulted from this relationship and fulfilled itself in it.

At the beginning of the 1980s Grotowski was still not speaking directly about the meaning of this type of relationship with his research. But he did so in February 1987 at a conference in Pontedera, when he spoke about the relationship between the teacher of Performer and Performer. 'I am *a teacher of Performer*', he said. 'A teacher – as in the crafts – is someone through whom the teaching is passing'. The teacher himself came to know this teaching, as Grotowski says mysteriously, 'by initiation or by theft'. The teaching mentioned here concerns knowledge – Grotowski calls the Performer a 'man of knowledge'.

[18] Jerzy Grotowski, 'Teatr Źródeł' (Theatre of Sources) arranged by Leszek Kolankiewicz, *Zeszyty Literackie*, no. 19 (1987), 102–115 (p. 113).
[19] Martin Buber, 'Jewish Mysticism' in Buber, *The Tales of Rabbi Nachman*, trans. by Maurice Friedman (New York: Avon Books, 1970), pp. 3–17 (p. 10).

A man of knowledge [*człowiek poznania*] has at his disposal *the doing* and not ideas or theories. The true teacher – what does he do for the apprentice? He says: *do it*. The apprentice fights to understand, to reduce the unknown to the known, to avoid doing. By the very fact that he wants to understand, he resists. He can understand only after he *does it*. He *does it* or not. Knowledge is a matter of doing'.[20]

Obviously the knowledge mentioned here is not scientific knowledge – instead it is more like the central notion of Gnosis: active knowledge, which is the sole path towards salvation.

In the version from the aforementioned conference in Toronto published in *The Grotowski Sourcebook*, Grotowski makes a distinction between *Gnosis* and *gnosticism*.[21] He regards the latter as very 'baroque' in its language and invention of levels of reality. In one sentence Grotowski speaks about early Gnosis and transmission attributed to the non-public teachings of Jesus. But perhaps he meant early Christianity, which was still mixed up with Gnosis, as was the case with the apocryphal Gospel of Thomas from the Nag Hammadi library. Grotowski viewed this gospel as a collection of practical tips.

There is a transcription of an extraordinary meeting that Grotowski held in March 1981, during this stormy period for Poland, with researchers of Polish Romanticism. It took place in Gdańsk, the city where the workers' movement of Solidarity had been born half a year earlier. The transcription was published simultaneously in three different unauthorised versions, and it reflects Grotowski's *orature* excellently.[22] It is still very little known in Poland, and is probably completely unknown abroad. The encounter took place at a very particular historical moment, and this may be why Grotowski said things he never mentioned either before or afterwards. I think that, of his texts, this is one of the most important.

He said then: 'In fact, Gnosis does not interest me at all. It is a system, one system among many. And every system is a Procrustean bed to which one must adapt'.[23] He must have meant this sincerely

---

[20] Jerzy Grotowski, 'Performer', trans. by Thomas Richards, in *The Grotowski Sourcebook*, pp. 374–78 (p. 374).

[21] Jerzy Grotowski, 'Theatre of Sources', in *The Grotowski Sourcebook*, pp. 250–68 (p. 261).

[22] Republished in Jerzy Grotowski, *Grotowski powtórzony* (Grotowski Repeated), ed. by Stanisław Rosiek,(Gdańsk: słowo/obraz terytoria, 2009). The English translation is to be published by Black Mountain Press in early 2010.

[23] *Ibid.*, p. 77 (version C).

because Gnosis interested him only as a practice. Or it interested him only in as much as it worked in the practice of such performing arts that he later called Ritual Arts. In fact, this brought his approach closer to Afro-Haitian vodou, which, above all, is practice and only practice – even if it becomes like a system on the pages of ethnographic studies, such as those of Maya Deren or Alfred Métraux. And it also brought it closer to Hasidism, which Martin Buber could not have introduced better through stories about the *Zaddikim*, through traditions in which the teaching is inseparable from action and events. According to Buber, to create or acquire a more or less systematic theory in our time is completely beside the point. The point is to get to know a reality which can help man remain in a state of readiness.[24] Grotowski probably shared this view. This is why he did not give his teaching a systematic form: neither scientific, nor gnostic. And such accounts as *At Work with Grotowski on Physical Actions* and *The Edge-Point of Performance* by Thomas Richards are the best testimonies of his teaching.

During the meeting in Gdańsk, which I have been speaking about here, Grotowski presented his gnostic world view for the only time in such a direct way. 'I think that the world in which I was born and where I live is not for life,' he said. 'It is as though we are expelled, as if we are born in this world but not of this world, and not for this world – I don't know if from another – but as if a lot can be found in this world'.[25] In this desperate recognition his imitation of the way of the Hasidim was consolidated. Grotowski said: 'For them God exploded with sparks, and the further they fly, the more they disappear, disperse; the Hasidim understood that the sparks need to be gathered up and shared with people – and so they wandered around for this reason'.[26] Based on this understanding, the world of nature and human experience is the stage where the exile of the soul is played out – and being so, it remains a mission for man, who should find sparks of God and should collect and return them during his exile. Later, in the text 'Performer', Grotowski would speak about this – after Meister Eckhart – as a 'breakthrough', the return of an outcast from exile in this world. [27]

[24] Cf. for example, Martin Buber, *Between Man and Man*, trans. by Ronald Gregor Smith (London: Routledge, 2002; 2nd edn), p. 135; Buber, 'Heruth and Religion', trans. by Eva Jospe, in *The Martin Buber Reader*, ed. by Asher D. Biemann (London: Palgrave Macmillan, 2002), pp. 125–138 (p. 126).

[25] *Grotowski powtórzony*, p.82 (version A).

[26] *Ibid.*, p. 39 (version C).

[27] Grotowski, 'Performer', p. 377.

Grotowski understood the mission imposed on man as being independent from current events of history. In Gdańsk, in the most heated period of contemporary Polish history, he suggested treating social turmoil as a period similar to the time spent in the transit zone at an airport. He then said: 'The Hasidim, St Francis, the madmen of Zen – they all resemble each other. It is as though everything has started from scratch, with people coming from the very heart of society and at the same time from its fringes'.[28] Turning points happen in the lives of societies, and at such times political matters are at stake. Often it is war, but at the same time – somewhere around the edges – people appear who refer specifically to spiritual sources, to the very origins of the human calling and mission. Perhaps it is the deepest manifestation of the relationship between Grotowski's work in his laboratories and the mainstream of social life, between knowledge and history.

Grotowski rejected Gnosis as a system. With Gnosis, he was interested in knowledge itself, which he considered a matter of doing. This brings to mind an association with alchemy, which Grotowski himself never mentioned, even though he suggested using the term *opus* in order to describe the work in Ritual Arts. As a matter of fact this was something which brings him closer to Carl Gustav Jung and George Ivanovich Gurdjieff: Gurdjieff presented his teaching to Ouspensky – and this is acknowledged in *In Search of the Miraculous* – as a kind of alchemy, while Jung drew a genealogical line which started in gnosticism and ran through alchemy and towards analytical psychology.

It is a well known fact that alchemists made many scientific discoveries, so popularly understood alchemy is regarded as pre-chemistry, an imperfect science – imperfect because alchemists gave themselves over to a world of fantastic imaginings of hermeticism, pointing to the conclusion that they were not aiming for chemical reactions. Alchemy everywhere – wherever and whenever it was cultivated – remains closely related to some mystical tradition or other. Chinese alchemy was related to Taoism, Indian alchemy to tantrism, Hellenic alchemy to gnosticism and the religion of the mysteries, Arabic alchemy to Sufism, and European alchemy of the Middle Ages and Renaissance to hermeticism and cabbalistic mysticism. Indeed, alchemy was a spiritual technique.

The alchemist performed operations above all on himself in his laboratory: on his psycho-physiological life, on his experiences. He did

---

[28] *Grotowski powtórzony*, p.74 (version A).

these operations with a rigour characteristic of scientific procedures and at the same time as an artist, drawing from gymnastic, choreographic and ecstatic techniques. In the Chinese esoteric alchemy of *neidan*, chemical substances were not employed at all, but operations were carried out in the body and psyche of the adept. This is where the *elixir vitae*, the elixir of life, was being prepared. However, in the main, alchemy was nothing but laboratory work. In this work the drama of the *psyche* was experienced as being inseparable from the drama of matter. This dramatic dimension can be seen best in Hellenic alchemy, where the initiatory scenario of the mysteries was projected onto laboratory procedures, which were the realisation of the drama of life and transformations of matter. Yet everywhere alchemy involved initiatory schemes: suffering, death and the resurrection of matter, analogous to the suffering, death and resurrection of the laboratory adept. The work of the alchemist sought to redeem the *anima mundi*, the soul of the world, imprisoned in matter. The ultimate aim of the *opus magnum*, the great work, was an *apocatastasis*: renovation, healing, restitution and liberation of the *anima mundi*. Just as Christ redeemed man, the alchemist's task was to ensure the redemption of nature. That is why alchemical operations were of soteriological value.

While searching for gold the alchemist was searching for his spiritual essence. This is why Jung interpreted the *opus magnum* as an individuation process and viewed the finding of the *elixir vitae* as attaining the Self. But this transformation did not proceed according to a natural rhythm. In alchemy, *transmutatio*, the transformation of matter and the transformation of an adept, were triggered off artificially in the laboratory. Hence the laboratory was needed, and alchemy deserved the title of art, or of artistry and craftsmanship. Jung distinguished between natural individuation, which happens voluntarily in the course of man's life, turning as he grows older, as is natural, to his inner life, and individuation triggered artificially, for instance by means of the initiatory techniques of mysteries and alchemy. Gurdjieff also spoke about the two ways of reaching the essence: the way of a 'citizen', who goes through the vicissitudes of life in his conscience, and the way of a 'sly man', who by all possible means – by initiation, or by theft – accelerates his transformation. This in fact is an art – an alchemical *ars magna*, a great art – and a laboratory is needed for this.

I think that this is the deepest and the most exact meaning of the term laboratory in the name of the Polish Teatr Laboratorium and in all subsequent laboratory works of Jerzy Grotowski. In his first manifesto 'Towards a Poor Theatre', in 1965, Grotowski spoke about his method – which suggested that it all boils down to the actor's physical exercises:

> Here everything is concentrated on the 'ripening' of the actor which is expressed by a tension towards the extreme, by a complete stripping down, by the laying bare of one's own intimacy – all this without the least trace of egotism or self-enjoyment. The actor makes a total gift of himself. This is a technique of the 'trance' and of the integration of all the actor's psychic and bodily powers which emerge from the most intimate layers of his being and his instinct, springing forth in a sort of 'translumination'.[29]

Something that Grotowski called at that time 'the most intimate layers of his being and his instinct' later received the more alchemical name '"density" of the body'[30] in his vocabulary. The actor's organism should eliminate any resistance to the inner process: 'the body vanishes, burns, and the spectator sees only a series of visible impulses'.[31] Later Grotowski called Ryszard Cieślak's accomplishments in *The Constant Prince* a '*carnal prayer*'.[32] He said that it was as though Cieślak in this role 'liberated himself with his body from the body itself, as if he liberated himself – step after step – from the heaviness of the body'.[33]

In this type of acting it was as though the actor radiated 'like figures in El Greco's paintings', as if it were possible 'to "illuminate" through personal technique, becoming a source of "spiritual light"'.[34] Grotowski describes here a transformation of an alchemical nature, which consisted in lifting up what is heavy and carnal towards light and spirituality. He described this transformation in *Performer* as passing 'from the *body-and-essence* to the *body of essence*'.[35] But in his opinion to make this transformation possible a precise 'structure' of actions is essential. *A series of actions* was the structure that he called, quite deliberately, an *opus*. Grotowski placed great emphasis on this.

---

[29] Grotowski, *Towards a Poor Theatre*, p. 16; original translation corrected.
[30] Jerzy Grotowski, 'From the Theatre Company to Art as Vehicle', in Thomas Richards, *At Work with Grotowski on Physical Actions* (London and New York: Routledge, 1995), pp. 115–35 (p. 125).
[31] Grotowski, *Towards a Poor Theatre*, p. 16.
[32] Grotowski, 'From the Theatre Company to Art as Vehicle', p. 123.
[33] *Ibid.*, p. 123.
[34] Grotowski, *Towards a Poor Theatre*, p. 20.
[35] Grotowski, 'Performer', p. 376.

One cannot work on oneself (to use the term of Stanislavski) if one is not inside something which is structured and can be repeated, which has a beginning, a middle and an end, something in which every element has its logical place, technically necessary. *All this determined from the point of view of that verticality toward the subtle and of its (the subtle's) descent towards the density of the body.*[36]

This is precisely why Grotowski needed laboratory work – a laboratory devised as a permanent empirical quest run with a stable team of apprentices.

This research was not of a scientific nature but rather resembled an alchemical art. In alchemists' practice, the laboratory, the place for experiments, was at the same time an oratory, a space for prayer. In the picture by Hans Fredemann Vries, published as a print in Heinrich Conrad Khunrath's *Amphiteatrum sapientiae aeternae*, we can see an alchemist's room divided symmetrically into two parts: a chapel and a working space, where these two operations – prayer and work – are carried out in tandem, both equally necessary for the completion of an *opus*.[37] Alchemists believed that by influencing matter in an *opus magnum* one can make an impact on spirituality; and vice versa: being subjected to spiritual processes one can transmute matter. Hence in the art of alchemy a laboratory and an oratory were two sides of the same coin. European alchemists were mainly Christian. Jung plausibly showed that their *lapis philosophorum*, the philosophers' stone, was analogous to Christ. Gurdjieff also considered his teaching an esoteric Christianity. But neither Jung, Gurdjieff nor Grotowski relied in their work on faith. Like Gnostics, they all relied exclusively on empirical knowledge. This is why they created laboratories – not churches and sects.

Alchemists tested gnostic and/or Christian truth in a practical way: 'the kingdom is inside of you, and it is outside of you. When you come to know yourselves, then you will become known'.[38] According to Grotowski, a man of knowledge understands only through doing. In the domain of the performing arts the man of knowledge

---

[36] Grotowski, 'From the Theatre Company to Art as Vehicle', p. 130.

[37] This engraving is reproduced in *The Cambridge History of Science: Volume 3 – Early Modern Science*, ed. by Katharine Park and Lorraine Daston (Cambridge: Cambridge University Press, 2006), p. 291 (fig. 13.1).

[38] 'The Gospel of Thomas (II, 2)', trans. by Thomas O. Lambdin, in *The Nag Hammadi Library in English*, ed. by James M. Robinson (Leiden, New York and Cologne: E. J. Brill, 1996) pp. 124–38 (p. 126).

is a dancer-priest and as such, through fighting with his habits, searches for the extremity of passivity in action; passivity that is repose – inner repose in movement (action). Outwardly his action of a dancer-priest does not lose any of its dynamics, whereas inwardly he becomes a carrier for a process of knowing himself (a knowing which is gnostic salvation).

The ethos of alchemists was extraordinary. The basic principle of alchemy was – as Michał Sędziwój (Sendivogius Polonus) put it: 'Nature is one, one is art, but there are different laboratory apprentices.'[39] For this reason alchemists – quite unlike philosophers or theologians – did not encourage polemical debates among themselves. There was a kind of professional solidarity among them. On the other hand, they did not feel the need to create brotherhoods (with the exception of Rosicrucianism). Alchemists worked in the privacy of their laboratories, each on his own process. And if they referred to tradition, they quoted only what they had accomplished empirically themselves.

But while they eagerly discoursed on the introductory phases of an *opus* they spoke vaguely or kept silent about its goal. Grotowski was the same – but then he did say why. I cite again:

> A man of knowledge [*człowiek poznania*] has at his disposal *the doing* and not ideas or theories. The true teacher – what does he do for the apprentice? He says: *do it*. The apprentice fights to understand, to reduce the unknown to the known, to avoid doing. By the very fact that he wants to understand, he resists. He can understand only after he *does it*. He *does it*, or does not. Knowledge is a matter of doing.[40]

Why was the Polish Teatr Laboratorium a laboratory? Firstly, to avoid being a repertory theatre, which was common in Poland. Secondly, to avoid being a theatre, to avoid the necessity of producing performances. But this was not a simple matter of trickery over an official name. The Teatr Laboratorium and Grotowski's later laboratories were laboratories in the very essence of his world view and through their likeness to the alchemical tradition. This is why his Teatr Laboratorium was first and foremost a laboratory in a literal sense. In the summer of 1970 Grotowski spoke about this quite directly: 'It is not so important to call it a laboratory, it is not important

---

[39] Michał Sędziwój, *Traktat o kamieniu filozoficznym* (Treatise on the Philosophical Stone), trans. and with an introduction and commentaries by Roman Bugaj (Warsaw: Państwowe Wydawnictwo Naukowe, 1971), p. 190.
[40] Grotowski, 'Performer', p. 374.

whether it is called a theatre. Such a place is necessary. If a theatre did not exist, another pretext would be found'.[41]

The word 'laboratory'

What does a non-random research with no direct goal mean, we asked ourselves as we listened to Kolankiewicz. We had entered the heart of the problem: a laboratory is a place where one has the chance to go down any road, to test any branch of the actor's art in a way that is not conditioned by having to prepare for a performance. It is a place where knowledge of the actor's art grows, not where this knowledge is applied. And Grotowski, through Kolankiewicz, was reminding us that it was a mysterious field and one that is little known. A field in which it is very rare to find true 'teachers of Performers'.

Zbigniew Osiński, the other Polish scholar addressing us, suggested that we should not only think about the metaphorical meaning of the laboratory formula, but that we should also carefully consider its *pragmatic motivations*. Laboratory was a name that Grotowski had invented, together with Flaszen, to prevent his theatre from having to be a run-of-the-mill repertory theatre, forced to produce performances at a rate established by external forces. Osiński recalled Grotowski's words:

> It was the epoch of Stalinism, with very harsh censorship, so all my attention as a director was focused on the fact that the performance could be censored but not the rehearsals. For me, the rehearsals were always the most important thing. It was there where this thing happened between one man and another, between an actor and me, and this thing could touch this axis, this axial symmetry, out of sight and beyond external control. And this has remained in my work. It means that the performance has always been less important than the work done in rehearsals.[42]

[41] Jerzy Grotowski, 'Co było (Kolumbia – lato 1970 – Festiwal Ameryki Łacińskiej)' ('That Which Was: Colombia – Summer 1970 – Festival of Latin America'), *Dialog*, no. 10 (1972), 111–118 (p. 117).

[42] From an interview with Grotowski in the film *Il Teatr Laboratorium di Jerzy Grotowski*, dir. by Marianne Ahrne (Pontedera Teatro for RAI, 1993). The interview was undertaken in French.

Barba told the story of how, in 1966, he had been offered as a home a disused pig farm in a town in Denmark. When he accepted the place, the farm and the pig pens, he immediately made it clear that his was not a normal theatre but a theatre laboratory. The town Mayor had asked him: 'What is a theatre laboratory?' His reply was simple: 'It's a theatre that does not put on performances every evening'. He also pointed out that the term laboratory had been affixed to Grotowski's theatre quite unexpectedly and almost by chance, one day when he had had to quickly fill in a questionnaire.

But what would someone unaware of the history of twentieth-century theatre think as he listened to these anecdotes on theatre laboratories, this loose way of mixing greatness with randomness and rubbish, this trite mixture of weighty questions and cunning ploys?

II

Conflicts within the 'collective mind'.
Discussion on Decroux and the theatre
as a non-religious abode. Also discussion on body
language, on the value of the laboratory
for self-knowledge and on its importance in the creation
of performances.

Two men of the theatre are chatting in a New York restaurant about what they have been doing in recent years. They haven't seen each other for a while, and have taken different paths in life. This is back in 1981. As always happens, one of the two is more willing to listen.

The listener is Wallace Shawn, a playwright and actor of both stage and film, who has acted in many Woody Allen movies. The other, the talker, is André Gregory, director and actor. Shawn says that it was Gregory, in 1975, who was the first to stage his play *Our Late Night* with his group the Manhattan Project. Gregory was already a well-known director, and some of his productions – *Alice in Wonderland, Endgame* and *The Seagull* – had been very successful. Ten or so years later Gregory would stage, in a run-down theatre, *Uncle Vanya* for just ten spectators, with Wallace Shawn playing the lead role. It was the result of a long period of rehearsal and experimentation from 1990 to 1994 and became a reference point for America's experimental theatre, even though the usual channels of communication and advertising were avoided. The performance would become known to the public at large thanks to a 1994 film directed by Louis Malle, *Vanya on 42nd Street.*

But back in 1981 the word was out that Gregory was going through a crisis. He had been out of artistic production for a long time. He had travelled down different paths, met Jerzy Grotowski in Poland, given workshops, acquired out-of-the-ordinary experiences, apparently quite alien to the theatre world. Now he was having dinner with his friend Wallace Shawn and was telling him what he had been doing away from the theatre.[43]

WALLY (*voice-over*): I was feeling incredibly nervous. I wasn't sure I could stick through an entire meal with him. He looked crazy to

---

[43] The conversation takes place within the semi-autobiographical film *My Dinner with André*, dir. by Louis Malle (Pacific Arts Video Records, 1981), in which the two screenplay writers, Shawn and Gregory, play two characters who could be themselves. Cf. Wallace Shawn and André Gregory, *My Dinner with André. A screenplay for the film by Louis Malle*, (New York: Grove Press, 1981), pp. 20–30.

me. (*Cut* to ANDRÉ's *face*.) He was talking about Jerzy Grotowski, the great Polish theater director – a close friend of his, and in a way his guru. After becoming the most respected experimental theater director in the world, Grotowski had dropped out of the theater, just a couple of years before André did. Grotowski had once been a rather fat man, who had worn black suits and a tie [...]

WALLY *looks up from his menu.*

(TO ANDRÉ): By the way, is he still thin?

ANDRÉ: What?

WALLY: Grotowski, is he still thin?

ANDRÉ: Oh, absolutely. [...].

Close-up on ANDRÉ's face, talking. As WALLY's voice over ends, ANDRÉ's voice slowly fades up.

ANDRÉ: So this was about five years ago, and Grotowski and I were walking along Fifth Avenue, and we were talking, and you see, he'd invited me to come and teach that summer in Poland – you know, teach a workshop to actors and directors or whatever. And I had told him that I didn't want to come, because, really, I had nothing left to teach. I had nothing left to say. I didn't know anything. I couldn't teach anything. Exercises meant nothing to me anymore. Working on scenes from plays seemed ridiculous. I didn't know what to do. I mean, I just couldn't do it. And so he said to me, 'Why don't you tell me anything you would like to have if you did a workshop for me, no matter how outrageous, and maybe I can give it to you.' So I said, kind of jokingly, although in retrospect it makes great sense, I said, 'If you could give me forty Jewish women who speak neither English nor French, either women who have been in the theater for a long time and want to leave it but don't know why, or young women who love the theater but have never seen a theater they could love, and if these women could play the trumpet or the harp, and if I could work in a forest, I'd come.' And we both laughed a lot.

And then a week later or two weeks later he called me from Poland. And he said, 'Well, you know, forty Jewish women are a little hard to find,' but he said, 'I do have forty women. They all fit pretty much the definition.' And he said, 'I also have some very interesting men, but you don't have to work with them. These are all people who have in common the fact that they're questioning the theater. They don't all play the trumpet or the harp, but they all play a musical instrument. And none of them speaks English.' And he'd found me a forest, Wally, and the only inhabitants of the forest were some wild boar and a hermit. So that was an offer I couldn't refuse. [...]

We worked for a week in the city before we went to our forest, and of course Grotowski was there […] I did hear that every night they conducted something called a beehive. And I loved the sound of this beehive, and a night or two before we were supposed to go to the country I grabbed him by the collar, and I said, 'Listen, this beehive thing, you know, I'd kind of like to participate in one, just instinctively I feel it would be something interesting.' And he said, 'Well, certainly, and in fact, why don't you, with your group, *lead* a beehive instead of participating in one?' And I got very nervous, you know, and I said, 'Well, what is a beehive?' And he said, 'Well, a beehive is, at eight o'clock a hundred strangers come into a room.' And I said, 'Yes?' And he said, 'Yes, and then whatever happens is a beehive.' […]

Well, one of the young women in our group knew a few fragments of one of the most beautiful songs of St. Francis. […] And that became our theme song, and I must play this thing some day, because you just can't *believe* that a group of people who don't know how to sing could create something so beautiful, but it was because we were really in great harmony. But I decided that when the people arrived for the beehive that our group would already be there singing this song, and that we would simply sing it and sing it and sing it until something happened.

WALLY: Uh-huh.

ANDRÉ: Because it was a very beautiful song. And one person wanted to bring her very large teddy bear, because she felt a little afraid of this event, and this teddy bear had been something that as a little child she had loved, and somebody wanted to bring a sheet. Somebody else wanted to bring a large bowl of water in case people got hot and thirsty. And somebody suggested that we have candles and that there be no artificial light, but candlelight.

WALLY: Mm-hmm.

ANDRÉ: So there was nothing but this song, a teddy bear, water, a sheet, and candles. Now, of course this was very similar, Wally, to the theater, because I remember, before this thing began, feeling sort of like an old actor who was about to go on stage but didn't really know his lines yet. And all the critics were going to be there. I was terrified. And I remember watching people preparing for this evening, and of course there was no makeup, there were no costumes, but it was exactly the way people prepare for a performance. You know, people sort of taking off their jewelery and their watches and stowing them away and making sure it's all secure. And then slowly people arrived, the way they would arrive at the theater, in ones and twos and tens and fifteens and what have you, and we were just sitting, and we were singing this very beautiful song, and people started to sit with us and started to *learn* the song.

WALLY: Uh-huh.

ANDRÉ: Even though nothing in what we did led them to do it. In other words, it could have gone in any other direction.

WALLY: Uh-huh.

ANDRÉ: You see. And after a while they were, whatever it was, a hundred and something people who were all singing this very beautiful song together, and we sang it over and over again. Now there is, of course, as in any improvisation or a performance, an instinct for when it's going to get boring.

WALLY: Ha ha.

ANDRÉ: So, at a certain point, but I think it may have taken an hour to get there, or an hour and a half, I suddenly *grabbed* this teddy bear and *threw* it into the air.

Gregory is playing the part of the 'American', talking about 'the beehive' and Grotowski's work through the eyes of a non-European, and adding a teddy bear to the singing. No matter: he is a good witness. But the most revealing thing in the film is his friend's expression: he had gone to the dinner quite reluctantly, then had grown more interested in the story, more and more understanding. As if he recognises places and problems familiar to him, even though they are solved in a manner that must seem strange to him. For Shawn, what Gregory is saying is comprehensible. He appreciates the doubts, the difficulties and the demands. He can understand to which questions the long trips and odd experiments recounted by Gregory are an answer. Perhaps the paths suggested by Grotowski to overcome his friend's *impasse* seem a little odd to him. But the problems are definitely *understandable*.

What Gregory is talking about is not a theatre laboratory. The subject is Grotowski's activities after his decision to abandon stage performing. But these activities can provide us with important pointers. Gregory's tale is falsely innocent, brazen in a way. But precisely for this reason it forces us to question the reasons why so many men and women of the theatre have looked at certain problems, apparently private in nature, and sought to work them out in the theatre, in the performances and in related activities, and not elsewhere.

It is in stories like the one above that we can see how 'our discussion' ended up dealing with areas, activities and problems that are, at face value, a long way from the theatre world.

The theatre as a non-religious abode

At the Aarhus conference Leszek Kolankiewicz had noted, talking about Grotowski, that the first transformation which occurs in a laboratory is the one effected by the alchemist on himself.

He has thus forced us to take up a challenging point of view from which to consider the whole of twentieth-century theatre: the discovery of the theatre as a place where it is possible to experiment on and transform one's inner self through knowledge of the other.

This subject was tackled by Ferdinando Taviani, an Italian theatre scholar and literary advisor to Odin Teatret for over thirty-five years. His ponderous argument marked a breakthrough in the discussion, which for a time seemed to be decisive.

He said that in terms of acquiring self-knowledge, theatre activity should be a particularly suitable tool, since it brings together both physical and mental work in an inextricable combination. This assertion was much more challenging than it first appeared, as we discovered later on. Many of the problems and features of theatre art arise from the difficulty in accepting the sense and the importance of the 'body culture': little do we understand what the body is saying, unless it is something relating only to the senses, and still less do we manage to recognise its importance.

Taviani, whose fondness of paradoxes and brilliant precise speaking can get his listeners to go along with him whatever he might say, gave us his point of view: namely, that of the theatre as a *non-religious abode*. Theatre could be a privileged place for a sort of spiritual research that cannot be pursued in a religious institution of any kind. We have to keep in mind that in 1970 Grotowski had declared that he would no longer do performances and was engaged in another type of research not aiming at a performance. However, this new research was developed starting from theatrical techniques. Its purpose was perhaps to make manifest one of the theatre's deeper meanings, also to those within that world.[44]

Theatre activity should be a particularly suitable tool. Yet European culture has traditionally kept it out of the array of spiritual vehicles. Prior to Stanislavski it seemed impossible to relate an actor's work to the vast themes of inner searching. […] Putting together metaphysics (the territory of the spirit so to speak) and acting techniques was out of the question. The secret revolution of twentieth-century theatre was that of infringing this taboo. Anyone who fails to understand this continues to belittle Stanislavski's science, linking it indissolubly with realism, to misunderstand Grotowski and as far as Artaud is concerned, to think he is only pretending to talk about theatrical fiction. […]
Sometimes those writing about the theatre like to wander off into the realm of esoterism, and by so doing do even more harm. Firstly, the usual harm caused by amateurs when they enter a field where deception may even be unconscious, and in which the rule, almost universally accepted, is that the more you know the more you keep quiet about it. Then there is the distraction, dragging attention away from an important and still under-exposed historical-cultural problem, which is not the overlapping of doctrines, religions and theatre

[44] In a conversation with Peter Brook in 1989, Grotowski commented on his 'absent presence' in the theatre, even in the period when he no longer did performances: '…these studies that I carry out, their conclusions, must serve theatre; the people with whom I work must learn the elements of craft in the performing arts; at the same time, my absence at the very centre of theatrical creativity must serve the presence of others. When I ask myself how I see this situation, I always remember the example of old Zossima, in *The Brothers Karamazov*. One day Alyosha asks Zossima, "What do you have in common with these people of the world, or with these peasants? Their life is different, and you are leading a life that is destined for the hermitage and for prayer". And Zossima replies, "No, you are wrong, that's not right. I do that in their stead, and they come here because they know that someone does this job in their stead". So if my absence from the place of theatrical creation serves the presence of others in this place, not in a metaphysical or metaphorical sense, but in the sense of craft, in this case the disappearance into the forest is justified. Otherwise, it is not justified.' Brook, *With Grotowski*, pp. 98–99.

but rather the theatre as a non-religious, non-doctrinal alternative vehicle, or abode, for the religious path. [...]

When spiritual excesses or practices make use of the theatre, it in no way means that a bridge has been built between theatre and religion, but rather that the theatre has the honour of being used *in place of a religion*. It might be said that in these cases, the most important aspects of the theatre are the work of the actor (i.e., working on actions as physical and mental scores) and silence: the possibility of not turning theatrical practice and experience into a doctrine. The *stage ritual*, which among rituals is perhaps the least dictatorial and the least full of overlapping beliefs or superstitions, may resemble a religious ritual only to a muddled mind. The more the stage ritual is conscious and precise, the greater the demonstration of its independence from the religious sphere.[45]

In one of the most important books on twentieth-century theatre, *Towards a Poor Theatre*, Jerzy Grotowski, interviewed by Eugenio Barba in the early 1960s, clearly outlined plans to build small theatres that might resemble new monasteries. This did not mean creating similarities between the life of an actor and that of a monk but entailed a much more sophisticated historical perspective, based on the awareness that nowadays the *devotion to the art* gives a social justification to an interpersonal research that was once justified and deemed to be socially useful only within the framework of religious devotion.

In short, the transformation spawned by Grotowski, passing from the performance phase and then the 'paratheatre' phase to what he called 'art as a vehicle', is actually not a 'transformation' at all but rather the recent and almost straight-line conclusion of an action announced from the outset and regularly developed step by step.

Historically, i.e., in the period since the late nineteenth century, Jerzy Grotowski is undoubtedly the most significant, coherent, secular and extreme figure in terms of how he lived the theatre. It was he who created the radical, indefinable and subtle value of the phenomenon that we generally indicate and camouflage – often even banalising – as the 'birth of stage direction'.[46]

---

[45] From this stance I believe that the historians of culture would find particularly useful the notion of theatre as an 'empty ritual', which crops up repeatedly in Eugenio Barba's writings, particularly in *The Paper Canoe. A Guide to Theatre Anthropology*, (London and New York: Routledge, 1995).

[46] Ferdinando Taviani, 'Quei cenni famosi oltre la fiamma' (Those Famous Gestures beyond the Flame), in Monique Borie, *Antonin Artaud. Il teatro e il ritorno alle origini. Un approccio antropologico* (Antonin Artaud. The Theatre and the Return to

The theatre laboratory was indicated not only as a place offering a path for individual transformation but also as the repository of a non-religious value: a value initially outlined by Grotowski, then developed by Taviani, and later reiterated and supported by the majority of the 'collective mind'.

Taviani and Grotowski were immediately backed up by Franco Ruffini, reaffirming the connection between the theatre (a certain type of theatre) and *value*, and taking up the problem of inner value with reference to Stanislavski. Later on we shall read in full Ruffini's speech at the Aarhus conference. But even before Aarhus he had said:

> There is no doubt that Stanislavski is a master of the theatre. But in what way must he be considered a *master*, referring not just to the realm of the theatre?
>
> There are two main reasons. The first is the way he solved the problem of *transmitting experience* through the written word. The transmission of experience is the key issue for every master, whose knowledge is not only discursive but *Knowledge* that seeps into the organism. It is not simply a theatre-specific problem. The second reason is the systematic and creative work he undertook on the edge, *between body and soul*, irrespective of its subsequent use in a performance setting.[47]

And here we arrive at the first real confrontation in our discussion.

The collective mind that was debating the question of theatre laboratories split into two factions on the question of body-soul and on the problem of the relationship between work on oneself and work on the performance.

Two values

I call it 'collective mind', but in actual fact it is the symbolic representation of a mental milieu. Earlier I called it 'us' and

the Origins: An Anthropological Approach) (Nuova Alfa Editoriale: Bologna, 1994), vii-xxxix (pp. viii-xi).

[47] Franco Ruffini, *Stanislavskij. Dal lavoro dell'attore al lavoro su di sé* (Stanislavski: From Work on the Actor to Work on Oneself), (Bari-Rome: Laterza, 2003), p. 3.

identified it with a few people of the ISTA staff: persons who share a professional imprinting and a twenty-year habit of discussing.

Faced with the prospect of the theatre as a non-religious abode and the image of theatrical work as not necessarily aimed at producing a performance, there was a split in this collective mind: on the one hand those increasingly interested in the radically new, spiritual and individual *value* emerging in the theatre through laboratories, and in particular through Grotowski's practice; on the other, those who did not want to stop asking questions about other matters, the technical and *practical* value of laboratoriality, and a work resulting in a performance.

What would be the point of the laboratory and our way of thinking about it, if we forgot about the performance?

But the problem of working on oneself was delicate and complex. Within the 'collective mind', it initially gained the upper hand.

Constructing performances and furthering knowledge

Eugenio Barba then intervened in an attempt to calm the atmosphere, asserting that 'a theatre laboratory has the vocation to construct performances (arranging an encounter with unknown spectators through the performance) just as much as a vocation to further knowledge on the foundations of the stage profession. A laboratory is alive in this tension or contradiction'. But they appeared to be overly subjective remarks, seeing that he (unlike Grotowski) and his theatre laboratory had stubbornly continued to create performances. The picture he was painting of the theatre laboratory was too much like a self-portrait.

During the course of the discussion he had also said that the notion of theatre laboratory 'is marked by the ability to distinguish, according to one's own experiences, what is useful to transmit, irrespective of the individualities of one's aesthetic choices'. And was not this a typical tendency of his and of Odin Teatret, albeit a tendency shared by Stanislavski? Wasn't it almost impudent for him to suggest this as a general rule for a theatre laboratory? His words therefore seemed too subjective and were not given the weight they might have had in other circumstances.

This was a specific case of a broader question, a difficult problem of method wrapped up in the illusion of familiarity. Eugenio Barba was the promoter, the provoker, the host and even an important subject of the discussion, all at the same time. These different roles, becoming entwined, were in danger of becoming muddled and belittled. Sometimes, frequenting the same people for a long time, mutual interests, solidarity and friendship cease to be tools of knowledge: when you cease trying to understand him, a friend is not usually asked questions but rather given advice. It appears to be a human problem, yet it is an error in a cognitive process: the loss, or the dwindling, of estrangement.

All of this has to do with a subject that is only apparently secondary: theatre and science. Or we might say: theatre science.

Remembering Grotowski's interest in Niels Bohr's Institute (and in the activity of his brother, a physicist in Poland), Barba suggested that when looking at the problem of theatre laboratories, it was also necessary to consider the relationship between theatre and science. He spoke about scientific research and behavioural science (strong traces of which remain in *A Dictionary of Theatre Anthropology: The Secret Art of the Performer*, his book, written in collaboration with Nicola Savarese and published all over the world)[48]. He recalled his own interest in studies on the human brain, guided by Danish psychologist Peter Elsass, and in the method of scientific research, a sphere of knowledge in which he was assisted by Jean-Marie Pradier,

[48] Eugenio Barba and Nicola Savarese, *A Dictionary of Theatre Anthropology: The Secret Art of the Performer*, ed. by Richard Gough, trans. by Richard Fowler (London: Routledge, 2006; 2nd edn).

a former psycho-linguist and later theatre professor at the University of Paris VIII. Barba spoke of the conferences organised by Pradier on the relationship between theatre and science, focusing primarily on biology-related problems. He had attended all of them alongside some of his actors during a period of intense research between 1979 and 1991. He recalled the importance of the collaboration between ISTA and specialists such as Henri Laborit, a French biologist and philosopher. He stressed the importance of these studies as regards the very concept of theatre anthropology and thus of ISTA. He talked about the dialogue maintained with scientists by Stanislavski and Meyerhold.

Seeking an area of research a considerable way from one's own, speculating, feeding off the discoveries made in this area and concocting keywords or slogans is a path that opens up exciting prospects. But as soon as the initial novelty wears off, one must know when to give it up. Basically this is a way of altering the usual images and metaphors of one's own field of work and of using other, estranging ones. Some of the discussion participants were impatient to turn to theatre science. Kolankiewicz patiently returned to the image of the alchemist's laboratory.

But Barba offered up an alternative to the tendency of identifying the theatre laboratory with 'work on oneself'. He suggested looking at the most subtle and unstable of disciplines: 'theatre science' – the science that seeks to investigate principles that, if not eternal, are at least recurring in the fragile art of the theatre. This science makes an attempt to systematise this art in formulas, theories and know-how that can be transmitted. The great masters of the early twentieth century all appear to be inspired by the same excitement, despite their radically different theories, as if they finally began to bring to light what actually governs the external appearance of the theatre.[49]

---

[49] Peter Brook is also aware of this association between theatre and science and emphasises it to throw light on certain traits of theatre research. He quotes Sta-

An illusion that has never been dulled and never confirmed.

Interlude: some thoughts on Decroux

In this stalemate situation, Marco De Marinis, an Italian scholar who has closely followed Barba's activity at ISTA and studied twentieth-century mime, came to the Aarhus conference in 2004 to speak about Decroux. De Marinis's talk served not only to give us an insight into Decroux but also to sum up and settle many issues either taken for granted or left unresolved.

Decroux is certainly a key figure, and often relatively neglected because, more than anything, it is difficult to pigeonhole him, unless a unique category is created for him. This also happens because, as De Marinis stressed, it is impossible to put him among the Studios of the early twentieth century or among the theatre laboratories of the second half of the century. He belongs to both categories in some ways and to neither.

But he was someone who had to be remembered, at that point of the discussion, because Decroux has always been considered as being devoted to his school and not overly interested in creating performances. De Marinis told us to beware of this simplistic view:

> In actual fact, as his pupils of several generations unanimously proclaim, Decroux was not only attracted to but actually obsessed by creation, from the start of his career to the close of his school in 1987 (when he was 89!). [...] The ounce of truth contained in these clichés relates to Decroux's difficulties as a stage actor, his relationship with the spectator, the gap between his extraordinary talent as a research-

---

nislavski: 'I am sure that [in theatre] between the great aspiration for quality and concrete work, there must be some precise elements. There must be a "science"'. Then Brook comments: 'And from start to finish, when he discovered emotional and then physical actions, he searched for the key in a scientific manner. [...] Grotowski created a science of the theatre. Thus it is possible to connect him to other, very different people who were also engaged in this way of "not going beyond". There is not only Stanislavski, but also Craig in England or Meyerhold, Brecht, Artaud...'. Brook, *With Grotowski*, p. 68.

er and his aspiration towards the absolute, on the one hand, and his modest abilities as a mime actor, on the other. It also refers to the fact that while creative work was fundamental for him, as I have already said, he considered it above all (if not only) a test bed for the knowledge acquired during the course of his extraordinary and very long journey through the unexplored land (at least when he began, in the 1920s)[50] of corporeal expressiveness and pre-expressiveness.[51]

De Marinis recalled the history of Decroux, the creator of corporeal mime, busy teaching in his Paris School right up until the 1980s.

He was educated in the great season of the early-twentieth-century avant-garde movement and began his career as theatrical creator, researcher and teacher in the second half of the 1920s. Decroux obtained greatest public recognition (albeit relative), first in France and then in the rest of the world, from the mid-1940s to the early 1960s. He taught almost uninterruptedly for over half a century, first at Dullin's Atelier Theatre and then at his own school.

De Marinis spoke about the breadth of his artistic and pedagogical work, which could not be contained within a single formula, and he warned us against speaking about Decroux in the singular.

This point touched upon a very sensitive problem, because practically no laboratory, in either the first or second half of the twentieth century, had remained faithful to its origins. The problems not only of plurality but also of decadence, old age, even death – glorious, anonymous or miserable – continued to gnaw away, perhaps unfairly but inevitably, in many people's minds.

---

[50] In a book from 1921, *L'oeuvre d'art vivant* (The Work of Living Art), Adolphe Appia speaks of 'The Great Unknown' with regard to 'our ignorance regarding our own body, our entire organism, *from an aesthetic point of view*'. Appia, *The Work of Living Art: A Theory of the Theatre*, trans. by H. D. Albright (Miami: University of Miami Press, 1960), pp. 68–78 (p. 68).

[51] I quote from the transcription of Marco De Marinis' address at the Aarhus conference, 'Étienne Decroux: why a theatre laboratory?', revised by the author.

De Marinis then spoke about the importance of Decroux's invention of corporeal mime:

> Decroux's corporeal mime was created not to *reform* the tradition of pantomime but to *revolutionise* the theatre. More precisely, it is a response (extreme, of course, as well as utopian) to the same question raised before by other pedagogue-directors (primarily his two mentors: Copeau and Craig) in their research in the early twentieth century: *how to make an art out of the theatre*. In other words, how to raise the theatre's status from that of a trade, pertaining to the sphere of entertainment and evasion, to that of cultural and artistic relevance, to an aesthetic creation'. Expressing the view shared by most of the masters of the early twentieth century that theatre is, basically, the *actor*, Decroux had worked to create an art of the actor, or in other words a *stage presence*, a body in action. It is only by starting from work on one's own *body* that one might hope to attain the status of art.

'What is art, what is an artist in Decroux's eyes?', De Marinis continued.

> For him, art requires the artist's complete mastery of his means of expression, of his material. Accordingly, the work of art represents the result of an unrestricted, voluntary and conscious intervention of the artist on his material, without being dominated by it, but instead dominating, transforming and minimising accidental interference.

In Decroux's opinion, the reason why our contemporary theatre has this shortcoming, preventing it from attaining the status of an independent art form, lies in the non-appreciation of the actor's *double handicap* as an (aspiring) artist. According to him the most serious aspect going against the creation of the stage actor, compared with all other forms of aesthetic creation that are not based on the use of the living human body, is mainly the fact that, as Meyerhold stressed, the 'artist' and the 'material' are one and the same. The second handicap is that this 'material' (the human body) already has a form, apparently unalterable, before the artist intervenes. Western theatre has taken this unfavourable characteristic as something that cannot be remedied, surrendering to the facts without a struggle. And De Marinis added:In order to be able to *really* be an artist, the actor has only one way, Decroux believed: he must take the road of 'body counterfeiting' and carry on until the end. Counterfeiting of the body means, again following the teaching of the early theatre masters, deconstructing and recomposing it, causing automatisms to cease.

The human body

This, I reflected as I sat at the Aarhus conference, had been the *theatre science* as hoped for, dreamed and sought by the early masters: the search for and acquisition of instruments to work on the human body, to turn it into a solid, reliable and *different* tool. This *science* represented the will and the illusion of early-twentieth-century directors to begin again from the most ephemeral and unstable of artistic means – the human body – to study its mechanisms, both visible and invisible, and then to change it from the core. The core being the skeleton and the soul of the actor.

The protagonists of the Great Reform had conducted basic research to make the human body *different*, enabling it to speak its language, which is the essence of the theatre, but which can easily become puerile, inadequate and muddled.

That was the purpose of all Studios, a term we used to indicate a more complex reality, made up of studios, workshops and special schools, such as that of Émile Jaques-Dalcroze at Hellerau or Decroux in Paris. They were places where 'different' bodies were created in an attempt to develop a body language that was not bumbling, over-simple or hidden beneath other languages.

They were of course laboratories for creating 'different' human bodies, I thought to myself, as De Marinis carried on speaking, but above all they allowed bodies to manage to think in their different languages, and actors to create different ways of thinking. Automatisms are not only in the body.

In all previous centuries the *social diversity* of the actor had usually been sufficient to give him an out-of-the-ordinary way of thinking.

Conclusions on Decroux

Finally, De Marinis touched upon what he believed to be most profound and significant in Decroux's teaching: its deeply political meaning. Although he had repeatedly brought up Decroux's obsession with performance, something he had maintained right up to the end, even though he had actually produced very few performances, his main teaching – according to De Marinis – went beyond the frontiers of the theatre:

> That the work of the actor is first and foremost a work on oneself is one of the great ideas proposed and implemented in twentieth-century theatre by Stanislavski and his successors, also based on important external inspirations: that of esoterical or in any case spiritual research, for example, conducted by 'life masters' such as Rudolf Steiner and George I. Gurdjieff, who all start off from the body and from movement.[52] [...]
> I believe that the actor's work on himself forms the backbone for the openly *political nature* ascribed by Decroux (an old anarchical trade unionist and, in the 1930s, a member of the agit-prop theatre and follower of the French *Front Populaire*) to his research on mime. He spoke of movement activists: 'Being in mime means being an activist, a militant of movement in a seated world'.[53] He also argued that the art of mime 'is political or Promethean, since it is opposed to the *religious* art', which is limited to contemplating or pretending to act

[52] Cf. Marco De Marinis, *In cerca dell'attore: Un bilancio del Novecento teatrale* (In Search of the Actor: An appraisal of Twentieth Century Theatre) (Rome: Bulzoni, 2000) pp. 183–225; Mirella Schino, 'Teorici, registi e pedagoghi', in *Storia del teatro moderno e contemporaneo* (The History of Modern and Contemporary Theatre), ed. by Roberto Alonge and Guido Davico Bonino, vol. III: *Avanguardie e utopie del teatro. Il Novecento* (Avant-gardes and Utopias in the Theatre) (Turin: Einaudi, 2001), pp. 5–97.

[53] Cf. Corinne Soum's address in *Le arti del gesto. Le trasversali* (Arts of the Gesture: Transversals), ed. by Ribes Veiga, (Rome: ELART, 1994). This volume contains the proceedings of the eponymous conference held in Mantova from 5–7 November 1993.

(such as dance that, for this reason, Decroux viewed as a basically religious art). Mime *acts* and *produces* realities rather than imitating them, it creates its own world instead of passively going into ecstasy over a world already created. So for him, mime is not only an art but a philosophy of life, a philosophy *tout court*, a veritable vision of the world, of the nature of the human being and his fate.[54]

If we remove the preaching emphasis (Decroux the teacher and orator could often be accused of this), what remains is what many other twentieth-century masters have discovered and practised:

– the ethical-spiritual (and thus also *political*) effects of the actor's technical work on himself;

– the possibility of using the actor's techniques as a means to achieve a *personal discipline*,[55] as in Grotowski's research into 'art as vehicle'.[56]

Recapping

In the meantime, both sides of the collective mind had put forward a hypothesis on the laboratory-performance relationship.

One side, interested in the inner value of the theatre, took a position that can be summarised as follows: within the problem of laboratoriality, what appear to be practical solutions regarding the actor's stage life also tend to exist on their own as another type of *value*, masked behind devotion to the art.

The other side said: Of course, we can accept the existence in some cases of this 'inner' use of the laboratorial zone. A private and individual use, designed to take a path towards inner value and self-knowledge. This was perhaps the most extreme (and thus most striking) aspect of late-twentieth-cen-

[54] Cf. Marco De Marinis, *Mimo e teatro nel Novecento* (Mime and Theatre in the Twentieth Century), p. 132.

[55] Ferdinando Taviani, 'Passaggi e sottopassaggi' (Passages and Underpassages), in *Drammaturgia dell'attore* (The Actor's Dramaturgy), ed. by Marco De Marinis (Bologna: I Quaderni del Battello Ebbro, 1997), 123–154 (p. 145).

[56] Cf. Grotowski, 'From the Theatre Company to Art as Vehicle'; Thomas Richards, *The Edge-Point of Performance*, interview with Lisa Wolford (Pontedera: Fondazione Pontedera Teatro, 1997).

tury theatre and the most hidden (and thus most surprising) aspect of the theatre in the first half of the same century. But another use is also made of the laboratorial zone. This relates not to the individual actor, his skills, abilities, inner life – indeed, not at all to inner value. It refers instead to the *scenic life* of the performance, its *bios* and that of the actor. And it undoubtedly refers to the spectator's presence.

They were two different though not incompatible stances. Yet once again, as already in the past, they were set in (violent) opposition to each other.

Thus the discussion on the relationship between laboratory and performance stalled on these positions. Kolankiewicz, Taviani, Ruffini and others, and above all Grotowski, were interested in highlighting the potential for self-knowledge inherent in the theatre. The Italian theatre scholar Fabrizio Cruciani had in his writings from the 1970s already noted that the founding fathers of the Great Reform had also sought in the theatre something that went beyond its existing boundaries. Grotowski had stressed that this lengthy process was possible while rehearsing, free from all censorship. He had also stressed that he had always been interested in this type of rehearsal time and not so much in the actual process of constructing a performance. Kolankiewicz had emphasised the *quasi* alchemical process of transformation inherent in the idea of the theatre laboratory, while Osiński stressed that the creation of a theatre laboratory had been crucial for Grotowski in casting off the fetters of a repertory theatre and the production rules of a socialist regime.

This led to a heated discussion – inspired mainly by Fabrizio Cruciani's writings about the relationship between *research time* and *performance construction time*, two tendencies deemed by some to be radically different.[57]

Nevertheless it was becoming ever more apparent, even to that part of the collective mind more interested in the the-

---

[57] We shall observe Fabrizio Cruciani's views more closely in chapter four.

atre as a non-religious abode, that the usefulness and sense of laboratorial practice could not be *limited* to research of a spiritual or inner nature. This would have led to the removal from the laboratorial question of key figures such as Meyerhold or Barba. Finally, it was clear that laboratorial paths were those that wandered furthest from work focusing on performance.

A space with bodies and shadows, or a mental space

I have used 'us' when describing the discussion on theatre laboratories, and I have spoken of the 'collective mind'. I have described its crises and its inner rifts. But I would not wish to give the impression of a group of people gathered together in a room – for a conference or simply a meeting – talking and talking until they become a collective mind.

That may have been true for some of us in conferences, meetings and debates. But some of the contributions I am reporting here came years before our discussion on theatre laboratories. Some of the most important voices – Jerzy Grotowski and Fabrizio Cruciani – were already deceased and participated through the written word, through books and the memory of their thoughts and ideas.

There can be no doubt that the actor's work on himself, which first came to the surface with Grotowski, was an important product of laboratorial practice.

But if one studies the past, to what extent has the shadow of Grotowski and his decision to abandon the performance side of the theatre, while remaining in the 'theatre orbit', weighed upon us? Anyone involved in the question of theatre laboratories has had to gauge the impact of his choice, becoming the filter through which we have looked at this question.

And while it is of course possible to discern the sense of inner value in the work of Stanislavski, Artaud or other directors of the Great Reform in the early twentieth century, we often view their activity through eyes conditioned by Grotowski.

Our very way of looking has been conditioned.

As I reflected on this, I found myself suddenly being pushed backwards in time.

A history of emotions

Theatre anthropology should also investigate another 'level of organisation' and deal with the history of emotions in the theatre. A history that, for once, does not focus on *how* to provoke emotion, but on *which* strings are plucked in a particular theatrical context. It should take into account which emotions are to be considered as 'right' and thus to be stimulated and why, and how they change and why, and in which historical and mental contexts. And what the emotions are that various audiences would hope for or demand, and how all this changes and is transformed, depending on contexts and points in time. Such a study would allow us to see wholly new zones of the theatre. There Natyashastra would certainly figure in this history, and doubtless Zeami too, but above all, and even more exotically, compared with theatre culture in the West, Denis Diderot, who depicted the possibilities of a new gamut of emotions between the stage and the audience in his novel-*cum*-drama *Le fils naturel* (The Illegitimate Son).[58]

It appears clear that the advent of Grotowski constituted a revolution in the history of theatre emotions.

Grotowski himself underlined the different kind of emotional involvement required of his actors. This is another purpose of the laboratory, to alter the emotional and existential involvement of the actor. But for the audience, too, after Grotowski's intervention, there was a transformation of the emotional sphere of the theatre experience.

[58] Cf. Mirella Schino, 'Diderot a Lampedusa' (Diderot to Lampedusa), *Teatro e Storia*, no. 28 (2007), 145–173.

With a Grotowski performance, the purely *affective* sphere, which seemed to be the only one in which the art of the actor could dominate, is put to one side. What for Grotowski seems to become the very essence of the theatre is the ability to develop a symbolic dimension and to create profound images.

This is the new strength of Grotowski's performances: with their specific language, and not only through the playscript, they could develop a symbolic dimension whose effect was much deeper than the mere verbal language of the text.

That was partly what had happened in the early years of the twentieth century with Stanislavski, Meyerhold, Copeau, Craig and many others whose activity was often confused with symbolism, expressionism and other stylistic categories. But with Grotowski's theatre – perhaps as a result of differences with the intellectual Brechtian theatre of the 1950s prior to him – this new symbolic dimension is clearly visible. We might presume that he was not the one to invent it, but he certainly was the one to *bring it out into the open*. After Grotowski the new cultural role of the theatre and of performance coincides with this dimension.

Moreover, there was another revolution, perhaps even more important, which may be appreciated more easily after the explanation of Decroux's work. With Grotowski's performances it became evident that *thought*, in the theatre, can basically be transmitted through the actors' bodies and the spectators' senses. Here I am talking about *thought*, not sensual stimuli or feelings but abstract problems and archetypal impulses.

Body language

The theatre has always been an ambiguous art: too corporeal, imprecise, apparently able merely to depict sensual emotions. The discovery that the body, and not the spoken word, was particularly suitable for expressing symbolic and abstract meanings had already been the great revolution of the Great Reform in the early 1900s. In the second half of the century, the theatre is expressly recognised as an art in which the 'body culture' has a special place: something much broader than plain physical expressiveness, with a complex non-verbal language and countless logical, sensitive, irrational and rational ramifications. Consequently the theatre also takes on the semblance of a place that is *particularly suitable* for developing the potential of the body, a special instrument for self-knowledge as well as abstract knowledge. This is true both for those who do theatre and for those who watch it.

Body language had always been considered a weakness of the art of the theatre, or just difficult to accept. But now it became its strength, at a time when the actor's body was no longer merely the instrument of a (still very important) sensual presence and was no longer viewed only from a genetic or anatomical perspective. It became a *body in movement*, considered and accepted as a *language*. A language that could not be translated but that was perhaps best able to express profound images.

Probably for the first time since Diderot's revolt, the emotions expressed by the theatre were no longer individual (even though Grotowski spoke a great deal about the spectator in the singular) but rather supra-individual. In the first phase of his theatrical work Grotowski called them archetypal. With Grotowski the theatre stressed, for the first time in black and white, that the subject matter was the zone accessed *through* a sensory and emotive experience, yet it did not focus on individual emotions and feelings. Rather it related to the supra-individual level of feelings, and thus to self-knowledge, but through 'the other'. It related to a type of research that we can certainly brand as spiritual but was carried forward and transmitted through the body.

For these reasons, I concluded in my own inner monologue, the role of the laboratorial zone is *evidently* essential for developing body movements on stage that are capable of arousing profound images, and of speaking with their mysterious language to the body and the mind of the spectator.

One might ask why, on the subject of the autonomous language of the body, the great lesson provided by the protagonists of the Great Reform was buried halfway through the century. We can answer that it was a period of historical disasters, such as have caused the disappearance of other civilisations.

But it was Grotowski who dusted down this lesson and rendered it evident. We also know the *way* in which the body became something other than a complex expressive tool. Eugenio Barba had this to say back in 1965:

> The systematic aptitude of the actor is connected to systematic and continual training, consisting of special lessons that are separate from rehearsals. The programme of exercises should not be thought of as a closed field. It is subject to continual change depending on the actor's theatre tasks and the progress he makes. The belief that a 'technique' (meaning an arsenal of accumulated skills) has already been prepared is wrong and in practice would lead only to a reiteration of platitudes (stereotypes).
>
> In actual fact, there is no fixed, well established technique. There are only technical hurdles as the actor advances in his craft, obstacles that have to be overcome continually by performing practical 'elementary' exercises. *The purpose of these exercises is not to broaden one's corporeal skills but rather to annul the body, in other words to eliminate its resistance in order to immediately realise one's psychic impulses.*[59]

Barba (and in this case one should say Barba and Grotowski, as we are quoting from the book that Barba wrote on Grotowski after collaborating with Teatr Laboratorium) also pointed out that the process of 'self-penetration' can be painful, and certainly disconcerting, in the actor's work. He stressed the importance of:

---

[59] Eugenio Barba, *Alla ricerca del teatro perduto* (In Search of a Lost Theatre) (Padova: Marsilio 1965), p. 117. Author's emphasis.

applying the brake on form, on artificiality. The actor, performing an act of self-penetration, starts off as if on a journey which he recounts to the spectator, in a sort of invitation, through reflexes of his voice and movements. The signs used by the actor must be articulate. Expressiveness is always connected to forms of contrasts and contradictions. Self-penetration that is not accompanied by discipline does not become a liberation but is a form of biological chaos. [...]

The theatre that seeks to provoke an experience of collective introversion must go back to its origins and, through a physical and direct contact between actors and spectators, become a collective ceremony. There cannot be a split between those who are there peacefully taking in the scene and those getting involved in the action. The stage-audience dichotomy must disappear. [...]

The commitment of such a theatre aims to place man's conscience in touch with his situation and his history, his dreams and aspirations, his cruelty and his candour, obliging him to face up to his responsibilities as a moral and social being.[60]

Barba's words here are youthful and in many ways rigid. But they contain valuable points. This way of stressing the risk of 'biological chaos', for example, is fundamental in a context as elusive and difficult as that of the theatre conceived as self-penetration.

The spectator

I thus ended my inner detour on Grotowski and his performances and returned to the problem of the relationship between laboratory and performance. As already mentioned (but perhaps we should repeat it here), the collective mind had taken up two different positions.

One half was interested in the laboratory phenomenon as detached from performance, heralding profound experiences for the actor, independent of the production of performances, indeed opposed to it.

---

[60] *Ibid*. p. 117.

The other half insisted on the relationship between laboratory and performance, arguing that in light of the 'inner-life' developments introduced by the first half of the collective mind, the laboratory-performance relationship could be seen in a new light, no longer in terms of an apprenticeship or pure and simple training. The relationship between theatre laboratories and the performance should be radically reviewed, since it was not so simple and was even contradictory, but *for this very reason* more interesting. Now it seemed that we could begin to make out the physiognomy and the relevance of this complicated relationship.

Grotowski (or rather Grotowski plus Barba) showed us:
– the knowledge-building process that could be created by the theatre
– the way this process of self-knowledge happened, i.e., through the body
– the part, the zone and the temporal area of the theatre where this process was taking place, i.e., the time of *preparation* of the performance.

With Stanislavski and Meyerhold preparation time had become important, and had consequently become longer. But again, it was with Grotowski, and right after with Odin Teatret, that all of this became explicit and evident. The attention that had until then been focused on the performance began to alternate with that focusing on the *preparatory path*.

The 'path' is that part of theatre work that *turns its back on performance in order to prepare it*. It must transcend the performance in order to give it real depth so as to prolong the journey needed for the preparation, thus widening the gap between *daily life* and *performance*. This gap is perhaps the zone where the actor embarks on his processes of self-knowledge, but it is certainly a vital zone as far as the performance is concerned, because it is in this gap that all the performance's flavours, moods and depth are formed.

Turning one's back

Laboratorial activity cannot just be a zone where theatrical knowledge is developed over a longer-than-normal time-frame. It is not even an area *parallel* to artistic creation, but it has a precise relationship with it: it turns its back on artistic creation, but only to get to this destination via a longer, more winding road. It establishes a mental and temporal distance. This distance has turned out to be fundamental in uncovering the most unexpected meanings of the performance and in constructing a body language with all its most unforeseeable and mysterious aspects.

The practical use of the laboratory is not that of improving the training of actors nor that of discovering gestures, ways of moving, new physical and verbal nodes. Rather it is the possibility of *widening the gap between daily life and performance*, but in a non-random mode. If we think of the 'path' as a way of creating this gap and of lengthening the journey required to prepare the performance, we can begin to *envision* its practical use.

Even spiritual values could emerge along this path – which is not simple physical training but may be viewed as a *bifurcation*, an extreme tension.

> Why are we concerned with art? To cross our frontiers, exceed our limitations, fill our emptiness – fulfil ourselves. This is not a condition but a process in which what is dark in us slowly becomes transparent. In this struggle with one's own truth, this effort to peel off the life-mask, the theatre, with its full-fleshed perceptivity, has always seemed to me a place of provocation. It is capable of challenging itself and its audience by violating accepted stereotypes of vision, feeling, and judgment – more jarring because it is imaged in the human organism's breath, body and inner impulses. This defiance of taboos, this transgression, provides the shock which rips off the mask, enabling us to give ourselves nakedly to something which is impossible to define but which contains Eros and Caritas.[61]
> [...]

---

[61] Jerzy Grotowski, 'Towards a Poor Theatre' in *Towards a Poor Theatre*, pp. (pp. 21–22).

The word research should not bring to mind scientific research. Nothing could be further from what we are doing than science *sensu stricto*, and not only because of our lack of qualifications, but also because of our lack of interest in that kind of work.

[...]

The actor is a man who works in public with his body, offering it publicly. If this body restricts itself to demonstrating what it is – something that any average person can do – then it is not an obedient instrument capable of performing a spiritual act. If it is exploited for money and to win the favour of the audience, then the art of acting borders on prostitution. It is a fact that for many centuries the theatre has been associated with prostitution in one sense of the word or another.

[...]

Just as only a great sinner can become a saint according to the theologians (Let us not forget the Revelation: 'So then because thou art lukewarm, and neither cold nor hot, I will spue thee out of my mouth'), in the same way the actor's wretchedness can be transformed into a kind of holiness. The history of the theatre has numerous examples of this.

Don't get me wrong. I speak about 'holiness' as an unbeliever. I mean a 'secular holiness'. If the actor, by setting himself a challenge publicly challenges others, and through excess, profanation and outrageous sacrilege reveals himself by casting off his everyday mask, he makes it possible for the spectator to undertake a similar process of self-penetration.

[...]

The difference between the 'courtesan actor' and the 'holy actor' is the same as the difference between the skill of a courtesan and the attitude of giving and receiving which springs from true love: in other words, self-sacrifice. The essential thing in this second case is to be able to eliminate any disturbing elements in order to be able to overstep every conceivable limit. In the first case it is a question of the existence of the body; in the other, rather of its non-existence. The technique of the 'holy actor' is an *inductive technique* (i.e., a technique of elimination), whereas that of the 'courtesan actor' is a *deductive technique* (i.e., an accumulation of skills).[62]

---

[62] Jerzy Grotowski 'The Theatre's New Testament', interview by Eugenio Barba, in *Towards a Poor Theatre*, pp. 27–54 (pp. 27, 32, 33, 35, respectively).

Scilla, 1996

I recall a session of the University of Eurasian Theatre at Scilla, in 1996, when all our internal discussion had revolved around Grotowski: not the qualities or peculiarities of the theatre man, not his qualities as leader and a teacher of Performers, but rather his influence on European and American theatre in the second half of the twentieth century. We discussed Grotowski as a model and point of reference. In 1998 Barba came out with the book *Land of Ashes and Diamonds*, which spoke about his Polish apprenticeship.[63] We commented upon the book. Then discussion moved on to the theatre laboratory, in which the 'Grotowski question' naturally played a part.

Looking back, it seems clear: we were moving around a stumbling block. We had ended up identifying it with Grotowski, but with one or two question marks. We couldn't even identify it with Odin Teatret or with any other precise theatre. There was no model as such. At the same time, despite all our contradictions and differences, when we spoke about 'theatre laboratory' we all seemed to know what it meant.

The origins of the theatre laboratory

The first laboratories to emerge in the second half of the twentieth century were Grotowski's Teatr Laboratorium (1959) and Barba's Odin Teatret (1964), as we all knew. Before them, there had been other phenomena that might be considered similar. For some of us these precedents were harbingers of a related phenomenon, while others did not agree. Yet it was clear that in the mid twentieth century there had been a turning point, a break from the past caused by the theatres of Grotowski and Barba. These two theatres, in the arro-

---

[63] Eugenio Barba, *Land of Ashes and Diamonds: My Apprenticeship in Poland. Followed by 26 Letters from Jerzy Grotowski to Eugenio Barba*, trans. from Italian by Judy Barba and from Polish by Judy and Eugenio Barba (Aberystwyth: Black Mountain Press, 1999).

gance of youth, appeared to be well aware of the novelty and importance of their work. But they could not have imagined the height of the tidal wave they caused, the effect of many different forces, demands, hopes and expectations, too many indeed to name here.

The presence in Western Europe of Barba's theatre and Grotowski's tours with his performances also had a secondary effect that could not have been imagined: the rediscovery of a connection going back to the *Wielka Reforma* and the great theoreticians and directors of the early twentieth century.

I have always thought of Barba as a 'Polish' director. When in 1961 Barba, still quite ignorant about the theatre, arrived in Poland with its extraordinary theatre culture, not only did he complete his apprenticeship there, but he also soaked up a way of thinking with respect to the history of the theatre and directing. When talking about the 'birth of directing', Polish scholars and theatre people use a less ambiguous formula than the French and the Italians: *Wielka Reforma*, the Great Reform. It was at the Warsaw theatre school in the early 1960s that Barba became aware of the existence of a *Wielka Reforma* and heard about the fundamental division that separated twentieth-century theatre – with Stanislavski, Meyerhold, Craig, Appia as well as Tairov, Vakhtangov, Leon Schiller, Osterwa, Piscator, the agit-prop groups et al. – from the previous centuries. But it was not only from lessons in the theatre school: the *Wielka Reforma*, and related names and topics, kept popping up in leading Polish magazines, such as *Dialog* and *Pamiętnik Teatralny*, as subjects for study and as role models for contemporary performances. In Poland the connection with such an intense and relatively close past appears to have remained incredibly alive and fervent.

In Western Europe the memory of the breakthrough of modern theatrical art was generally quite dim compared with Eastern Europe. Dust had quickly settled over the picture, we might say. There had been a dramatic severing caused by

Nazism, fascism and World War II, then the separation of the two blocs, divided by the Iron Curtain.[64]

On the other side of the Iron Curtain things had gone a little differently. In the 1920s, after the Russian revolution, for a few years something had occurred which had never been seen anywhere: a global transformation of the theatre. And its essential traits, findings, values and techniques had been transmitted. This transmission was one of the merits of the revolution – at least as long as it was tolerated by Stalin.

Even when this was all dismantled in the Soviet Union and in the bloc under its control, a sense of continuity remained. Barba is, to all intents and purposes, as far as his education is concerned, a director of Polish origin, who grew up in a milieu that carried on the work of the early twentieth century theatre reformers. Now we can see it even more clearly through the work not only of Grotowski and Barba but also of great artists from Eastern Europe, directors such as Kantor, Nekrošius and Vasiliev.

When in 1964 Barba left Poland and went back to Oslo,[65] and when Grotowski's performances started touring abroad, only then did Western Europe begin to learn about the *Wielka Reforma*. Barba added something too: the idea that the great masters of the past were still alive, that we could easily learn from them, not in an abstract manner or in search of utopias but simply from a practical and technical point of view. Providing they were studied in depth.

[64] On this subject Peter Brook recalls: 'When I began to work in the theatre in England, I had a lot of luck. There was no school there, no theory. Everything was practical. In the English theatre of that time, which was often boring and nearly moribund, there were many good actors. But no one ever admitted that theory could exist. For my part I had vaguely heard mention of a certain Stanislavski: when I opened his book, I found it so heavy and solemn that I immediately put it to one side. And I was the only one to have read at least three pages! At that time, no idea from the "continent", as we say, made any impact in England'. Brook, *With Grotowski*, pp. 64–65.

[65] Barba left Norway in January 1961 for Poland where he attended the Warsaw theatre school and met Grotowski, staying until April 1964 when he returned to Oslo and founded Odin Teatret.

In recent years, I have been using the word 'Disorder' more and more when speaking of the theatre craft, aware that it creates confusion. For me it has two opposite meanings: the absence of logic and rigour characterising nonsensical and chaotic works or the logic and rigour which provoke *the experience of bewilderment* in the spectator. I ought to have two different words for this. Instead I use an orthographic trick – the difference between small and capital letters – to distinguish disorder as a loss of energy, from Disorder as the irruption of an energy that confronts us with the unknown. [...]

When I think about the extremism of their thought, the protagonists of the theatre revolt in the twentieth century, from Stanislavski onwards, become for me *maîtres fous*, masters of Disorder.

In a climate of aesthetic, technical and economic renewal, they raised questions which were so absurd that they were met with indifference and derision. Since the incandescent core of these questions was wrapped in well-formulated professional theories, these were considered as attacks against the art of the theatre, or 'utopias', which is a harmless way of saying that we do not need to take them seriously. Here are some of these cores:

– to look for *life* in a world of papier-mâché
– to let the *truth* stream into a world of disguises
– to reach *sincerity* through pretence
– to transform the training of the actor (an individual who imitates and represents people different from himself) into a path leading towards the *integrity* of a New Human Being.

Some of the masters of the extreme added insanity to insanity. Unable to understand that those 'utopias' were unachievable, they realised them.

Let's imagine an artist today applying for a grant from the Ministry of Culture to research the Truth through theatre. Or the director of a theatre school writing in its programme: here we teach acting with the aim of creating a New Human Being. Or again, a director who demands from his actors the skill to dance in order to mirror the harmony of the Celestial Spheres. It would be permissible to consider them as nutcases. Why, then, do theatre historians describe Stanislavski, Copeau and Appia as if their mad questions were noble utopias and original theories?

Today it doesn't cost anything to see in their apparent madness a sensible reaction to the strains of an epoch that was jeopardising the survival of the theatre. It is easy, today, to recognise perspicacity, coherence and cleverness in the *bewilderment* that the masters of Disorder brought to the theatre of their time. They rejected its centuries-old organisation, overturned hierarchies, sabotaged the well-tested communicative conventions between the stage and the audience, cut the umbilical cord with literature and surface realism. They brutally stripped the theatre down and reduced it to its essence. They justified themselves with a paradox: they gave life to performances that were unimaginable in their extremism, originality and artistic refinement in order to deny that theatre is *only* art. Each of them, with different words, stressed that the theatre's vocation was to break intimate, professional, ethical, social, religious or cultural chains.

We are used to reading the history of modern theatre upside-down. We don't start from the incandescent cores of the questions and the obsessions of the masters of Disorder but from the reasonableness or the poetry of their printed words. Their pages have an authoritative and persuasive tone. But for each of them there must have been many nights of solitude and fear when suspecting that the windmills they fought against were invincible giants.

Today we see them portrayed in picturesque photos: intelligent faces, well-fed and ironically placid like Stanislavski, suggestive, begging kings like Artaud, proud and aware of their own intellectual superiority like Craig, eternally frowning and pugnacious like Meyerhold. It is impossible to sense in each of these bright spirits the incapability to forget or to accept their own invisible chains. We are unable to feel that their efficacy derives in part from the strain of tearing themselves away from a condition of impotent silence.

Art which is capable of provoking *the experience of bewilderment*, and thus of changing us, always conceals the zone of silence that has produced it. I think about this sort of silence that is not a choice but a condition suffered as an amputation. This silence generates monsters: self-denigration, violence towards oneself and others, gloomy sloth and ineffective anger. At times, however, this silence nourishes Disorder.

The experience of Disorder doesn't concern the categories of aesthetics. It happens when a *different reality* prevails over reality: in the universe of plane geometry a solid body falls. As when unexpectedly, like lightning, death strikes a beloved one, or when in a split second our senses ignite and we are aware of being in love. Or when in Norway, as a recent immigrant, I was contemptuously called 'wop' and a door was slammed in my face.

When Disorder hits us, in life and in art, we suddenly awaken in a world that we no longer recognise and don't yet know how to adjust to.[66]

From this side of the Iron Curtain, the sense of continuity from the *maîtres fous* to the theatre of the 1950s and 1960s had faded. Not the memory of Copeau, of course, and not the sense of theoretical importance of the 'quixotic' Craig. In France there was Nina Gourfinkel and in Italy Angelo Maria Ripellino, with their books on Stanislavski, Meyerhold and on Russian theatre of the early twentieth century respectively. But on the other side of the Curtain there was another awareness: that of a disturbing phenomenon but which in some way had an integral unity, physical but interested in the spoken word, cultural but obsessed by dance.

A few years later, Grotowski's performances, followed by those of Barba, the Living Theatre, Peter Brook, the American avant-garde and many others, began to travel around Europe.

Thinking back about the immediate *recognition* in Western Europe on the part of theatre people and scholars about the worth of Grotowski and Barba, I cannot help asking myself: over and beyond the undeniable quality that struck many people all over Europe, what else did they see in the performances of the two 'Polish' artists?

I am convinced that people like Peter Brook, Renée Saurel, Marc Fumaroli or Charles Marowitz saw another quality, a particular nuance of physical work: *a difference*.

This *difference* marked a turning point for so many theatre artists, both old and young. It was not the birth of laboratoriality, but it was proof of the existence of a 'laboratorial' phenomenon. This discovery caused a veritable change in the history of the theatre: the birth of numerous other theatres

---

[66] Eugenio Barba, 'Children of Silence: Reflections on Forty Years of Odin Teatret', from the programme of the performance *Andersen's Dream* (2005). Also published in *The Drama Review*, 49. 1 (2005), 153–61.

that were expressly and deliberately 'laboratorial'. It was a real historical and unexpected breakthrough. Indeed, how could Grotowski and Barba have planned it that the needs of so many theatre people would be immediately recognised in their theatres?

The turning point

It was pointless to ask oneself which was the superior model, whether Grotowski's Teatr Laboratorium and his choice to abandon the production of performances, or Barba's Odin Teatret, because the question had a double core. It was a pairing of two strengths.

On his own, one director would not have been able to cause a similar intense and visible wave, complex, multifaceted and not limited to a single model. On his own, one director would never have been able to create new values and techniques and, at the same time, to articulate such different tendencies and needs. That had proved impossible in the past for theatre artists of the stature of Meyerhold and Craig. For their example and their words to become effective, as indeed they did, an entire *network* of great theatre people was needed, some of these lending their support, others voicing their dissent.

Something similar happened midway through the twentieth century. Even though the network created was not as powerful and extensive as that at the turn of the century, it did have all the force of a particularly strong pairing, one that in Italy was called the 'Grotowski-Barba axis'.

If we fail to consider this *pairing*, we will be unable to appreciate the relevance and influence that these two directors and their theatres have had, also with respect to directors and theatres that have produced equally famous, if not more famous, performances and other life and theatre models that are equally, if not more, incisive, interesting and anomalous.

The Grotowski-Barba axis

Throughout the first phase – the theatre phase – of Grotowski's presence in Europe, Barba's support and actual presence had been crucial. The two theatres, Teatr Laboratorium and the newly created Odin Teatret, had always been radically different, yet also companions. One might say they presented themselves to the world with what seemed to be a common survival strategy, one supporting the other.

There was this aspect of a friendly pairing that made the examples proposed by the two groups more compact and inescapable. It was an alliance between two theatres that was both defensive and aggressive, strategic, political, spiritual and theoretical. It related to the way of organising tours and disseminating theories. They forcefully put forward the model of a master-pupil relationship that was basically alien to European theatre, and fascinating. Grotowski's first seminars were organised in 1966 in Holstebro, at the newly formed Odin Teatret. Even though they were for a limited number of participants, these practical working meetings became an essential point of reference for Europe's leading theatre minds. The final part of this book will include a description of one of these seminars.

In February 1966 Odin Teatret had organised the first tour abroad of Grotowski and Flaszen's Teatr Laboratorium 13 Rzędów to Sweden, Denmark and Norway. In 1968 Odin Teatret Forlag published *Towards a Poor Theatre*, Jerzy Grotowski's book that would go on to become one of the most important texts for late-twentieth-century theatre. Barba edited the volume, which was published as a monographic issue of Odin Teatret's journal *Teatrets Teori og Teknikk*.[67] In addition to other people's contributions, in particular Ludwik Flaszen, it included a Barba interview with Grotowski and

---

[67] Jerzy Grotowski, *Towards a Poor Theatre*, ed. by Eugenio Barba (Holstebro: Odin Teatret, 1968; *Teatrets Teori og Teknikk* no. 7).

writings by both Barba and Grotowski.[68] It is tangible evidence of this pairing.[69]

Grotowski's presence could be felt at all the events organised by Barba: the international meetings of the 'Third Theatre', then the sessions of ISTA. In Bonn (1980), then in Volterra (1981), Grotowski had been an integral part of ISTA. It had been the same a few years previously, in the major group theatre meetings arranged by Barba in Belgrade and in Bergamo in 1976 and 1977.

Grotowski had given up doing theatre, but he regularly attended festivals and theatre conferences. The questions he was asked, his very presence, were the confirmation of his position as a leading authority.

Sometimes Grotowski's absence was actually like an unusual 'presence', felt even more than if he were present. In Peru in 1988 Barba had staged a special day, 'Homenaje a Grotowski', during a meeting of theatre groups in Huampanì, organised by Mario Delgado and his group Cuatrotablas, and by the Peruvian Motin (Independent Theatre Movement) groups. On 26 November all the groups had travelled to the archaeological site of Cajamarquilla, which they reached after a two-hour hike, in order to create a spectacular 'architecture' consisting of fragments of performances of all the groups and dedicated to the absent Jerzy Grotowski. In 1989 Odin Teatret organised, together with producer Pietro Valenti, a 'Latin American project' in Italy, with the participation of Raúl Osorio's TEC (Teatro experimental de Chile), Compañia de Claudio de Girolamo, also from Chile, Galpão from Brazil, Yuyachkani and Cuatrotablas from Peru, as well as the Mexican scholar and publisher Edgar Ceballos. The programme included a meeting of Latin-American artists with Grotowski himself in Pontedera.

---

[68] A few years earlier, in 1965 as we have seen, Barba's book on Grotowski's theatre, *Alla ricerca del teatro perduto* had been published in Italy and in Hungary, with a French typewritten version circulated among scholars and theatre artists in Europe.
[69] Cf. on this point Franco Ruffini, 'La stanza vuota. Uno studio sul libro di Jerzy Grotowski' (The Empty Room. A Study on Jerzy Grotowski's Book), *Teatro e Storia*, no. 20–21 (1998–99), pp. 455–85.

Barba's performances and Odin Teatret's tours were often meeting places for Grotowski's nomadic followers.[70]

All of this was taking place at a particularly favourable moment in time, a period of great change. It was the 1960s, and in many parts of the world people felt impelled to find new ways of doing theatre. This had a global diffusion and was a crucial influence for over twenty years.

It is in this bubbling context of expectancy that one must try to imagine the effect that Grotowski and Barba had, not only in terms of survival strategies and the consolidation of their two theatres, or of their way of conceiving and doing theatre, but also as something broader, that went beyond their intentions. Indeed, not even the strength of this pairing would be enough to explain their historical influence, which was much greater than what a single theatre, or two allied theatres, could possibly have exerted. This coming together of two forces would not in itself have been sufficient. But this pairing was, for the whole of Western Europe, an important means for transmitting the memory of the vision and the accomplishments of the great masters of the past, a memory that had survived chiefly in Eastern Europe.

On the subject of laboratoriality, Barba's and Grotowski's joint influence marked a crucial breakthrough, going well beyond the influence of theatres of similar artistic merit, and of much greater fame, such as Brook's, for example.

Therefore it is necessary to consider the two theatres as if they were a *single* entity, of which Grotowski and Barba and their respective theatres are its two poles.

A two-headed model

Teatr Laboratorium and Odin Teatret presented themselves as two closely related theatres. They were unusual, with

---

[70] On 21–22 February 2009 Odin Teatret organised in Holstebro a 'Banquet for Ludwik Flaszen and Jerzy Grotowski to mark the 50th Anniversary of their Teatr Laboratorium'. On this occasion, Leszek Kolankiewicz, in his speech, recalled how 'Holstebro and Odin Teatret were always considered home by the Grotowskians'.

new, interesting features and many aspects in common. But they were also very different, often expressing opposing and sharply contrasting points of view. Their alliance had been seen as so close as to constitute a veritable pairing. In this way, as a pair, they had made a breakthrough. At the same time, their very differences had prevented the crystallisation of a *single model*.

They were two inextricably linked but opposing poles of the same phenomenon, and for that reason they were able to generate so much energy.

This explains why theatre laboratories go about their work in all manner of forms: their working method is never based on a single model.

The two poles

In this pairing Grotowski came to represent the pole of inner value andthe tendency to shy away from artistic creation. Barba was the pole representing the existential and political value of the theatre, for both the actor and the spectator. He also represents the possibility that the time of the performance – and not just the time devoted to the theatre – might become a moment and a place of knowledge. The two different ways of conceiving the theatre by two great directors were perceived as, and *became*, the two living poles of a single and specific way of conceiving and living the theatre. The tension between these two poles constituted the space for laboratoriality.

This is how the two polarities of a single entity were viewed both by those looking from afar, sometimes with a hostile gaze, and by the entire movement that came to be formed around these two theatres. Of this paradoxical single entity, Barba came to represent the pole of vital energy, of a call to arms, an appeal for new dignity for the school-less theatres, the theatres without a home, the theatres of the 'nameless', the community theatres that focused on social issues. Grotowski was able to tune into the growing propensity towards spiritual searching and to give this movement fresh legitimacy.

These two poles were not two alternatives but a single tension.

Within this tension between the two poles of a single entity there reappeared, all mixed together, spiritual and existential values, greater focus on the spectator, work on oneself, interest in technique and its transmission, research into a theatre science, an obsession with and a detachment from performances. At Odin Teatret there appear not to have been many specific paths of self-knowledge, except perhaps at the outset, and in any case they were not considered as being of sufficient interest to investigate further. As far as Grotowski is concerned, focus on performance techniques lasted longer than any real interest in the performance itself. But for the pairing it is important, essential indeed, that there were both poles, and the tension they generated covers all of these values.

The fact that the two theatres representing the two poles are so different has prevented the formation of an actual model, or prototype. I am not talking here about Teatr Laboratorium or Odin Teatret being imitated, which of course they have been. I am talking about a prototype: a means of comparison, something that makes it possible, through a similarity of characteristics, to define whether or not a theatre is a theatre laboratory (one famous example might be the Living Theatre, albeit somewhat anomalous for the subject we are discussing).

The Grotowski-Barba pairing could not have produced models, as the two theatres were too dissimilar. Yet their complementary nature could and indeed did produce a *laboratory dimension*: a *new mental horizon* for theatre-makers and new hopes and expectations for theatre-goers.

A mental horizon is not a model: it has neither the clarity nor the precision. It is vague, confused, imprecise and it breaks into pieces, figuratively speaking, if you try to put it down on paper. What is more, in recent years this horizon seems to have become even less visible and on the point of disappearing completely.

This is how the Grotowski and Barba pairing ended up being the *core* of the laboratory question, in other words a point of transition and transmission from the problems faced by the protagonists of the Great Reform in the early twentieth century to the most pressing dilemmas of the second half of the century. Due to its unusual nature, this pairing built the pillars of Hercules for the world of theatre laboratories in the late-twentieth century. It determined the particular hue of theatre problems relating to laboratoriality like no other great experimental theatre, no matter how much interest the latter may have had in laboratory activity or how effective they may have been from an artistic viewpoint.

Now we can finally read the letter that Barba, in March 2004, towards the end of our discussion, addressed to the speakers at the Aarhus conference on the subject of theatre laboratories, setting down his own doubts and uncertainties.

Why a theatre laboratory?

The aim of the symposium *Why a Theatre Laboratory?* is to raise a number of questions. The symposium is not a review of the most important historical and contemporary examples, nor does it propose a phenomenology or praise that specific theatre genre.

Do theatres which have defined themselves or which we consider as 'laboratories' share something in common? Or is it just a matter of a recurring name?

Is it possible, by comparing the practice of such different theatres, to sketch the profile of a shared idea, a destiny, a social position, an attitude towards the craft and the art of theatre? Or are we, on the basis of our personal experience, merely projecting a non-existent category on the past and the present?

We have chosen a few examples from Europe. They are very different both from the point of view of the historical period in which they were active as well as of the culture in which they were rooted. We

have cast a stone – the same question – in each of these small ponds:
Why can we call that particular theatre a theatre laboratory?
But I am not totally sure that this is the right question to ask. And if
not, why not?
There are pertinent questions, inappropriate questions and also
paradoxical questions. We have rejected the apparently safe path:
the path which might have attempted to give a theoretical definition
of the qualification 'laboratory', and later verify its possible application to any of the examples provided by European theatre in the
twentieth century.
By following the path of paradoxical questions, we run the risk of
searching for what is uncertain by means of the uncertain. But the
straight path which claims to start from the certain, often leads
sure-footedly to the vast icy sea of tautology.[71]

The examples chosen by Barba for questioning the theatre laboratory were: Konstantin Stanislavski, Vsevolod Meyerhold, Jacques Copeau, Étienne Decroux, Jerzy Grotowski,
Peter Brook, Ariane Mnouchkine's Théâtre du Soleil and
Odin Teatret. There were also general contributions on the
situation in Asia and South America, and Richard Schechner
spoke about the United States. The choice of these figures,
and the absence of others, such as Craig, Dalcroze and Vakhtangov, was obviously random. But overall, the programme
was a good representation of a shared and widely held belief,
at least within the study and working milieu where Barba was
posing his questions, that there existed not only a laboratoriality that had flowed throughout the twentieth century but
even a continuity between historical phenomena of the start
of the century and theatre laboratories that came into being
after the breakthrough made by Grotowski and Barba.

As I said, it was a widely-held view. But then an objection
began to be heard, first in the form of a question, then more of
a belief: did the Studios supporting the great theatres of Stanislavski, Meyerhold, the schools of the famous 'small' theatres

[71] Eugenio Barba, 'Letter to the Speakers', unpublished correspondence, March
2004.

of Copeau and Dullin and then the closed fortresses of the theatre laboratories in the second half of the century really form part of the same phenomenon?

And if one can really talk about different phenomena, what were the differences?

And what sense would it make to distinguish between the two phenomena?

Thus it was that the discussion entered a new phase.

III

1. In the first half of the century
*A closer look at Konstantin Stanislavski's
Opera-Dramatic Studio (by Franco Ruffini)
and Vsevolod Meyerhold's Studios
and Workshops (by Béatrice Picon-Vallin).*

2. In the second half of the century
*Jerzy Grotowski's and Ludwik Flaszen's Teatr
Laboratorium (by Zbigniew Osiński and Ugo Volli)
and Eugenio Barba's Odin Teatret
(by Nando Taviani).*

One must take a long, close look to understand the special nature of what is happening in the laboratory zone of the theatre. So at the risk of interrupting the flow of the discussion, the time has come to examine carefully some of the places in question and their activities.

We will home in on the various Studios and theatre laboratories through the voices of some of the Aarhus conference speakers. This chapter does not include the situations that lie outside the geographic area on which our discussion focuses (in Aarhus Richard Schechner spoke about the situation in the US, Raquel Carrió about that in Latin America, while Nicola Savarese described the situation in Asia). This book does not cover all the proceedings of the conference. Also left out, according to the same logic, which gives precedence to only four cardinal points of reference, are the analysis of figures such as Decroux, given by Marco De Marinis, and of Peter Brook and Ariane Mnouchkine, who were the subjects of talks by Georges Banu and Béatrice Picon-Vallin during the conference.

The chapter is in two parts, mirroring the two halves of the twentieth century that we are questioning. It should be viewed as an interlude, an essential detour to look at the actual work of the individual subjects of our discussion and to discover the face of laboratoriality. This chapter is the pivotal point of our discussion, and thus of the whole book. It is also a pause in the tale.

1. In the first half of the century

What was going on in the theatrical homes of the great directors of the early twentieth century, in their separate spaces, be it Studios, workshops or schools? Franco Ruffini on Stanislavski and Béatrice Picon-Vallin on Meyerhold look back at that work.

In his talk on Stanislavski, Franco Ruffini focused in particular (but not only) on the Opera-Dramatic Studio of 1935. He described a laboratory-type work hinging on the relationship between music and the actor's art, an area in which Stanislavski appears to have forced himself to choose the essential elements of his old theoretical, and above all practical, researches. Ruffini also mentions fundamental points, useful for exploring the multifaceted laboratory sphere. These can be summed up as follows:

a) The importance of the shift away from the company (or from the class of a theatre school) to the theatrical community.

b) The problem of a path (and thus of a guide) that is not only theatrical but also spiritual in nature. In other words, a path that extends beyond the realms of the performance.

c) The shift from the construction of a performance to the need to build for oneself a different space in which to seek creative states conducive to constructing not only a new actor but also a new human being. This is how laboratorial work goes beyond the purely theatrical dimension.

d) The problem of youth as a necessary requirement for embarking on work to radically renew the actor's art.

e) The drive to leave behind performance and move beyond it. Theatre and performance, Ruffini argues, are not the same thing: the theatre includes the performance, but the two are not synonymous.

I believe questions on the relationship between (artistic) youth and old age and between theatre and performance are the thorniest and certainly the most disturbing.

For the past twenty years Franco Ruffini has been a point of reference for the 'invisible' young theatre groups in Italy. He is a theatre scholar specialising in studies on Artaud, Stanislavski and Italy's Renaissance theatre. He has been following Barba's work for over thirty years and also that of Grotowski, especially after the foundation of the Workcenter in Italy, about which he has often written.

Allow me to add that among the Italian scholars appearing here, especially Franco Ruffini, Ferdinando Taviani, Fabrizio Cruciani, Nicola Savarese and myself, there has been an affinity for many years, with a tendency to share working and critical methods. This has led some people to believe that this quintet was actually a sort of 'school'. A part of this book ends up by being, perhaps unintentionally, testimony to a tiny, compact and unruly working milieu, with a penchant for debate and contradiction. I cannot help but wonder whether the mixture of unity and fractiousness is the quintessence or the parody of what we call laboratory.

The second essay is on Meyerhold and on his penchant for founding new Studios. Four in particular are emphasised: the Studio in Borodinskaya Street, the KOURMASTSEP Laboratory, his actor's school and the Workshops of 1921–22. Béatrice Picon-Vallin suggests that to these should be added at least the 1905 Studio, created by Stanislavski within the Art Theatre and directed by Meyerhold.

Over the years Béatrice Picon-Vallin has become Meyerhold's spokesperson in Europe. She has translated his writings, reconstructed his performances, studied his creative processes, his pedagogy and experimentation. Her contribution has been fundamental in informing the theatre world about probably the best director of the twentieth century.

Béatrice Picon-Vallin stresses that, in Meyerhold's eyes, no matter how urgent and relevant the artistic creation was, pedagogical activity and pure research were always crucial, sometimes also a compensation chamber. It was not so much the idea of pedagogy that interested him – even though he ascribed great importance to it – as the degree of unrestricted experimentation afforded to him by the Studios: 'I am not a teacher,' Meyerhold said, 'I am an explorer of new shores on the ocean of the theatre.'

Experimental as well as pedagogical work appears to have flowed parallel to that of performance production, as if the creation of performances and continuous laboratorial experimentation were the two rails of the great director's working track. We might say that the Red Queen's race, for directors like Meyerhold, worked first of all like a form of internal stimulation. It was a moment of pure research never really detached from the parallel creation of performances, and it allowed a gathering of materials irrespective of the themes or texts he wanted to put on stage. In this unceasing work it is difficult to separate what is intended for performance creation from pure research.

FRANCO RUFFINI

Stanislavski's Extremism

What is a theatre laboratory, irrespective of periods, names and proceedings? Is it a study centre for performance, an avant-garde theatre, an advanced actor training school?

A theatre laboratory may be defined as a theatre in a state of effervescence. It cannot exist without theatre or without the work allowing it to move to a higher temperature. But it is something else.

Artaud

Artaud was notoriously alien to theatre experimentation, the avant-garde and pedagogy, even more so in his last years.

During the days of madness and the mental hospital, electroshocks and hunger, from 1937 to 1948, when he died – stripped of free will, thought and feeling – he simply took to the extreme his long-held belief that one can rely only on one's body, as he describes it with anatomical rigour: the limbs, external and internal organs and everything else. There is nothing but the body. He realised however that the body, left to the automatism of its organs, is reduced to an 'overheated factory' that 'expels filth'. They are his words. The limbs move, the lungs breathe in and out, the stomach digests, the liver secretes, each organ having a specific function. And the final product of all this activity is 'shit'.

The theatre conceived by Artaud is an appropriate point of departure for discussing the actual nature of the theatre laboratory: *a laboratory that builds a human being liberated from automatisms, using the tools of the theatre and starting off from the body alone*.

One might argue that Artaud is an extremist. That is true.

But the theatre laboratory has to be observed from the viewpoint of extremists. Otherwise it would fade away into a series of individual cases which, by indicating what makes them different, risks missing what actually unites them deep down. An extremist is not someone who exaggerates and talks nonsense about things. Quite the opposite: he is someone who reasons about things in a logical yet intransigent manner, seeking to uncover what lies beneath the surface.

An extremist's eyes focus on the essential. The masters of the theatre laboratory possessed such a gaze. Focusing on the essential is not a continuous process. There is a *break in the gaze*, an interruption. The break occurs in the gaze, and alters the nature of the observed phenomenon.

Put more bluntly: by stressing the essential, one revolutionises it.

In the footsteps of the First Studio

Before the official opening of the First Studio, in September 1912 – first in the former Lux cinema, then in the Hunting Club in Tverskaya Street – Stanislavski had attempted for two years to teach the 'system' to the actors of his Art Theatre. The experiment had been a complete failure. Stanislavski then decided to establish the Studio in a different location, using different methods from those of the Art Theatre.

'Attempt to use the "System" in life' is the name of the chapter of the Russian edition of Stanislavski's book on attempts made within the Art Theatre. It is followed by a chapter entitled 'First studio'.[72] In the 1924 American edition the chapter

[72] Cf. Konstantin Stanislavski, *Sobranie sočinenij v vos'mi tomach. 1, Moja žizn' v iskusstve* (Selected Writings, Vol. 1: My Life in Art) (Moscow: Iskusstvo, 1954) and

on experimentation was entitled 'The First Studio', and the following chapter 'The Founding of the First Studio'.

Stanislavski himself explained the reason for the change in titles: 'laboratory work cannot be done in the theatre itself, with its daily performances, its concerns over the budget and the box office, its heavy artistic commitments and the practical difficulties of a large enterprise'.[73]

In the Russian and new English versions, this begins the chapter 'First studio' (in the corresponding chapter of the original English version this statement is missing).

There was a break in Stanislavski's gaze. While working on the Russian edition, he realised that the First Studio began only when it became detached – not only physically – from the Art Theatre. What in the English version were already credited as being Studio activities were traced back to what they had really been: experiments. Invaluable and courageous, but part of the 'Before'.

Prior to the laboratory there had been the territory of experimentation. But experimentation in itself does not constitute a theatre laboratory.

From the class of a theatre school or a company to the theatre community

The first revolution produced by the break in the gaze is the shift from the theatre company or the class of a school to the *theatre group* or *theatre community*, as it was called by some of the people involved as well as by leading historians.[74]

The notice put up by Stanislavski to seek applicants for the First Studio in September 1912 was in no way the same as recruiting actors to form a company or as an examination

---

Konstantin Stanislavski, *My Life in Art*, trans. and ed. by Jean Benedetti (London and New York: Routledge, 2008), pp. 297 and 301.

[73] Stanislavski, *My Life in Art*, p. 301.

[74] Cf. in particular Fabrizio Cruciani, *Teatro nel Novecento. Registi pedagoghi e comunità teatrali nel XX secolo* (Twentieth Century Theatre: Pedagogical directors and theatrical communities in the twentieth century (Rome: Editori & Associati, 1995; revised edn.).

for admission to a school. With that notice Stanislavski was searching for fellow travellers with whom to explore an unknown territory, jeopardising the performance side of the theatre. The long duration of rehearsals, which characterised experimentation, brought about a breakthrough in quality. It became the 'adventure of the rehearsals'.[75]

A theatre community is not just a company or a school class.

A theatre community continues to have the size of a company or a school class. Indeed both types, as far as dimensions are concerned, are 'chasing' each other, are in dialogue and influence each other, just as in Alice's Red Queen's race. It is not possible to know who is behind and who is ahead. They are different, yet they are in the same race.[76]

When operating only as a company or as a class, the company and the class become the ballast of the theatre community. This is what happened with the First Studio, especially after the success of *The Cricket on the Hearth*, staged on 24 November 1914. The community went back to being a company, albeit a leading one, or the class of a school, albeit a leading school.

Leopold Sulerzhitski, to whom Stanislavski had entrusted the Studio, wrote in an unsent letter dated 27 December 1915 that the First Studio had become 'a big institution... Any dream or any hope of utopia is removed, only 'work' remains,

---

[75] 'Rehearsals are a great adventure', says Grotowski. 'Rehearsals are not only a preparation for the opening, they are for the actor a terrain of discoveries, about himself, his possibilities, his chances to transcend his limits'. Jerzy Grotowski, 'From the Theatre Company to Art as Vehicle', in Richards, *At Work with Grotowski on Physical Actions*, pp. 115–35 (p. 118). The idea of rehearsals as an adventure is implied or expressly declared in all of Grotowski's writings.

[76] Mirella Schino spoke about Alice and the 'Red Queen's race' (from *Through the Looking-Glass* by Lewis Carroll) in her speech entitled *Theatre Laboratory as a Blasphemy* at the Aarhus conference. Schino's intention is to insert the theatre laboratory in a dialectic with the theatre as the production of performances. My aim, however, is to distinguish the two areas; but differentiating means neither separating nor opposing, of course. Schino presents an outline of the theatre laboratory problem in *La nascità della regia teatrale* (The Birth of Theatre Directing), (Rome-Bari: Laterza, 2003).

good or bad… but there are no more dreams'.[77] For the 'good old Suler' (as Stanislavski called him)[78], the adventure of the rehearsals of the First Studio had ended with honours but also with the constraints of the performance.

From director to spiritual guide

The second revolution of the theatre laboratory bears the name of Sulerzhitski in his activity in the First Studio. Defining this revolution in more general terms, we could speak of the emergence of a *spiritual guide*.

Stanislavski was rarely present at the First Studio and, significantly, mostly when performances were being rehearsed. More than as a master, he went there as a guest director. The role of spiritual guide had already been assigned to Sulerzhitski and could not be shared.

The spiritual guide of a theatre community is not merely the director of a company or a school.

The spiritual guide of a theatre community often acts as director. But the director is responsible for the performance, while the responsibilities of the spiritual guide extend beyond stage production, sometimes even going against the interests of the performance. Whereas the responsibility of a school director centres on the teaching side, the responsibility of a spiritual guide covers the general education of the pupils.[79]

The Red Queen effect holds true too for the director and the spiritual guide.

---

[77] Sulerzhitski's letter is published almost in full in *Il teatro possibile. Stanislavski e il Primo Studio al Teatro d'Arte di Mosca* (The Possible Theatre: Stanislavski and the First Studio at the Moscow Art Theatre), ed. by Fabio Mollica (Florence: La casa Usher, 1989), pp. 191–194.

[78] Stanislavski, *My Life in Art*, p. 267.

[79] In his notes for the new school, Copeau writes that there had to be 'an *integrated company* … under the direction of one man'. Extracts published as Copeau 'The Manifesto of the *Vieux Colombier*' trans. by Joseph M. Bernstein, in *Actors on Acting*, ed. by Toby Cole and Helen Krich Chinoy, pp. 217–18 (p. 217); author's emphasis. The text is published in full as Copeau, 'An Essay of Dramatic Renovation: The Théâtre du Vieux-Colombier', trans. by Richard Hiatt, *Educational Theatre Journal*, vol. 19, no. 4 (1967), 447–54 (p. 452). Copeau writes 'school', but he was thinking of laboratory, as can be seen by the activity of Les Copiaus a few years later.

From creation to the creative state

On the subject of the First Studio, Stanislavski insisted on pursuing the goal of the *'creative state'*. He complained that during his 'experiments' the experienced actors considered his exercises as new clichés to be added to the old ones. Already-trained actors, he said, would consider his teaching as a theory. They did not realise that 'what I told them cannot be understood and absorbed in one hour or twenty-four but must be studied systematically and practically for years, for a lifetime', in order to absorb it and maintain it as if it were 'second nature'. They thanked him and heaped praise on him, but Stanislavski concluded sadly: 'that praise did not cure me'.[80]

From the letter to the 'spirit'

Sulerzhitski also wrote, in the unsent letter to Stanislavski of December 1915:

> My goal is to create a *commune-theatre* [...] with the great tasks of a *temple-theatre* [...] I particularly liked the nature of the land you bought at Evpatoria for the Studio, desert-like and arid, where we would have had to work hard to construct a *common home*.[81]

Stanislavski too recalled the Evpatoria project, calling it a 'spiritual order of actors'.[82] It never came to full fruition, but from the summer of 1912 Sulerzhitski went there every year to spend his holidays with a group of students from the Studio. They did everything that was written down in the original project: working the land, building their own homes, welcoming spectators as guests. Stanislavski remained distant, even circumspect. He did not take part in the Evpatoria holidays until 1915. It was not his utopia but Sulerzhitski's, and its failure was a foreboding of his own death.

Today, utopia has become an unutterable word. In its weakest version, it means a dream without any foundation in real-

---

[80] Stanislavski, *My Life in Art*, pp. 297–300.
[81] Cf. *Il teatro possibile*, pp. 191–92; author's emphasis.
[82] Stanislavski, *My Life in Art*, p. 304.

ity, in its strongest it signifies ethical tension which, in fact, means nothing at all.

Instead of utopia, therefore, we shall say *anagoge*. In medieval interpretation of a text, the anagogic meaning is the fourth meaning of words. After the literal, moral and allegorical meanings, the anagogic meaning expresses the 'spirit' of the word, and of the thing it represents, to the letter. The commune-theatre, the temple-theatre, the common home and the spiritual order of artists are the anagogic meaning – the spirit – of the theatre laboratory.

Copeau too, in his 1916 project, spoke of his school as a 'veritable *school for actors*', a 'contingent of new forces'.[83] Elsewhere, he calls for the creation of a *fraternity of players*'.[84] The community of actors-workers would go on to fulfil his vision in Burgundy in 1924. The way he recalls it after the event, in 1927, greatly resembles the description that Stanislavski had provided about the Evpatoria commune.[85] Copeau might have read this, since *My Life in Art* came out in 1924. In any case, even if he had not written it himself, he subscribed to the description. And for his part, Grotowski talks about 'comrades-in-arms'.[86]

Are they dreamers without any foothold in reality? No, they are extremists. Focusing on the essential, they simply see what the theatre laboratory represents in spirit and, equally simply, they describe it. It is not the fault of Stanislavski, Copeau or Grotowski if historians, in compliance with the principle of neutrality, refuse to be extremists. They have interpreted *literally* those descriptions of temple-theatres or confraternities of artists as not being founded on reality, instead of being the

[83] Copeau, 'An Essay of Dramatic Renovation', p. 452; emphasis in original.
[84] Cited in James Roose-Evans, *Experimental Theatre: From Stanislavsky to Peter Brook* (London: Routledge, 1996), p. 88.
[85] Cf. Jacques Copeau, 'The Vieux Colombier School in Burgundy', in *Copeau: Texts on Theatre*, ed. and trans. by John Rudlin and Norman H. Paul (London And New York: Routledge, 1990), pp. 48–51, This is the text of one of three lectures given at the American Laboratory Theatre in January 1927.
[86] Grotowski states: 'I don't want disciples. I want comrades-in-arms. I want brotherhood-in-arms'. 'Reply to Stanislavsky', p. 32.

spirit of theatre laboratories, so founded on reality that they are able to transcend it in order to affirm their foundation.

From literalness to the spirit: with this revolution, the creative state is also proposed as a human condition beyond the actor.

In the footsteps of the First Studio it could be said that this is an essential definition of the theatre laboratory: *a theatre community which, under the wings of a spiritual guide, works to embody the creative state as if it were second nature, as actors but also as human beings, in order to become capable of living outside the clutches of automatism.*

Stanislavski's theatre laboratories: music

In December 1915 Stanislavski began to conduct exercises at the First Studio, with the singers of the Bolshoi Theatre. He began to see more clearly the primary role of tempo-rhythm. Tempo-rhythm guides not only the exterior actions of the singer, but also potentially his inner actions. And when great music takes to the fore, the inner action is that of a genuine feeling.[87] The tempo-rhythm of great music, like the tempo-rhythm of a genuine feeling, is the *right tempo-rhythm*. But the actor-who-sings is unaware of this. Satisfied with *bel canto*, he does not even wish to learn it. The music guides his movements, but he does not know how to turn those movements into actions justified from inside, heart-felt[88]. The ac-

[87] 'How do we organise Studio teaching with you? By means of rhythmic exercises we try to reach a harmony of body movements with your parts, your musical organs. But where have we got this musical sense from? We started from the rhythm, the word and the sound, from the life that the composer dressed in sound. These sounds, by virtue of his genius and the fire in his heart, have been merged with the rhythm with which a certain character lived, in his awareness'; Konstantin S. Stanislavskij, *L'attore creativo*, ed. by Fabrizio Cruciani and Clelia Falletti, trans. by Clelia Falletti (Florence: La Casa Usher, 1989), pp. 142–43. This is a clear definition of 'great music' and of its ability to contain – in the right tempo-rhythm – the truth of human passions.

[88] Stanislavski expressly tells his singers: 'To bring music, singing, speech and action into a single whole, you need more than outer physical tempo and rhythm, you need inner, mental tempo and rhythm'; Stanislavski, *My Life in Art*, p. 332. Pavel Ivanovich Rumyantsev, a baritone who joined the Opera Studio in 1920 at the age

tor-who-speaks, on the other hand, can mobilise his inner life thanks to hard practice of 'real action', but he does not have the music to guide him.

The actor-who-speaks is not a diminished singer: he is only the latter's missing half. And vice versa, the singer is the missing half of the actor-who-speaks.

The work to 'graft' the actor-who-sings into the actor-who-speaks is concentrated on physical action. Segmentation into 'supplementary actions' – each justified by a relative task – helped the actor not to drift away from the present moment in time. Now exterior rhythm, caused by segmentation, has the task of equating itself with inner rhythm, recording possible time lags, and making due modifications. And so on: from exterior to inner action, and then from the inside to the outside. Until tempo-rhythm becomes the *right tempo-rhythm*.

For the actor-who-speaks, exterior tempo-rhythm is the equivalent of music. When it becomes the right tempo-rhythm – a perfect matching of the external and internal, body and soul – the music becomes great music. The actor's movement becomes dance, the words uttered by the voice become poetry. Together, dance, poetry and music express the 'truth of human passions'. In this process the exterior tempo-rhythm is the trigger and the constant monitoring tool.

The discovery of music was the true revolution of the 'system'.

But physical actions, like music, would have to wait many years before they would find their theatre laboratory. Stanislavski had few years left to live, being in a permanent state of convalescence after the double heart attack of 1928.

---

of twenty, insisted on this point in *Stanislavski on Opera*: 'Stanislavski did not recognize any beauty in gesture or pose for its own sake; he always insisted on some action behind it, some reason for a given pose or gesture based on imagination'. Rumyantsev quotes Stanislavski summarising that: 'Action is all that counts, a gesture all by itself is nothing but nonsense'; Constantin Stanislavski and Pavel Rumyantsev, *Stanislavski on Opera*, ed. and trans. by Elizabeth Reynolds (London and New York: Routledge, 1998), p. 6.

Around the 'sick armchair'

In the autumn of 1935, Stanislavski drafted a letter in reply to Stalin who, two years previously, had proposed that the status of the Art Theatre be changed to that of Great State Theatre and Actor Training Academy. Stanislavski replied that it was impossible to keep both things together. The artistic tradition of the Art Theatre should be preserved and developed but, with regard to the training of actors, for most veterans and youngsters working in the Art Theatre, 'greater creativity, which places greater demands on them as people and artists, is an unnecessary nuisance'.[89]

Stanislavski himself had 'turned to youth' and with these youngsters founded a few months previously – in July – an Opera-Dramatic Studio. In the meantime he kept on writing the book about the 'system', with the intention of transmitting the experience of his life in art.

The Opera-Dramatic Studio was an extreme theatre laboratory. Its present was the future. The breakthrough was moral in nature. The name, in itself, was the expression of his intent. It initially appeared to be a simple extension of the Opera Studio at the Bolshoi. It was, in actual fact, the revelation of the essential. With this name Stanislavski meant that the actor-who-sings would no longer be the missing half of the actor-who-speaks. They would be the same thing, with the same *risky possibilities*, only under the guidance of different forms of music. Notes, metronome, melody, or rather physical actions with their tempo-rhythm.[90] This projection towards the future formed the present of the Opera-Dramatic Studio.

---

[89] 'Stanislavski to Stalin: Autumn 1935' in *The Moscow Art Theatre Letters*, ed. and trans. by Jean Benedetti (London: Methuen Drama, 1991), pp. 353–55 (p. 354).

[90] The central role of tempo-rhythm in Stanislavski's last Studio may be seen in the enthusiastic and insistent testimony of Toporkov. He writes: 'rhythm, tempo, tempo-rhythm, rhythm-tempo fall frequently from the lips of directors, actors, theatre scholars and critics' But no one – including him, and naturally excluding Stanislavski – would have 'a precise definition of what these words mean'; Vasili Toporkov, *Stanislavski in Rehearsal: The Final Years*, trans. by Jean Benedetti (New York and London: Routledge, 2004), p. 28.

The students worked in Stanislavski's flat in Leontev Street, around his 'sick armchair'. Quasi-acrobatic work was often involved. Against such a backdrop of dynamism and youth, and the usual good humour, Stanislavski's face must have been a stark contrast! Suffering, and the self-will to carry on despite everything, had distilled from the master the 'spirit' of the spiritual guide. Compassion, euphoria and a sense of a mystery had distilled the spirit of a community from the group of students.

Stanislavski had said: 'Stage action, like the spoken word, must be musical'.[91] They were dramatic actors, but they had to 'sing' their physical actions.[92] Their guide was continually searching for this from them, without ever being satisfied with half successes. The only measure allowed in the Opera-Dramatic Studio was the extreme measure.

They followed the instructions as they had done from the start, when Stanislavski had warned them: 'If you want to study, then let us make a start; if you don't, let us part without ill feeling. You will go back to the theatre and carry on your work, and I will form another group and do what I believe to be my duty towards art.' They had stayed. More than a formal agreement, theirs had been a pact for life.

They were not the disciplined pupils of a school, nor members of a company busily preparing for the first night. In the first meeting of the work for *Tartuffe*, which kept them busy in the final period of the Studio, Stanislavski had made it clear: 'I have no intention of putting on a performance, I am no longer interested in theatrical glory. For me to put on one production more or one production less has no meaning for

[91] Stanislavski, *My Life in Art*, p. 332.

[92] Toporkov states that Stanislavski 'tried to achieve, if we may so express it, good "diction" in physical actions'; Toporkov, *Stanislavski in Rehearsal*, p. 113. Toporkov meant 'good diction' in the sense of music, saying he was able to form an idea of tempo-rhythm since, as a former musician, he had a certain familiarity with such exercises: 'I realised it was something akin to exercises for the violin, or technical music exercises – etudes – in general. I knew that, as a former musician' p. 63. 'Singing the actions' may be considered synonymous with dance.

me. What is important for me is to communicate my store of knowledge to you.' What they were called upon to work on was the creative state. Stanislavski had warned them that 'without such study you will go up a blind alley'.[93]

In a scene of *Tartuffe*, relatives are discussing how to rescue Marianne from Orgone's plans for her to marry Tartuffe. The pupils discuss the 'agitated tone' of the situation, but Stanislavski forces them to concentrate on the action of rescuing and hiding and to find the right tempo-rhythm. This prompts an exercise in which, with Molière temporarily put to one side, they all seek concrete ways of hiding Marianne from an imaginary madman who, armed with a knife, is trying to kill her.

They seemed to be playing like children. In actual fact, they were working on the creative state, as if it were second nature, based on the 'musicalisation' of the body.

The study of music

In the autumn of 1918, Elena Malinovskaya, director of the state academic theatres, had suggested that the Art Theatre collaborate with the Bolshoi Theatre, creating a Studio. Nemirovich-Danchenko and Stanislavski agreed to the suggestion. But while Nemirovich-Danchenko worked within the Bolshoi, Stanislavski worked separately in two rooms reserved for rehearsals. Later he moved to his own flat, in Leontev Street, which would be his last theatre laboratory. The Music Studio of the Art Theatre, created in 1919 by Nemirovich-Danchenko, had no ties with Stanislavski's work.[94] As with the First Studio, there was a separation at the outset of the Opera Studio too.

Stanislavski chose the youngest singers to accompany him in this adventure. One of the group, Konkordia Antarova,

---

[93] Toporkov, *Stanislavski in Rehearsal*, p. 105.

[94] In 1924 the Opera Studio was definitively separated from the Bolshoi, and named the Stanislavski Opera Studio. In 1926 it became the Opera-Theatre Studio, then in 1928 the Stanislavski Opera Theatre.

transcribed the 'conversations' of the first four years. Some quotes, among the many available, will be sufficient to pinpoint what the nature of the Studio was to have been for Stanislavski and his students.

'The Studio is a little like the entrance to a temple of art'. If the master were to turn teaching into a 'very boring despotism with no happy laughs during exercises, then the Studio would never become a temple of art'. We have already come across this expression – the 'temple-theatre' – when Sulerzhitski had uttered it about the First Studio, with nostalgia for the 'anagogic' version of Evpatoria. 'Whoever he may be in the private sphere, the student-actor, as soon as he enters the Studio, becomes a member of the new family.'[95] Sulerzhitski had said 'common home': the spirit is one and the same.

The first six conversations carry on in this tone, insisting on the real goal of the Studio, irrespective of the techniques adopted. The 'life of the artist is founded on his creativity'; 'you must prepare yourself for this high mission, for creative work'; 'the Studio must reveal to the student, one by one, the mysteries of creative work'.[96]

There are 'seven steps' to access those mysteries: watchfulness, mental alertness, courage, creative calm, heroic tension, fascination and joy. Courage, Stanislavski explains elsewhere, is the ability not to block the action due to rational calculation but to let it flow organically.[97] Fascination is nothing other than sincerity.[98] For anyone who reaches the final step – man

[95] Stanislavskij, *L'attore creativo*, pp. 54, 70 and 78, respectively.

[96] *Ibid.*, pp. 53, 59 and 68, respectively.

[97] Toporkov, *Stanislavski in Rehearsal*, p. 109. '[Stanislavski] warned us many times against a coldly rational approach to creative work. He required action not to talk. "When an actor is afraid to demonstrate his will, when he has no desire to create, he starts talking"'.

[98] *Ibid.*, p. 112. Toporkov cites Stanislavski: 'Genuine, human behaviour, sincerity of experiencing, that is to say, those qualities which are the most truly persuasive in the theatre, which hook an audience and influence their hearts and minds, are the qualities and the art that are personal to great artisits and are an example to us'.

or actor who speaks or sings – it is as if he has become another man. 'A second birth', Stanislavski now says about 'second nature'.[99]

Community, spiritual guidance, second nature as a creative state: on stage and, through stage art, in life. The Opera Studio at the Bolshoi was a true theatre laboratory.[100]

'When the Opera Studio was born', Stanislavski recalls in his autobiography, 'I had agreed to lead it with much hesitation. Subsequently, seeing how useful it was to me in my profession, I realized that music and singing would help me find a way out of the *blind alley* into which my research had led me'.[101]

Stanislavski was able to ask more of the singers than of the actors-who-speak. With music, and with mastery of the creative state, there was what he himself called 'crossing the Rubicon'.[102]

Now we have, so to speak, crossed the Rubicon and can proceed with our creative work. We will no longer deal with the work of the actor on the part or on himself, rather with the problem of where to place all the energies and attention in the work on the role, without there being a conflict between your 'I' and your 'if I', i.e., the role.

---

[99] Stanislavskij, *L'attore creativo*, p. 76.

[100] As with the First Studio, we will not focus on the exercises performed in the Opera Studio. But one at least should be mentioned. In the fifteenth lesson, an exercise is described for developing focus. Although the description is long and detailed, the exercise was basically that of harmonising the breath with various movements of the arms and fingers, until movement is carried from the breath and vice versa: movement and breath thus become one; cf. Stanislasvkij, *L'attore creativo*, pp. 97–98. Rumyantsev also describes similar exercises, remembering them as being monotonous and energy sapping. Stanislavski showed 'enthusiasm and joy' when leading the exercises. He demanded the same attitude from the performers. And he received it; cf. *Stanislasvki on Opera*, pp. 4–7. Singers standing in a circle, presumably stunned, go from monotony to enthusiasm and to joy, moving their fingers and breathing: this is a revealing image of the working climate of a theatre laboratory.

[101] Stanislavski, *My Life in Art*, p. 334; author's emphasis.

[102] Konstantin Stanislavski, *An Actor's Work*, ed. and trans. by Jean Benedetti (London and New York: Routledge, 2008), p. 358.

Further explanation was forthcoming: the actor must carry 'all his energies, feelings and thought, expressed in the physical action, to the highest level allowed by the truth of the performance'. He gives the example of the actor, seated and in silence, his posture must be 'totally relaxed'; if he sticks his head out from behind a bush, 'his head must stick out as much as possible'.

He examines an actor's performance: 'Has he correctly thought about the problems, and solved them correctly? Yes. Is his body free from impediments? Yes. Does the artist's life flow within the creative circle? Yes, again.' So what is missing that we can find in the genius actor? What is missing, he answers, is *heroic tension*.

The *heroic condition* is the final step of the creative state.

The heroic condition starts with the body which must be *extremely* relaxed yet *extremely* tense. Tense yet relaxed: the heroic condition is a question of proportion, of 'evidence of the most extreme tension'.[103]

Then, from the body, it goes to the heart and to the head.

> Let us imagine you have to do a dramatic scene with your sister, who has taken away your husband with whom you have lived for twenty years…
>
> How will you be able to give some life to the scene? When will you be able to reach the heights of creative art? Only when you have crossed the Rubicon will you have forgotten yourself and risen to higher sentiments: only when you have discovered the facts that mitigate your sister's guilt, and when you begin to wonder when and where you have wronged your husband. Then, emerging from you, a wave of goodness and not of curses will flow into the part, as well as the energy arising from the heroic tension of the female heart and of forgiveness.[104]

The actor's task gained in quality. Whereas the creative state committed him to *precisely expressing* the character's

[103] Stanislavskij, *L'attore creativo*, XIX, pp. 116–17; author's emphasis.
[104] *Ibid.*, XIX, pp. 118–19.

passion, the heroic condition calls on him to *objectively express* compassion for the human condition. Stanislavski says so explicitly:

> Everything that is incidental, conventional, must be eliminated from the qualities of the role. You have to discover the essential in each quality, only the organic nature of a passion, and not the *casual hint given in the text* to this or that sentiment and to the resulting action.[105]

Superficially, we identify the hero thinking only of the modes of heroic action: the hero as an intrepid individual, extremely courageous, almost with a love of risk for risk's sake. The hero is this too, but first it must be someone who takes upon himself a condition that transcends his personal situation – the condition of a people, of a social group, of a shared ideal – that may be seen as objective. If he acts in his own name only, he is the tragic caricature of a true hero.

There is a double vector in the hero's action. One that goes inward, towards the action for its own sake and its protagonist as an individual. The other that goes outward, towards that which the action represents for everyone, irrespective of the particular individual who performs the action. The heroic action is not enough in itself, yet the hero cannot evade it, at the risk of losing the vector that enables his transcendence.

Coming out of the performance

An actor who is unable to enter a creative state is in danger of dying; an actor who is unable to enter a heroic condition is in danger of dying for no reason. But in the theatre, acrobat or hero, death is 'as if'. One might wonder what the risk is, without the 'as if', for the actor who represents 'only the organic nature of a passion, and not the *casual hint given in the text* to this or that sentiment or to the resulting action'.[106]

---

[105] Stanislavskij, *L'attore creativo*, XX, p.121.
[106] Richards, *At Work with Grotowski on Physical Actions*, p. 101.

The answer was given by Grotowski, in words and with his work. Thomas Richards says that Stanislavski's work referred to:

> physical actions within the context of the common life of relations, people in 'realistic' circumstances… [but the] art of the actor is *not* necessarily limited to realistic situations, social games, daily life. Sometimes, the higher the level and the quality of this art the farther it distances itself from the realistic foundation, entering into realms of exceptionality… It is precisely this that has really *always* interested Grotowski in his work with the actor.

Again, directly from Grotowski himself:

> The human being in this type of *inner maximum* makes signs, rhythmically articulates, starts to 'dance', to 'sing'. Not common gesture or daily 'naturality', but a sign that is proper to the primal expression of human beings.[107]

Stanislavski would have agreed in full. At least Stanislavski the music researcher. He had said that he would no longer have focused on 'the actor's work on the role'. They would have tried to go, Grotowski believes, beyond the 'realistic foundation'.

Historically, from Stanislavski to Grotowski, there is a shift from the actor who brings a proof of truth to a character, to the actor who brings a proof of truth to the human being 'in the inner maximum'. In Stanislavski's trajectory there is a shift from the creative state to the heroic condition.

The risk is identical: that of *leaving behind the performance*. Where extremes are jumbled – goodness and cursing, revenge and forgiveness – the danger is that the character, the piece of life depicted by the text, disappears, to be replaced only by 'life taken as a whole'.

[107] Grotowski cited in Richards, *At Work with Grotowski on Physical Actions*, p. 104; translation modified in Richards' book. Cf. Grotowski, *Towards a Poor Theatre*, pp. 17–18.

The lessons at the Bolshoi continued from 1918 to 1922. The heroic condition occupies three full lessons (XIX – XXI) and remains a leitmotif right to the end. It is, without any doubt, the crowning moment of the teaching. *My Life in Art* was published in 1924 and then in a second edition in 1926. *An Actor's Work* was drafted from 1930 to 1938. But there is no further trace of the heroic condition, either in his autobiography or in the part of the book on the 'system' dedicated to tempo-rhythm, i.e., to the problem of music for the actor-who-speaks.

Whether, for Stanislavski, it was the heroic condition that prevailed over the risk of leaving behind the performance or vice versa, essentially the same question remains open. If *in general* it was the heroic condition that prevailed, why did Stanislavski let the matter drop? And if *in general* it was the risk that prevailed, why did Stanislavski place the heroic condition in such a central, relevant and demanding position for future developments in his pedagogical work? As might be expected, it is the 'general' view that muddies the waters. Simply, and precisely, the stakes were worth the risk when music was present. They were too great when music was absent.

This, while it explains the facts, does not offer the reasons behind it. Thomas Richards writes:

> A further difference between the work of Stanislavski and that of Grotowski ... concerns the 'character'. In the work of Stanislavski, the 'character' is an entirely new being, born from the combination of the character, written by the author, and the actor himself. [...]. In the performances of Grotowski, however, the 'character' existed more as a public screen that protected the actor. [...] One can see this clearly from the case of the Constant Prince of Ryszard Cieślak. The 'character was constructed through the *montage* and was mainly destined for the mind of the spectator; the actor behind this screen maintained his intimacy, his safety.[108]

---

[108] Richards, *At work with Grotowski on Physical Actions*, p. 98.

If the intention is to allow the actor to come out of the character and, at the same time, the montage of the character's actions is 'mainly destined for the mind of the spectator', the director must answer for the performance. Grotowski said so expressly.

If not the director, then the music: Stanislavski said so, although not so directly. For Stanislavski, music was the equivalent of the director for Grotowski. For Grotowski, through directing, and for Stanislavski, through music, it was the same wager: coming out of the performance without losing the performance.

Theatre, performance, theatre laboratory

Coming out of the performance means, first of all, allowing the performance to come out of itself. Like the action of the true hero, in some performances too it is as if there were two vectors: one moving inwards, obliging the spectator to look where he is able to see; the other, driving him to look beyond. There is no need for demonstration; this belongs to the experience of any demanding spectator. These two vectors are very closely linked: the performance cannot come out of itself if at the same time it does not affirm itself. But that is not enough.

The director's, or the dramaturgical, composition flows, as does great music. Protected by that screen, the actor or the singer who has acquired the will and the talent may abandon the character, transcend it and move towards the human condition in its universality. On the other hand, while the performance engages the actor in the artistic experience, the spectator who feels this need may be totally involved in a life experience.

Wasn't this the miracle of Cieślak's and Grotowski's performance?

Wasn't this the miracle of Maria Callas's performance?

Grotowski's abrupt declaration, in 1970, when he announced that he would no longer direct, caused many to believe that leaving the performance behind means abandoning it. This should not be what we can learn from Grotowski. His gesture calls into question the relationship between theatre and performance.

What did Grotowski do with his 'stage exit'? He abandoned the activity as director but he did not discard the instruments of *performing arts*, according to his terminology. He retained the same aim of giving to the spectator-participant that life experience which he had been given, in full, with *The Constant Prince*. Grotowski left the performance side but remained inside the theatre, giving up the *performance form*.

Twentieth-century theatre has clearly shown that performance and theatre are not synonymous. But taking this assumption further, too often it has been concluded that performance and theatre are opposites. Theatre is not the opposite of performance. To be precise: the theatre *includes* the performance but *does not imply it*. That means it can cancel performance, or at least suspend it, whilst maintaining, using and fine-tuning all of its instruments.

Since it includes the performance without implying it, theatre may be defined as *that which goes beyond the performance:* in space, in time and in terms of function.

In space and time – this means going beyond the mere event. It inscribes theatre in a knowledge – which according to Stanislavski means 'being capable of' – that is long-term, despite the regular staging of performances. Theatre Anthropology, with its research into the pre-expressive principles of the actor, primarily serves the theatre and only secondarily its performances. The upheaval of this hierarchy has generated a lot of strife. Who cannot remember a host of bad performances, which attempted to force onto the stage the principles of Theatre Anthropology?

In its function the theatre goes beyond the performance, freeing up action for the stage also as a laboratory of action for life.

BÉATRICE PICON-VALLIN
Meyerhold's Laboratories

*I often wake at night in a cold sweat thinking that I have become
banal, that everything in life is going too well for me, that I will die
under a thick quilt, that I have stopped being an innovator.*[109]

Vsevolod Meyerhold, 1937

One should not attempt to put all the Russian and Soviet
theatre laboratories from the early twentieth century into
the same category, since they did not all operate in the same
manner. Indeed, Stanislavski's and Meyerhold's laboratories
were not like each other at all. The Art Theatre was an institution that built around it some Studios which, while they were
places for conducting research, also served, while acting as an
external institution, as a means of survival, in a sort of ecosystem created by the *mother home*.

The different Studios and laboratories created by Meyerhold were not always tied up with a particular theatre, since
he himself did not have a theatre until 1921. When they are
subsequently closely bound to his theatre, which had different
names, the laboratories live on the inside and are intended to
develop in a scientific manner the actors' technique, the directing methods of this theatre and research methods for the notation and study of performances. In short, to train actors and
directors, and not to create independent performances. Each
research Studio (those of Michael Chekhov, Evgeni Vakhtangov and Les Kurbas[110]) has a different face and a different way
of working. They are similar in their desire to found the theatre
of the future on new bases; what sets them apart are the methods adopted to attain this as well as the breadth of their goals.

[109] Meyerhold cited in Aleksandr Gladkov, *Meyerhold speaks/Meyerhold rehearses*,
ed. and trans. by Alma Law (London and New York: Routledge, 1997), p. 100.
[110] Les Kurbas (1887–1937), known as the 'Ukrainian Meyerhold', founded the Be-
rezil Theatre in Kiev in 1922, which was defined as an experimental theatre with
workshops, a course in theatre direction, a museum, an amateur stage and a stage in
which work with people from the country was undertaken.

The artist.
A 'Picasso of the theatre'

Vsevolod Meyerhold (1874–1940) is a leading figure and one of the greatest directors of the twentieth century. Rejecting the theatre of his time, and confronted by Stanislavski, who opened the way to re-materialising the stage by focusing on a realistic environment and psychology, Meyerhold puts into practice his take on dematerialisation, which privileges the invisible and the world of dreams while at the same time opening up onto a political and thought-provoking theatre. He took part in some of the most radical theatre adventures: Symbolism, Constructivism and the Russian Revolution. Executed in 1940, this Communist artist who, according to Vakhtangov, 'provided the roots for the theatre of the future', disappeared from the Soviet and European stages and from the normal process of transmission in history.

In the 1970s this indefatigable and daring experimentalist was gradually restored to his rightful place. His works, abounding with fertile contradictions, seem to be split by the schism that the 1917 Soviet revolution represented, but their coherence is linked to a very high esteem for the art of the theatre and to the will to develop a complex and poetic scenic language.

Meyerhold was attuned to the conflicts of a troubled era. He gave them shape in a non-mimetic theatrical language by working directly on scenic material in which words are only one element. Each sign possesses multiple facets that mirror and focus the complex stage relationships between literature, music, painting, movement, vocal art and cinema. Whilst imposing the seal of his personal view, where the theme of destiny which dominated the 1910s was followed by the tragicomedy of imposture, Meyerhold sought a specific style for each author he directed.

In the beginning he was open to European plays that he introduced into Russia. Later his repertoire favoured national dramaturgy, reinterpreted according to a 'fantastic realism'.

Through the theatrical treatment he gave to classical texts, he contributed to the emergence of a new Soviet dramaturgy. His theatre does not seek to be a reflection of life but to take part in its transformation. It is founded on the associative interaction between the performance and the audience. If Stanislavski represents the paternal founding figure of modern theatre, Meyerhold reinvents the artist, the inventor and the revolutionary. His work is intimately linked to the Utopian adventure of 1917, embodying its foreboding, elation and disenchantment.

Starting in 1908, and until the day he died, Meyerhold reflected on the training of the actor and of the director. The actor's gestures and movements are seen as the very matrix of acting, and his directing activity was filled with projects, researches and pedagogical initiatives.

At a time when the body was glorified by a growing passion for sport and for Olympic competition, the actor saw his status transformed. To embody Meyerhold's idea of a theatre of the mind, the conjunction of extra-linguistic means of expression (lines, movement, rhythm, colour) is sought not so much in the expressiveness of the face, which may disappear beneath the mask, as in that of the body. Compared with the little-developed bodies of Wagner's operas or the ill-defined figures of the Symbolists – the result of randomness and emotion – Meyerhold followed Appia in stating that the actor's body had to become, like the set design and the music, a work of art.

Meyerhold's laboratories

The Studio Theatre was the first 'theatre laboratory' in Russia, a place for research created in 1905. Stanislavski called over his old actor Meyerhold, who after three years working at the Art Theatre had established his own company in the provinces in order to follow his own path. Meyerhold began by imitating his master, before exposing his group to contemporary European writing. 'Studio' is a term that is very specific to Russia, indicating a theatrical place where young actors work with a master. This Studio Theatre, which would be followed by four Studios associated with the Art Theatre, was thus run jointly by Meyerhold and Stanislavski. The goal was to work on the Symbolist repertoire, not with the 'old and jaded actors of the Art Theatre' but with new actors. The term 'new actors' would recur in all of Meyerhold's enterprises. Meyerhold defined this first research place as a 'hermitage of schismatics'. The actors of these Studios had to be fanatics, to be able to live in a cell as if in a monastery. The experience ended badly. The two artists realised that their paths were totally different, and it was clear to Meyerhold that the art of the theatre had to be totally recreated. He would go on to seek new places, new Studios.

In 1907 another Studio was conceived, called the 'Music and Drama Studio', to be run by the director and two composers. This studio remained on the drawing board, but the following year the Studio in Zhukovski Street opened. The Studio focused on the importance of music in the theatre, and Meyerhold began to collaborate with the composer Mikhail Gnesin, with whom he worked until 1935. Gnesin attempted to give actors a musical score to manage the pitch of the voice separately from the emotions, which disturb diction. For Sophocles' *Antigone* he composed a 'half-spoken, half-sung' score, played at the Studio, which astounded Aleksandr Scriabin. In addition to 'choral and musical declamation in drama', a second discipline was added: 'plastic gymnastics'. Here, the Studio was a place for teaching and research. This would be the main trait of Meyerhold's Studios. In his quest for new training for actors, it was the very definition of director that was up for discussion: for Meyerhold, the director is the figure who has to train new actors capable of carrying out his designs.

His laboratories had different names, but all of his work was supported by activities performed in these places of research: in St Petersburg, the Zhukovski Street Studio, and more importantly the Borodinskaya Street Studio (1908–17), then the advanced course in theatre direction (KOURMASTSEP) and the Actors' School (1918–19); in Moscow in 1920–21 the Actor's Technique Laboratory at the First RSFSR Theatre, in 1922 the GVYRM and GVYTM (Advanced State Theatre Workshops), finally in 1923 the GEKTEMAS (Experimental State Theatre Workshops), TIM (Meyerhold Theatre) and GOSTIM (Meyerhold State Theatre). There was also the NIL, the Scientific Research Laboratory for the study of theatre performance and notation. It should be noted that in the mid-1930s Meyerhold considered a theatre laboratory to be a place where techniques and exercises are invented that can then be used in workshops to systemise and improve training. One should also remember Meyerhold's regret that he did not have at his disposal a similar laboratory, available to physiologists, with whom he maintained a constant dialogue.

Borodinskaya Street Studio (1913)

In the autumn of 1913, after a stay in Paris, Meyerhold managed to open a Studio in St Petersburg, in Borodinskaya Street, bringing together some of the people the director had worked with since 1908, as well as new arrivals, students from various disciplines and professional actors. This Studio was described by Vladimir Soloviov, who collaborated in it, as a 'scenic laboratory intended to verify, mathematically, the theatre's past and to prepare the material that the stage master will use in the future with his pupils'. It was also called a 'poor space', of the utmost simplicity, something required for Meyerhold's mental equilibrium, as he was very much isolated inside the Imperial Theatres where he directed.

In 1914, in a public conference discussing the question 'What is this Studio?', the answer given by Meyerhold was clear: 'This Studio is a laboratory that seeks to obtain new scenic knowledge. We do not know the face of the theatre we are going to find, but we are going towards the Theatre'. It was not at all the idea of a 'monastery Studio'. It appears that the laboratory-Studio was, around 1910, the subject of permanent enquiry for Meyerhold and his team. Every six months, *The Love of Three Oranges*, the journal published by the Borodinskaya Street Studio, posed the question: 'What is this Studio?' The discussion centred on the status of the place and on its activity. The laboratory-Studio was a formula in flux, which had to evolve because it was subject to contradictory tensions: a place of transmission and a place for research, theatre of the future and of old theatres (the 'genuinely theatrical theatres'), research into new forms and the awareness that there is no progress in art.

In the St Petersburg Studio, which would be operational from 1913 to 1917, Meyerhold gave a class, from 1914, on 'Technique of scenic movement'. He collaborated closely with Soloviov, a specialist of *commedia all'italiana*, conducting with members of this acting Studio – both professionals and amateurs – an in-depth research using a so-called 'objective' method on commedia dell'arte texts and scenarios.

Meyerhold discovered Japanese theatre, the dance of Isadora Duncan, Jacques Dalcroze, Loïe Fuller. He became keen on the circus art. His critical reflection on scenic movement materialised with the preparation of exercises or pantomimes, mostly constructed on commedia dell'arte improvisations, accompanied by music (on the piano, like in a dance school). These exercises deepened relations between the actor's movements and the form and dimension of the scenic space, according to the 'starting from the ground' principle of Guglielmo Ebreo of Pesaro. This fifteenth-century Italian choreographer is the author of a dance treatise in which he lists, among other qualities, the dancer's ability to gauge the real and the potential properties of the surface on which he must perform in order to adjust his steps.[111]

The actors' movements on stage are complex steps, like in a choreography. They are geometric, depending on the even

[111] Guglielmo Ebreo of Pesaro, *De pratica seu arte tripudii: On the Practice or Art of Dancing*, ed. and trans. by Barbara Sparti (Oxford: Clarendon Press, 1999).

or odd number of participants. The actor is invited to have an expressive walk, the tips of the toes pointing outwards and constantly skipping, so that he is always ready to react quickly to his fellow actors. Each etude and pantomime – for example, *Harlequin, the Vendor of Bastinados; The Wandering Conjurers; The Two Esmeraldinas; The Snake-Woman; Bird and Cat* – include physical activities (jumping, falling, running, slapping), acrobatic and juggling elements, handling of different objects, most of which traditional (bow, stick, rod, ball, basket, sword, pike, fan, hat, cloak, veil, fabric, etc.). Other exercises aimed to provoke vocal expression as a direct consequence of muscular tensions: movement, as it is practised, involving the whole body, even for a single gesture, may result in an exclamation and a spoken word. Finally, movement is conceived in terms of its relationship with time, or rather with rhythm, materialised from a constant musical backdrop, which does not have a psychological function.

The body is viewed as a material to be moulded and perfected, so that it becomes an instrument that serves not so much a director as an actor-musician. Recourse to commedia dell'arte does not lie in the desire for ethnic-iconographic restoration but is a strategy in the struggle against psychologism, in which the name of Gordon Craig is often invoked. In its use, there is the conviction that it is not so much a forgotten genre but one of those rare moments of theatre in which, like in a chemical precipitate, the secrets of the stage and of the craft pertaining to the actor's condition are deposited. These secrets need to be revealed to twentieth-century theatre, understood, deciphered and brought up to date in precise formulas similar to algebra. These secrets must be assimilated, not in order to go backward, but to go forward and to put an end to the tyranny of the 'speaker' or the 'gramophone actor'.

Working on historical materials and texts, the Meyerholdian actor tangibly walks in the footsteps of actors of the past, to ensure the right way of walking, actually and figuratively:

progressive, autonomous and sure-footed. Meyerhold indicates here his utopia: 'to discover the laws of the theatre'. He fosters a fruitful dialogue with 'genuinely theatrical' traditions, of which the commedia dell'arte, studied not as a rigid entity, but in its historical variations, is an embodiment. One must also seek a unified interpretation regarding the set of performing arts not limited to Western culture, but including the circus and oriental theatre. It is a question of rediscovering these hidden or rejected traditions, in an attempt to 'transmit the past to the present'.[112] But turning to the past does not in this case mean trying to return to the past.

The Studio's pupils, actors for a modern-day carnival, capable of transmitting know-how that is dormant yet vibrant, bestow on the Meyerholdian actor his definitive status as *homo ludens*. In short, displaying life on stage does not mean miming or copying it, but enacting it.[113] On stage the main thing is 'to live in an expressly theatrical state of mind',[114] 'in joy', 'in a world outside which [the actor] cannot exist, even if he has to die on stage'.[115] Far from entering inside the skin of his character, he must try to leave it, see and admire himself from outside in the very process of his acting. Emotions on stage can perturb and disturb precision, joy, brilliance. Finally, the script is the decorative element covering the theatrical skeletal frame, constructed by the work of the body in space: 'the words are but patterns on the canvas of movement'.[116] In the Studio, *Hamlet* is staged in the form of a pantomime, but it is a provisional situation: the goal was to act out the play in full in the future, without leaving out a single scene.

In Meyerhold's experience from this period there was both a romantic and a scientific conception of the actor and his

---

[112] Moscow, RGALI: Russian State Archive of Literature and Art (previously TS-GALI: Central State Archive of Literature and Art) 963, 726.
[113] *Ibid.*
[114] RGALI, 998, 1, 715.
[115] Cf. Vsevolod Meyerhold, *Écrits sur le theatre: tome 1*, trans. and annotated by Béatrice Picon-Vallin (Lausanne: L'Age d'Homme, 2001; revised edn.), p. 213.
[116] *Ibid*, p. 177.

labour, tied up with the theatre and para theatre works of Gozzi, Hoffman and Callot, leading to research on form or style, the technical mastery of clearly identified and formulated principles, a body trained in various sporting and acrobatic disciplines, forged in the classroom of scenic movement. It is an artificial body, constantly requiring two-pronged action, in terms of rhythm, design and space on the one hand, themes and style on the other: rapid reactions (constant alertness to fellow actors), but also pauses; a global dynamic design as well as the introduction of breaks and segments at odds with the general line of movement; finally, the spatial distribution, on a number of levels, of the raw materials of acting (stage elements, stairways) and the poetics of contrasts, as well as attempts at tragicomedy (the grotesque).

Mimicry based on the impersonation of living people is replaced by inventive creation. The multifaceted actor is a 'juggler of the scene' who gets his body into shape thanks to his cultural background (visiting the Hermitage Museum, learning the theories of versification, *solfeggio* and rhythm). The natural body (prosaic, ethereal or idealised) is contrasted with a body that might be defined as 'versified'. Theatricality is not organised around a fictitious character but around the actor himself, considered as the 'producer' of this fiction, starting with his actual life and his acting work.

The KOURMASTSEP laboratory (1918–19)

From 1913 to 1917, under the pseudonym of Dottor Dapertutto, Meyerhold studied in his Studio in St Petersburg the technique of scenic movement, starting with scenes composed by his pupils, scenarios from the commedia dell'arte or mute fragments of Shakespeare's *Hamlet*. 'Technique of scenic movement' was the title of his course in Borodinskaya Street. In 1914 he stated:

> The role of scenic movement is more important than that of other elements of the theatre. Thus even if theatre were deprived of the

spoken word, the costumes, the footlights, the curtains, even the theatre building, as long as the actor and his well-mastered movements remain, the theatre remains a theatre.[117]

For the Meyerhold actor of the 1910s, priority was given to movement, defined in relation to the type of space available and the objects handled, soft or rigid, real or imaginary, and developed in a counterpoint relationship with music. Meyerhold's interest in the relationship between the actor and music remained throughout his experimentations, both while directing and in his Studio activities.

In 1916, Meyerhold spoke of the need to work on the actor's body as 'treating the material (to perfect physical elasticity)'.

The February Revolution reinforced the political position that Meyerhold had taken since the war began, and, with its elementary violence, the Revolution seemed able to create a new audience and a 'new theatre, a genuine theatre for the people'. Meyerhold's relationship with the February and October revolutions was primarily through the theatre. It was an ethical and aesthetic relationship: revolution on the streets, revolution on stage. In August 1918 Meyerhold joined the Communist Party.

But while Meyerhold stressed the importance of 'moments of creative self-activity of the masses' and imagined the future of the theatre in terms of 'myth-creation' and 'genuine improvisation', he knew that his theatre for the people had to *learn* before it could *do*.[118] More than ever, Meyerhold considered the actor and the director as being in possession of professional expertise and believed that improvisation arose from a knowing combination of learnt and known fragments. This led to the urgent need to train instructors for theatre

---

[117] From Meyerhold 'Love of Three Oranges', cited in *Écrits sur le théâtre: tome 1*, p. 238.

[118] Meyerhold, cited in *Shemy k izučenija spektaklja* (Schemas for the study of performance) (Petrograd: TEO NARKOMPROS, 1919), p. 36.

groups that were spreading like wildfire in factories and in the army. But while committed to this teaching activity, Meyerhold firmly rejected any existing form of professional theatre as well as all forms of amateurism. He imagined, through theatrical *brigades* whose leaders would be trained by him, forms of popular feasts, the return of the jester, of the itinerant theatre freed from its century-long yoke. In that period of transition Meyerhold was active in the midst of these contradictions.

In those months, surrounded by his old Studio companions, such as Aleksei Gripich, he enthusiastically organised courses for instructors (June-August 1918) and above all the KOURMASTSEP[119] (autumn 1918 – March 1919), a course that was both experimental and oriented towards very practical and immediate ends. This teaching activity, to which Meyerhold was devoted with great passion and energy, took place despite the political climate, in the midst of a civil war and difficult material conditions. Its most original feature was the intention to train not only future actors but also future directors, stage designers and theatre technicians, and to provide them with a common base from which each student, in his own area of expertise, could think of the theatre not as the sum of different artistic disciplines but as 'an independent art'. To highlight the subject of his courses, Meyerhold coined the term *scenovedenie*: scenology, or stage science. Recruitment was different from that of the Studio, of which these courses were however an extension. For Meyerhold it was a question of 'fostering participation in the creative process of new forces coming from the democratic masses'.[120]

With pedagogy comes research. These courses were a laboratory for Meyerhold, who turned teachers and students into researchers. Meyerhold's courses included lessons on the history of the theatre, set design, scenic or drawing techniques

---

[119] Advanced theatre direction course.
[120] From 'KOURMASTSEP Programme', 27 August 1918, in *Vremennik TEO: vol. 1*, (Petrograd: TEO NARKOMPROS, 1918), p. 17.

(given by the great painter Petrov-Vodkin). The dream was to turn these courses into a scientific institute on the art of the theatre. This was indeed the first school for theatre directors in Europe.

As mentioned above, in defining the subject of these courses, Meyerhold coined the new term *scenovedenie*, stage science, a discipline that was basically comparative and interdisciplinary in nature. Within the framework of contemporary creation, he sought to study the theatre according to theatre practices, from an historical and technical perspective, closely linking dramaturgy, directing and set design, and always centring them around the acting of the actor. The golden rule was:

> submission of anything done on the stage to theatre laws, needs and tasks. In theatre there is no place for an art that is born outside the theatre, catering to tasks other than those of the theatre. [...] The theatre cannot be the place where technicians, writers and painters come together just to show off their know-how. Now theatres themselves must create their own artists.[121]

Meyerhold insisted on the novelty of this approach, with the theatre considered as an independent art, even though he made reference to Gordon Craig's school in Florence.

Meyerhold was also interested in a theory of theatrical creation. He got his pupils to make drawings with comments on the production of a performance and the way it works with the audience. These 'performance study sheets' register the activity of the different members of the 'union of partners' and define their interactions.[122] Geometric patterns, circles, squares, parallelograms (the representation of which uses the laws governing these figures), symbols, dotted lines, segments and use of lighting: these sheets are usually less simplistic than the drawings of future semiologists. The main thing is

---

[121] From 'KOURMASTSEP Programme', 27 August 1918, p. 17.
[122] Cf. *Shemy k izučenija spektaklja.*

the way each sheet *constructs* (the term was in common use
in that period) an analysis of the performance in its creation
and its functioning: emphasis on the 'group of creators', the
fields they represent, the elements of theatrical creation they
are working with and the channels of perception of these elements.

The Actor's School (1918–19)

The actor remained the key element of these courses because,
as we can read in the notes made by his students, 'the orchestrated score of the overall performance is the carpet on which
to lay one's art'. Meyerhold, together with his pupil Leonid
Vivien, organised an Actor's School (1918–19), in which he
continued to dedicate a lot of time to the study of gymnastics,
aimed at developing not so much muscular force as elasticity and skills (acrobatics with sticks and bottles, work with
apparatus, jumps, gymnastics with fellow actors). The scenic
movement class itself, entailing specific exercises, reinforced
the material of the pupil who had been trained in the gymnastics, fencing and dance classes and by participating in group
sports. Work focused on regulating movement, understanding rhythm, the sense of tempo, seeking to establish a link
between emotion and movement.

In a second phase, scenic movement was studied as an
impulse for the spoken word. Meyerhold viewed anatomical work as the basis for actor training, just as Noverre had
done for the choreographer, since 'if an actor does not know
anatomy, no psychological study can save him'. The actor's
body, agile and in form, is also an adventurous body, a model
of audacity.

The Workshops (1921–22)

Meyerhold was already a legend: 'The father and the grand-
child of youngsters', as Viktor Shklovski named him; 'the eternal rebel', Don Quixote, Savonarola or Christopher Colum-

bus of the theatre, as others called him. He then focused on teaching and research activity.

In the autumn of 1921, Meyerhold had to endure the closure of his theatre and the death of a dear friend, poet and playwright Aleksandr Blok. This was for Meyerhold, who from then on was known as the *Master*, a period of absolute youth. Surrounded by the 'theatre guard', his pupils and disciples, some very young (17–18 years old), Meyerhold organised in an old secondary school the State Higher Theatre Direction Workshop (GVYRM). It was a sort of two-storey working commune: Meyerhold had his living quarters upstairs, while there were two workrooms and a foyer downstairs. Because of transportation difficulties almost all the students slept where courses and meetings were being held. The Workshop for directors was linked to the Laboratory of actor's techniques (which was to become Meyerhold's Free Workshop). The fusion of the two groups would result, in the spring of 1922, in a single Workshop whose name was GVYTM (State Higher Theatre Workshop). Right from the outset it was clear how important the relationship between student directors and student actors was, so much so that they all took part in the second set of Meyerhold's courses, dedicated to scenic movement and biomechanics.

Pedagogy, in combination with research, was of the utmost value to Meyerhold and his experimental activity. It was not secondary to theatrical work; indeed, it was fundamental, parallel, intended primarily to meld together a group that could give life to a theatre akin to what he was looking for. 'Everybody learns here, both pupils and teachers', the actor Erast Garin wrote.[123] Meyerhold sought to radically transform the actor's psychology. His Workshops resembled a factory of new actors, indeed of new men, men of their time.

Meyerhold prepared with his *laborantins*, Valeri Inkizhinov and Mikhail Korenev, a set of biomechanical exercises

---

[123] Erast Garin, *S Meyerhol'dom: Vospominanija* (With Meyerhold: Recollections), (Moscow: Iskusstvo, 1974), p. 44.

that were the result of researches conducted since 1913, with the contribution of American objective psychology, especially William James's theory of emotions. Linked with the political, social and ideological context of the time (Taylorisation, Americanisation), biomechanics is also closely related to research on theatre traditions. One of its essential principles, the *otkaz* (refusal) – a preparatory counter movement preceding the main movement – was discovered in the Borodinskaya Street Studio. The study of biomechanics was also in tune with the most advanced research of contemporary physiologists and reflexologists. Meyerhold read the work of these researchers, corresponded with them and sent them invitations. References to I. Pavlov, V. Bekhterev and E. Sepp fill the programmes of courses from 1920 to 1933 when, in an internal symposium on 'The method of creation of the Meyerhold theatre', the director asserted the validity of biomechanics and the importance of the brain as an initiator of tasks and guide of movement, both in life and on stage.

This type of pedagogical activity was closely tied up with research. This would result in the third performance-manifesto of the October period, *The Magnanimous Cuckold* (1922). Most of these exercises were performed by two groups facing each other. But more important still than the description of these exercises, often performed to music, are the notes on Meyerhold's views on the subject of biomechanics, taken by his assistant Korenev and kept in the Russian State Archive of Literature and Art (RGALI) in Moscow.[124]

The following text, taken in shorthand, was from a course given by the great director in October or November 1921. Meyerhold stressed the need for the individual training of the actor, in solitude, in a personal or 'private' studio, during which he can 'recreate a body' through a building up of awareness, the focus resting on himself, extended in space, handling objects typical of the theatre.

[124] Cf. Vsevolod Meyerhold, *Écrits sur le théâtre: tome 2*, ed. and trans. by Béatrice Picon-Vallin (Lausanne: L'Age d'Homme, 2009).

In the previous course, the director had conjured up the concept, taken up by Craig, of the *Über-Marionette*. He underlined that 'in itself the naked body means nothing' on stage, and that the costume, like the objects knowingly handled by the actor, 'become a part of his body'. This is the individual research that a theatre Studio must foster, as part of an experience lived almost totally within the group (exercises were performed in pairs or in groups), defined by relations with others: with the world, with society, with one's companion, with the group, with the audience. Finally, in order to perfect 'the only production tool available to him', the actor, who must seek to rationalise his acting activity, is given as a model a vision inspired not by the theatre but by life:

No craftsman, no professional, can make progress with the mastering of technique if he does not have a room at his disposal. The tailor or the carpenter have around them their own specific tools. You immediately know if you are in a hairdresser's or in another craftsman's workshop. But when you are with an actor, you might think you are with a travelling salesman. There may be one or two clues: portraits of Duse, Kachalov or Stanislavski, or a student's desk.

So what should an actor's room be like when he is preparing for a part at his home? An empty room; small and empty. No furniture, no flower-decked wallpaper. Plain, white walls. A white, empty room. Gymnastics apparatus in one corner. Something soft on the floor. But not carpets: a wooden platform, that can be washed with water. That is very important, because on stage the foot must not slip, and the figure of the actor must be firmly anchored to the ground. The first thing in this room is to be sure of not falling [...]. A bare floor, therefore, or covered with rush matting. No mirror in the room but in the bedroom. It is important for the actor to see himself when he wakes up, his hair ruffled, untidy. Thus he can quickly see his features, the curves of his body. And when he tidies himself up, and straightens out all his deformities, he must remember the moment before that. If he stretches, he must remember, while he is stretching, that moment of monstrosity.[125]

---

[125] Meyerhold, 'L'atelier de l'acteur', in *Écrits sur le théâtre: tome 2*.

'I am not a teacher', Meyerhold wrote in 1917, 'I am an explorer of new shores on the ocean of the theatre'. In his search for a 'new theatre', the director would develop a second major activity, parallel to the construction of performances, in which pedagogy and research were very closely connected. It was an activity he would remain particularly fond of even when, after 1921, his school would adopt different names and he would prepare the leaders of a separate group, and even when Studio, school and theatre were no longer clearly separated.

Music

Meyerhold's work on music and on the actor-musician went hand in hand with his research on the body.

A director-musician, an actor-musician, or an actor-composer, an actor-poet: from 1922 onwards Meyerhold used a terminology that was half-Pavlovian, half-musical, to describe the biomechanical actor. Biomechanical preparation was compared to practices intended as exercise for the player and his instrument. But in this too, if the relationship can work metaphorically, the musical model, regarding both directing and acting, is based on ideal technical understanding, controlled and progressive training, a single set of laws and a single vocabulary. And a reality for acting. As his own director, the actor based his acting on the music chosen by Meyerhold, which provided him with references and a canvas on which to sketch his acting part. As Meyerhold explained:

> A character pronounces a phrase that marks the end of a given fragment of acting, and during this time a certain music begins to be heard. This musical piece defines the start of another fragment. Thus, based on this musical track, you construct another acting fragment, which does not resemble the previous one.[126]

---

[126] RGALI, 963, 1341. Cited in Aleksandr Fevralski's notes on Meyerhold's course at the GEKTEMAS Actors' Faculty (18 January 1929).

He made the actors work with music during both biomechanical preparation and on stage, to get them used to keeping time under close control, defined not only by meter but
also by rhythm. Meyerhold compared this musical work with
that of the circus acrobat. The music gives to the acrobat's
most dangerous number the aid of a precise calculation for
sectioning and performing movements. The minimum devia-
tion from this calculation or the minimum alteration in the
music might be disastrous. Work with music gives the actor
an awareness of theatrical tempo, helps him to memorise
the text and its spatial score. To further stress this musical
work, the reference to the circus acrobat is supplemented by
Meyerhold with more erudite references: the opera singer
Chaliapin, whom he had recently seen in the performance
of *Boris Godunov* in 1911, and oriental theatre actors, the
Japanese Sada Yacco and Hanako and later on the Chinese
Mei Lanfang, who would perform in Moscow in 1935. Seeing the sense of rhythm displayed by the latter, Meyerhold
stated: 'We do not have a sense of tempo. We do not know
what it means to economise it. Mei Lanfang counts in quarters of a second, we in minutes, without even counting the
seconds.'[127]

The importance attached by Meyerhold to the actor's
rhythm while acting certainly goes back to the start of the
century. The reading of Georg Fuchs in 1906 offered him
some initial theories for what he had tried out at the Theatre Studio. He would later be rebuked, in the 1930s, for his
interest in rhythm, linking it to Symbolism. But instead of
developing the spiritual essence of the rhythmic matrix, Meyerhold saw a living force that struggled against the monotony
of the metronome,[128] or, speaking in the style of art theorist

---

[127] Vsevolod Meyerhold, 'On the Mei Lanfang tour (14 April 1935)', in *Tvorčeskoe
nasledie V. Meyerhol'da* (The Creative Legacy of V. Meyerhold), (Moscow: VTO,
1978), p. 96.
[128] 'The interval and time on stage', Meyerhold's course at the GVYRM (19 November 1921), in *Tvorčeskoe nasledie V. Meyerhol'da*. This part of the course was
translated into French in Béatrice Picon-Vallin, 'La musique dans le jeu de l'acteur

Nikolai Tarabukin, an organic movement that is opposed to mechanical movement marked by meter.[129] By taking jazz to the theatre, Meyerhold adopted as his own a new plastic-musical experience 'whose finest details', André Coeuroy wrote in a study on jazz, published in 1926, 'translate all the subtle similarities and all the deviations between the rigidity of meter and the oscillation of rhythm'.[130]

Meyerhold believed that music had to form part of the actor's education, since it is able to develop his taste and organise his body. He recommended that his actors go to many concerts, and frequent libraries, museums and exhibitions. In Meyerhold's various Studios music was always one of the subjects to be studied. In 1908 a project entailed a school in which the first-year course, the same for both musicians and actors, required everyone to learn *solfeggio* at the piano, plus singing and diction.[131] In 1921–23, at the GVYTM, in the same way, music occupied an important place in the syllabus (*solfeggio*, harmony, theory of form, counterpoint). And in the late 1920s there were courses in the history of music at the GEKTEMAS, rehearsals using music and the preparation of actors accompanied by pianists from the theatre. This all helped to develop the musicality of acting, allowing Meyerhold to sense, in 1931, a theatre with a new architecture, inspired by the perfect construction of a boat, with the participation of no other than 'the actor, the light and the music'.[132]

Certain phases of acting are constructed like constants: repetition of a fragment of acting or of a posture which, in other contexts, just as in music, is never repetition but deep study and at the same time a signal for an association. The actor-mu-

---

Meyerholdien', in *Le Jeu de l'acteur chez Meyerhold et Vakhtangov* (Paris: Librarie Klincksieck, 1981), pp. 35–56 (pp. 42–43).

[129] Cf. Nikolai Tarabukin, *Opyt Teorii Zivopisi* (Moscow: Vserossiiskii proletkul't, 1923).

[130] André Coeuroy and André Schaeffner, *Le Jazz* (Paris: Éditions Claude Aveline, 1926), pp. 31–32.

[131] RGALI, 998, 2855. School project.

[132] RGALI, 998, 674. Meyerhold's address to NARKOMPROS (13 June 1931).

sician dialogues with the music produced on stage, responds to it with his acting and may even play an instrument on stage. He must be able to intervene at the right moment, as required by the overall movement. Finally, without music, he may construct his acting on temporal fragments of varying length and on combinations thereof: regardless of gestural expressiveness, which in this case is secondary to acting, what produces meaning is the relationship between durations, calculated in seconds, and contrasting times, which give sense to the action.

The Meyerhold actor is ideally, like the actor Sergei Martinson, 'he who dances his parts'.[133] Inspired by the oriental theatre model, all of Meyerhold's performances have moments when theatre dance expresses emotions or complex mental and physiological states, with no words being spoken, concentrating tragicomic situations in violent outbursts: dance to the rhythm of tap (*The Magnanimous Cuckold*), classical dance (*Teacher Bubus*), abstract dance of the poet V. Parnach (*D.E. – Give Us Europe!*), Spanish dance of the prostitute (*The Last Fight*), the desperate dance of the engineer (*The Mandate*). There is no performance in which Meyerhold fails to use the society ball or dance floor, for which he sometimes collaborates with choreographers. These dances, having binary, ternary or quaternary rhythms – waltz, gallop, furlana, gavotte, polka, polonaise, *kamarinskaya*, can-can, foxtrot – provide a precise plastic-rhythmic form for everyday situations or psychological relations, and make it possible to raise the original anecdote behind the play to a symbolic vision, turning it into a ritual.

The allocation of parts became orchestrated, so to speak. During rehearsals for *Boris Godunov*, Meyerhold said to the company: 'Now, in the new theatre school, there are orchestral roles: who's going to be the first violin, the bass, the horn? This is a problem that we are the only ones to pose'. The actor's speech tends towards a sort of free recitative in which

---

[133] Boris Alpers, *Teatr Revolyutsii* (Theatre of the Revolution) (Moscow: Teakinopetchat, 1928), p. 42.

the voices, like bodies, come together, oppose and then respond to each other, with an alternation of solos, duets, trios, quintets and choruses.

Towards the end of the 1930s, Meyerhold spoke about his relationship with music:

> I work ten times better with an actor who loves music. You should accustom actors to music right from school. Everybody appreciates the use of 'atmospheric' music, but not many realise that music is the best organiser of time in a performance. Acting is, for the actor, his duel with time, metaphorically speaking. And in this, music becomes his best ally. It may not even be audible, but it must be felt. My dream is a performance that is rehearsed based on music, and acted without it. With and without music: since the rhythm of the performance will be organised according to the laws of music, and each actor will carry it inside.[134]

Meyerhold's research in his various laboratories attached growing importance to the role of the actor and laid the foundations for the training of directors. The documents bearing witness to this research, mostly stored in state archives, are however inaccessible or at least difficult to access, meaning that they have not been passed on to future generations. The often tragic fate of his students has also been kept quiet. But these documents are very precise tracks to be followed. Eisenstein, who helped to rescue these records, called them a 'treasure'. And for us they certainly remain a treasure.

2. In the second half of the century

Opening this second part of Chapter 3 is Zbigniew Osiński's response to Barba's question: 'Why may Grotowski's theatre laboratory be defined as such?' Osiński's intervention at the

---

[134] Aleksandr Gladkov, *Teatr: Vospominanija i razmyšlenija* (Theatre: Recollections and Meditations), (Moscow: Isskustvo, 1980), p. 282.

Aarhus conference supplements Leszek Kolankiewicz's answer to the same question (which is found in Chapter 1).

Professor Zbigniew Osiński of the University of Warsaw could, like most of the scholars participating in the Aarhus conference, be defined as a fieldwork historian. In 1984, when Grotowski was in exile in the USA and Ludwik Flaszen and the actors closed the Teatr Laboratorium in Wrocław, Osiński prevented the authorities from taking over the historical premises by creating the Centre for Study of Jerzy Grotowski's Work and for Cultural and Theatrical Research, which he directed for many years (now called the Grotowski Institute). He is the most important among the first generation of scholars who studied Grotowski, a generation which not only cultivated and cared for the memory of the Polish director but also shared his life and work. We owe to Osiński all fundamental writings on Grotowski.

It should come as no surprise that the biographical text on Grotowski that follows next is an entry from the *Dizionario dello spettacolo del '900* (Dictionary of Twentieth Century Theatre) published in Italy in 1998. In his text, Ugo Volli skilfully condenses essential information on one of the twentieth century's masters who consistently devoted himself to the 'work of the actor on himself'. Grotowski transformed this aspect of the actor's craft into an artistic apprenticeship, using art as a vehicle to transcend the dimension of the performance in a sort of yoga developed according to the knowledge and tradition of theatre in the West.

Ugo Volli is a professor of semiotics at the University of Turin and a theatre critic. He followed for several years the experiences of paratheatre in Grotowski's second phase. He knows the theatre not only as a professional spectator but also as a field researcher: he has collaborated with the centre of active culture 'Il Porto', an international group in Volterra, Italy, founded by people who had been part of the team of Grotowski's Theatre of Sources project. Volli also belonged to the core of scholars who collaborated with Eugenio Barba in the years when ISTA was founded.

Writing close up about Odin Teatret, Nordisk Teaterlabo-ratorium, Ferdinando Taviani is a theatre scholar whose fields of study are commedia dell'arte, the actors' culture, minor-ity theatre in the twentieth century, the relationship between literature and performance and the history of Luigi Pirandel-lo's theatre. Since the 1970s he has been a leading light for research as well as group theatre in Italy and elsewhere. In this book, however, he is of special interest for us for another reason: he has been the literary advisor of Odin Teatret since 1973 (and this is why, as a member of the theatre, he writes under a different name – Nando instead of Ferdinando). Tavi-ani is a researcher of Odin Teatret but also a part of it. In his two articles here, he applies a dual perspective to our subject: both as a scholar and as a member of a laboratory.

ZBIGNIEW OSIŃSKI
Jerzy Grotowski and Ludwik Flaszen

In 'Lettre à mes amis historiens', Eugenio Barba wrote: 'It is evident that my personal history and the forty years with Odin Teatret determine my way of seeing. It is no accident'. Each of us speakers could say exactly the same thing. What we can do here is to try to give our own testimony. That's all.

Why did Jerzy Grotowski found the Teatr Laboratorium with Ludwik Flaszen? Firstly, it should be clarified that it was Grotowski who took the decision to change the name of their avant-garde 'Teatr 13 Rzędów' in Opole to 'Teatr Laborato-rium 13 Rzędów' in 1962, three years after he and Flaszen had taken it over. Of course Flaszen fully accepted this and justified it publicly, but the practical activities were shaped first and foremost by Grotowski together with his actors and the architect Jerzy Gurawski.

Responding with Leszek Kolankiewicz to Eugenio Barba's question, we mentioned three basic reasons for adopting the name 'laboratory'. Firstly, *pragmatic reasons*. Secondly, *the situation in the domain of the art of the theatre in Poland and in art generally at that time*. Thirdly, *personal dispositions*: specifically, Grotowski's *laboratory background*.[135] I will briefly describe them here.

From today's perspective, the most important seem to be the *pragmatic reasons*. If Grotowski had not adopted the laboratory formula, he and his team (operating as an official, professional state institution under the Ministry of Culture in Warsaw and, accordingly, under the appropriate regional authorities in Opole and from 1965 in Wrocław) would have had to produce: 1) a *repertoire plan*, which meant the preparation of a predetermined number of premieres in the season: eight to twelve new performances (at least one of them being a Soviet or Russian drama or a play from one of the Communist bloc countries – the choice depending on current political trends); 2) a *performance schedule* containing at least six shows a week; 3) an *audience attendance plan*; 4) a *business plan*. Every state theatre had to balance its accounts with the funding body.

In practical terms, the status of a laboratory meant that the institution was free of these obligations and provided a chance for creative freedom. Briefly speaking, the conditions for the creation of such performances as *Akropolis*, *The Tragical History of Dr Faustus*, *Hamlet Study*, *The Constant Prince* and *Apocalypsis cum figuris* would not have existed without a laboratory. Also the Grotowski that we knew would not have been possible, since his creative possibilities would have been limited beyond compare.

The second reason for the adoption of the name laboratory was the specific situation found in the theatre and in art gen-

---

[135] Cf. Leszek Kolankiewicz and Zbigniew Osiński, 'Jerzy Grotowski and Ludwik Flaszen', trans. by Grzegorz Ziółkowski and Kris Salata, in 'Why a Theatre Laboratory?', *Peripeti*, no. 2 (2004), pp. 41–44.

erally. Grotowski was among those theatre artists who were fully aware of the backwardness of this domain of art in relation, on the one hand, to other artistic disciplines (especially music, literature, fine arts and architecture) and, on the other, to the natural sciences. In other words, he was beset by the feeling that theatrical art was anachronistic compared to other arts. He said and wrote this many times, including during personal meetings with me, which began in November 1962 in Poznań. He said again and again that for him it was much easier to communicate with representatives of the sciences than with those from the humanities. It is worth noting that in this respect he was not the first nor the only one among theatre people – above all among those who created theatre laboratories before him. At the beginning there was the feeling that the art of the theatre was anachronistic in three ways: in relation to other domains of art, to the sciences, and simply in relation to life. Moreover, Grotowski constantly thought that this situation should be changed by focusing creative practice on the art of the actor, as it is the immediate contact between two human beings – the actor and the spectator – that remains the ultimate and irreducible opportunity for the theatre. And he concentrated all his efforts on this task.

Since we are here in Denmark, it is worth remembering that the Bohr Institute in Copenhagen was one of the points of reference Grotowski often returned to in his laboratory work. In the chapter 'Methodical Exploration' in *Towards a Poor Theatre*, one can read: 'The Bohr Institut has fascinated me for a long time as a model illustrating a certain type of activity.'[136] At the same time, the creator of the Teatr Laboratorium never identified art with science but indicated certain parallels between them and the possibility of mutual inspiration.

Such a diagnosis and therapy for the theatre were Grotowski's mode of self-definition in relation to the existing theatre and

---

[136] Grotowski, *Towards a Poor Theatre*, p. 127.

other artistic disciplines. They were also a practical indication of the territory of his identity and of the institution he guided.

Thirdly, and last but not least, we have to take into account Grotowski's *personal predispositions*, his affiliation with something that I would call a laboratory background in the domain of theatre art. After graduating from high school he faced the problem of choosing which subject to study. Eventually he decided to study acting at a drama school because of his personal circumstances. Many years afterwards, Grotowski spoke about this:

> I chose three subjects: theatre school, with the intention to continue to study as a director, medical school thinking about psychiatry, Oriental studies with the idea of concentrating on traditional Eastern techniques. The order of the entrance exams was such that the exams for the theatre school were first. This alone decided that I became the holder of a diploma which gives me the right to work in the theatre. If the entrance exam to medical school had been first, I would probably have become a psychiatrist; if it had been the exam for Oriental studies, I would have studied Eastern traditional techniques. Yet I am convinced that one way or another I would eventually have found myself in the same place where I am now. Obviously my vocabulary would be different, because now I am marked by my theatre experience, even though I went beyond the theatre. I suppose that, similarly, I would have gone beyond traditional psychiatry or oriental philology anyway.[137]

A penchant for contradiction, which reflected his attitude towards man, the world and nature, had already appeared in Grotowski in his childhood, which he spent in a village, both during and after the war. It later became an essential feature of his thinking. It was also during his childhood that his understanding of the human logical process first appeared. An anti-discursive and antithetical way of thinking characterised him. In the text 'Theatre and Ritual' (1969), he formulated the following in reference to the Teatr Laboratorium actor:

---

[137] Jerzy Grotowski, 'Teatr Źródeł' (Theatre of Sources), p. 105. This passage does not appear in the English language version published in *The Grotowski Sourcebook*.

But following the way of structure, one needs to reach this real act in which a contradiction is inherent. It was of great importance to understand that these contradictions are logical. One should not strive towards avoiding contradictions; on the contrary, the essence of things is included in contradictions.[138]

And ten years later he confessed:

You are right if you think that there are many contradictions in what I am saying. I am aware that I am contradicting myself in what I say, but please remember that on a basic level, I am a practitioner. And practice is contradictory. This is its substance. So if I am contradictory, I am so as a practitioner. I cannot theorise about practice. I can only talk about my adventure, with all the contradictions which were there and which are there. When for example I say that something is not logical, I want to say that it is not the result of using logic. I always speak in a pragmatic way. And can it then be said that this is illogical? When you do something, you do not set yourself questions about logic.[139]

In Grotowski's understanding, this paradoxical logic – based on the principle of complementarity (and-and), and not on the principle of exclusiveness (either-or) – reflects the contradictions inherent in the very substance of the profession he practiced and which he always understood as a vocation.

Grotowski studied acting at the State Higher Theatre School in Kraków during one of the worst periods of contemporary Polish history. The years 1951–55 were the peak of the Stalinist period in Poland, with the severest repression and persecution. All aspects of public and, to a large extent, private life were controlled. From the very beginning of his studies Grotowski belonged to the Students' Science Circle, and

[138] Cf. Jerzy Grotowski, 'Teatr a rytuał' (Theatre and Ritual), *Dialog*, no. 8 (1969), pp. 64–74 (p. 71). Reprinted in Jerzy Grotowski, *Teksty z lat 1965–1969. Wybór* (Texts from the Years 1965–1969: A Selection), ed. by Janusz Degler and Zbigniew Osiński (Wrocław: Wydawnictwo Wiedza o kulturze, 1990), pp. 61–86 (p. 71).
[139] Jerzy Grotowski, 'O praktykowaniu romantyzmu' ('On Practising Romanticism'), *Dialog*, no. 3 (1980), 112–120 (p. 120).

in the third year he became its chairman.[140] He led practical work on Stanislavski's 'method of physical actions'. Essentially, it was classical self-study work consisting of rehearsals with students of the same age and younger colleagues. Forty years later, in 1993, in a film made by the Swede Marianne Ahrne in Pontedera, the last film in which he participated, Grotowski said:

> It was the epoch of Stalinism then, with very harsh censorship, so all my attention as a director was therefore focused on the fact that the performance can be censored but not the rehearsals. For me, the rehearsals were always the most important thing. It was there where this thing happened between one man and another, between an actor and me, and this thing could touch this axis, this axial symmetry, out of sight and beyond external control. And this has remained in my work; it means that the performance has always been less important than the work done in rehearsals.[141]

It was in the Students' Science Circle that Grotowski read Vasili Osipovich Toporkov's book *Stanislavski in Rehearsal: the Final Years*, published for the first time in 1949. This book, written by an outstanding Russian actor, director and teacher, is regarded as the most important source of knowledge on Stanislavski's work in the last period of his life, especially on the method of physical actions. For Grotowski, it served as a guidebook in everyday work with actors, and this seems to me to be the reason for his special attachment to it.[142] It simply worked in practice, so for Grotowski it was not important that in those years Toporkov's book was regarded by many people as one of the versions of a Stalinist interpretation of Stanislavski. Grotowski could find in it what he most badly needed and what remained obscure forever for others as well

---

[140] Cf. Zbigniew Osiński, 'Pierwsze laboratorium teatralne Grotowskiego. Studenckie Koło Naukowe, 1951–1959' (Grotowski's First Theatre Laboratory. Students' Science Circle, 1951–1959), in Osiński, *Grotowski. Źródła, inspiracje, konteksty*, pp. 43–72.

[141] *Il Teatr Laboratorium di Jerzy Grotowski*, dir. by Marianne Ahrne.

[142] Cf. Osiński, 'Pierwsze laboratorium teatralne Grotowskiego'.

as for his colleagues. This constitutes one of his secrets: he could find a real treasure in the place where others did not look or could find nothing.

Throughout his life, he was characterised by a passion for specifically understood and practised research work. By creating an artistic institution in the framework of a laboratory, Grotowski opened up for himself and his group the possibility of doing research for its own sake, and also of creating the most important performances and other projects of the Teatr Laboratorium. Under Polish conditions at that time, it was unique and extraordinary and, as later turned out, it was also unique in world theatre.

The idea of a theatre laboratory or artistic laboratory was always very close to Grotowski, as it conditioned the essence of his work regardless of whether or not this was reflected in the official name of the institution led by him (as in Opole and later in Wrocław) or not (as in the USA and in Italy). Laboratory work embraced the values which Grotowski not only accepted but also created, making a long-lasting contribution in this area.

It could be said that Grotowski strove in his own particular way towards the 'disenchantment' of the actor's profession. This meant that acting is above all a craft, a job like any other. Hence he passionately fought against actors' folly and megalomania. And he did this in the simplest way: through hard, precise and systematic daily labour.

As early as 1966 Peter Brook wrote the words which entered into the canon of twentieth-century theatre thinking:

> Grotowski is unique. Why? Because no-one else in the world, to my knowledge, no one since Stanislavski, has investigated the nature of acting, its phenomenon, its meaning, the nature and science of its mental-physical-emotional processes as deeply and completely as Grotowski.
>
> He calls his theatre a laboratory. It is. It is a centre of research. [...] In Grotowski's theatre as in all true laboratories the experiments are scientifically valid because the essential conditions are observed. In

his theatre, there is absolute concentration by a small group, and unlimited time.

[...]

With a proviso. This dedication to acting does not make acting an end in itself. On the contrary. For Grotowski acting is a vehicle. How can I put it? The theatre is not an escape, a refuge. A way of life is a way to life. Does that sound like a religious slogan? It should do. And that's about all there was to it[143].

Thus it is no coincidence that Grotowski regards himself as an inheritor and perpetuator of Konstantin Stanislavski who initiated the tradition of Studios and laboratories in the twentieth century.

I will focus now on providing the answer to the first of the twelve questions posed by Eugenio Barba in his 'Letter to the Speakers':

> The name theatre-laboratory does not have to be related to theatre research, avant-garde theatre, experimental theatre, third theatre, theatre project, etc. The fact that many theatre laboratories were in the past and are also now avant-garde theatres does not necessarily mean that the avant-garde must be related automatically to a laboratory.

Tadeusz Kantor's art provides one of the most distinctive examples of this situation. Kantor was described as 'an eternal avant-garde artist', and he called himself the 'only authentic' avant-garde artist. This example also includes a reflection that relates to our subject.

We may all agree that the theatre laboratory consists of a stable team of people working according to methods adopted from science. Such a team works in a certain domain for many years. Usually this domain is the actor's art. The result of this work is an *Opus*, which is similar to ancient and medieval alchemy, which was not called an art for nothing.

---

[143] Peter Brook, 'Preface', in Grotowski, *Towards a Poor Theatre*, pp. 11–13 (pp. 11–12).

Leszek Kolankiewicz speaks about this. It is worth noting that Grotowski in his Workcenter in Pontedera called *Action* an *Opus*. Etymologically, a laboratory means a workshop equipped with the appropriate apparatus designed for carrying out research and experiments.

Hence there is the essence of a laboratory and there are specific 'realisations' each time. Thanks to them the essence gains a concrete shape, and there are also multiple determining factors of this essence.

I propose to use the term theatre laboratory, with its descriptive and typological meanings and not as an evaluative one. From an evaluative perspective, theatre laboratories would be seen as something better in their nature than non-laboratory theatres. Mixing up these two perspectives and ranges – descriptive and evaluative – can amount to essential misunderstandings.

Moreover, theatre laboratories are a quite recent phenomenon, which is characteristic of the twentieth century, and for a long time geographically limited, above all to European theatre. Beyond Europe, theatre laboratories appeared as a side-effect of cultural importation.

In the Polish context, only two groups in the twentieth century can be classified as theatre laboratories, and they regarded themselves and were commonly known as such. In the first half of the century there was the Reduta Theatre directed by Juliusz Osterwa and Mieczysław Limanowski, which operated between 1919 and 1939, and in the second half the Teatr Laboratorium, led by Jerzy Grotowski and Ludwik Flaszen from 1959 to 1984.

Obviously a question should be asked: would the creation of the Teatr Laboratorium in 1962 in the small Silesian town of Opole have been at all possible without Jerzy Grotowski? His persistence and uncompromising nature, which has long since become legendary and a part of theatre history, his creative and artistic radicalism connected with a clear-headedness and exceptional ability to move in the complicated meanderings of the reality of that time – were all these his personal traits, or are they features that belong to people from a certain background? The names which could be recalled here would first of all be the names of the heroes of our encounter: Konstantin Stanislavski, Evgeni Vakhtangov, Vsevolod Meyerhold, Juliusz Osterwa and his Reduta in Poland, and amongst the living: Peter Brook, Eugenio Barba and others.

The work of Grotowski was accompanied in Poland by ignorance and silence on the part of the traditionally-oriented theatre milieu, and also, from time to time, by local intrigues and smear campaigns, as well as attempts to liquidate his theatre. Grotowski has described this situation clearly enough:

> For many years, this particular phenomenon follows us in everything we do and, I have to say, also in my personal activities. It is openly or less openly expressed, and always in the same terms: impostor, charlatan.[144]

However, it should be stressed that from the very beginning, Grotowski was understood and supported by some remarkable representatives of the so-called ordinary theatre in Poland. But there were exceptions, and this fact should not be overlooked.

Polemical reactions came above all from artists leaning towards the avant-garde and from outstanding creators like Tadeusz Kantor and Włodzimierz Staniewski. The former questioned the idea of a laboratory in art, which resided at the opposite extreme from his artistic interests. In Kantor's opinion, true art and true artistry cannot accept 'experiments'; therefore research in this field should be abandoned. This is something that differentiates art from science, and they should not be identified with one another. Art is above all the result of the artist's gift, and the creative act is the repetition of divine

---

[144] Jerzy Grotowski, 'Jak żyć by można', *Odra*, no. 4 (1972), 33–38 (p. 34). This fragment does not appear in the English version: Jerzy Grotowski, 'How One Could Live', *Le Théâtre en Pologne/The Theatre in Poland*, 4–5 (1975), 33–34.

creation. The talent of the artist is decisive in measuring the value of a work of art.[145]

Tadeusz Kantor's conversation with Marian Sienkiewicz about his artistic traditions, published in November 1974 in the weekly *Literatura*, is the most exhaustive of his pronouncements on this subject. One of the questions to the artist was: 'Is an experiment avant-garde?' In response, the artist quoted the following fragment from his manifesto written four years earlier:

We don't recognise such terminology and situations as atelier or workshop, research, experiment, laboratory, etc. that are so fashionable now. Art is an incessant discovery of the 'new' and the 'impossible'. It discards what was before, it is an uninterrupted and alive development and change.

The notions of atelier and workshop contain all the characteristic features of academism. They appear and receive value just as the idea freezes and loses any perspective for development. From the start they are driven by a specialist narrowing of horizons and relations with the totality of art and life, and they are connected with the search for support and rescue in canons, quasi sectarian recipes, with the disappearance of invention and imagination.

In art, a clear and new idea always equals a 'perfect' means of expression. In authentic art it is 'miraculous' that revelation equals perfection. [...] Creativity is not testing, it is a decision, a 'discovery' 'Discovery' in art happens in completely unexpected, often scandalous and ridiculous conditions. It happens in an instant.

Besides, a 'discovery', or rather the creation of a 'new sensibility', may happen only in the field of friction among many contradicting ideas, in the furnace of topicality and, so important today, beyond the small backyard of professionalism, by *annexing* 'foreign' territories, through *going beyond* professional borders, through 'treason', in what was regarded until today as the core and specific focus of a certain domain. Any creation of artificial and safe *sanctuaries* for a work of art has nothing to do with the avant-garde.[146]

---

[145] Cf. Zbigniew Osiński, 'Kantor i Grotowski: dwa teatry, dwie wizje' (Kantor and Grotowski: Two Theatres, Two Visions), in Osiński, *Grotowski. Źródła, inspiracje, konteksty*, pp. 381–386.

[146] Tadeusz Kantor, 'Świadomość sztuki. Rozmowa z Tadeuszem Kantorem' (Awareness of Art. Conversation with Tadeusz Kantor), interview with Marian Sienkiewicz, *Literatura*, no. 46 (14 November 1974), p. 3.

In Tadeusz Kantor's opinion, laboratories, Studios, workshops or ateliers are some kind of artistic sanctuary. His remarks refer not only to theatre but also to art in its totality. Many times and on different occasions the artist recalled Witkacy's words, included in his thoughts 'O artystycznym teatrze' (On the Artistic Theatre): 'In art one cannot probe; one has to create, whilst being, so to speak, tightly buttoned-up.'[147] In this way, Kantor radically distanced himself from the whole twentieth-century tradition of Studios and theatre laboratories, above all from the Teatr Laboratorium of Jerzy Grotowski, as he was often asked about this during press conferences and in interviews.[148]

It is significant that among those artists whom Kantor regarded in different periods as being part of his tradition, he never mentioned the founders of theatre laboratories such as Konstantin Stanislavski, Leopold Sulerzhitski, Juliusz Osterwa's and Mieczysław Limanowski's Reduta, Jacques Copeau, Étienne Decroux, Jerzy Grotowski, who I have already mentioned, and also, for different reasons, Antonin Artaud. Instead he kept referring to Edward Gordon Craig, Stanisław Wyspiański, Vsevolod Meyerhold (who fascinated him above all as one of the greatest avant-garde artists and also as an ethical example, a man who was ready to pay for his art with his own life), Aleksandr Tairov, Kazimir Malevich, Vladimir Tatlin, Leon Schiller, Andrzej Pronaszko and the artists of the Bauhaus. This chosen tradition is telling us something, directing us towards something.

Perhaps he spoke most directly about this to a journalist whose opinion was that his theatre, Cricot 2, operating 'on the margins of the official theatre movement', was precisely 'a terrain of artistic research, a laboratory theatre.' Kantor re-

---

[147] The phrase 'tightly buttoned-up' is a Polish idiom suggesting a state of readiness and preparation. Cf. Stanisław Ignacy Witkiewicz (Witkacy), 'O artystycznym teatrze', in Stanisław Ignacy Witkiewicz, *Dzieła zebrane: 'Teatr' i inne pisma o teatrze* ('Theatre' and Other Writings on the Theatre), ed. by Janusz Degler, (Warszawa: Państwowy Instytut Wydawniczy, 1995), p. 389.
[148] Cf. Osiński, 'Kantor i Grotowski: dwa teatry, dwie wizje'.

sponded: 'Art is not probing but is a process and a situation in which there is only one and irrevocable solution'.[149]

In the presence of his collaborators, Tadeusz Kantor sometimes used the malicious term 'ambulatory theatre' instead of laboratory theatre, thinking of course about Grotowski. He stated firmly that one should be an avant-garde artist for one's whole life, not only when young.

It is well-known that Włodzimierz Staniewski belonged to the artistic team of the Teatr Laboratorium in Wrocław from 1971 to 1976. In 1977 he founded the Centre for Theatre Practices, 'Gardzienice', and remains its director. It seems that for him the most important thing was the social aspect of theatre work. This is his statement which defines his relationship to Grotowski's work:

> Nevertheless those experiments had a laboratory character. They were closed, separated from the social context, referring mainly to psychology, to intimate experiences, to the exploration of the inner life of an individual. [...] I think that using psychologism in theatre is a big mistake. [...] [It] may lead to something awful and agonizing. [...]
> I don't try to appeal to the individual, personal experiences of the actor, I don't penetrate his soul. I would not exploit an important, individual, personal experience of the actor in order to create a stage structure out of it. And this is what Grotowski did with Ryszard Cieślak in *The Constant Prince*. He often repeated that they drew material for the role from an ecstatic experience from Ryszard's early youth. I think that such a game may lead to risky things, to volatility, to disorientation, and maybe even to self-destruction.
> In my theatre it is completely different. [...] Ours is not a psychological theatre. I try to escape from psychology and psychoanalysis. [...] I try to lead the person I am working with in such a way so that he/she sees her/himself as a small part of nature, which responds to all this, which is 'in response' to everything that plays around and about.[150]

---

[149] Tadeusz Kantor, 'Autonomia teatru. Rozmowa z Tadeuszem Kantorem' (Theatre Authonomy: Conversation with Tadeusz Kantor), interview with Jerzy L. Ordan, *Fakty*, no. 9 (1976), p. 9.

[150] Włodzimierz Staniewski, 'Goście Starego Teatru. Spotkanie jedenaste: z Włodzimierzem Staniewskim rozmawiała Małgorzata Dziewulska. Kraków, Stary Teatr,

Staniewski cuts himself off from a laboratory in the name of 'objectivity' and 'social concerns', which are understood as possibly common and comprise the external verification of criteria for evaluating artistic phenomena. Grotowski's Teatr Laboratorium became for him a synonym of sectarianism in the domain of theatre art. I regard such a firm critique of the idea and practice of a laboratory, on the part of one of the former members of the team, as an example of a critique from the 'inside'.

As can be seen, Grotowski's laboratory was and is subjected to attacks in many different ways also by some representatives of the theatre's avant-garde. He was blamed for underestimating talent in art, for carrying out some kind of sectarianism which shows a lack of sensitivity in relation to the real social context, for being non-authentic, for a lack of objectivity, and even for being completely unable to be objective.

I recalled here Kantor's and Staniewski's positions as *an expression of the creative attitude* declared by these artists. An answer to the question of the extent to which such a reflection agrees with their own artistic practices, deserves a separate and extensive study. In my opinion, the Centre for Theatre Practices 'Gardzienice' actually performs classical laboratory work, but in a completely different way than Grotowski used to do. I could also speak about some laboratory elements in the case of Kantor's Cricot 2. I have an ally in terms of such an approach. Ludwik Flaszen posed a question in his presentation at the international symposium 'Theatre Laboratories and Studio Theatres in Europe in the Twentieth Century: Techniques and Values. Reconnaissance', organised by the Grotowski Centre in April 1997 in Wrocław:

> ...but what about Kantor for example? Would it be completely absurd to add to the name Cricot the word 'laboratory' or 'studio' al-

19 czerwca 1994' (Guests of the Stary Teatr, Eleventh Meeting: Włodzimierz Staniewski in conversation with Małgorzata Dziewulska. Kraków, the Stary Theatre, 19 June 1994), *Teatr*, no. 12 (1994), pp. 10, 13–14.

though of course … this great artist would burst into scornful laughter at the thought of such an operation? Nevertheless it would be a shame to eliminate Kantor from the circle of our thinking. Like many others – secret allies – for whom the title of our symposium would not be suited at all.[151]

The name theatre laboratory was always problematic. It is problematic now, and it probably will be in the future. Some theatre artists for instance work in a laboratory way, but for many different reasons they are not called creators of theatre laboratories and/or do not want to be perceived in this way. Here are three very different examples from Poland: Tadeusz Kantor's Cricot 2, the Centre for Theatre Practices 'Gardzienice' directed by Włodzimierz Staniewski, and Krystian Lupa, who operates within the framework of 'ordinary' theatres like the Stary Teatr in Kraków and the Teatr Dramatyczny in Warsaw. One of the most outstanding Polish theatre directors, Konrad Swinarski, did the same before Lupa, in the late 1960s and early 1970s in the Stary Teatr. He was a friend of Grotowski's who thought highly of him. Swinarski (1929–75) died prematurely in an aeroplane crash flying to Damascus.[152] However, it was Juliusz Osterwa who introduced laboratory experiences to ordinary theatres in the mid-1920s, regarding this as one of the basic tasks of his Reduta Theatre; he used to call it 'interlocking the Reduta

[151] Ludwik Flaszen, 'Kilka kluczy do laboratoriów, studiów i instytutów' (Some Keys to Laboratories, Studios and Institutes), *Dialog*, no. 7 (1998), 108–117 (p. 108). Cf. French edition: Ludwik Flaszen, 'À propos des laboratoires, studios et instituts', ed. by Monique Borie, trans. by Magdalena Marek, *Alternatives théâtrales*, nos. 70–71 (2001), 63–69 (p. 63).

[152] Cf. Jerzy Grotowski, 'Z korespondencji Jerzego Grotowskiego do Barbary i Konrada Swinarskich' (From Jerzy Grotowski's correspondence with Barbara and Konrad Swinarski), *Teatr*, nos. 1–3 (2000), pp. 71–72; Zbigniew Osiński, *Teatr Dionizosa. Romantyzm w polskim teatrze współczesnym* (Theatre of Dionysos: Romanticism in Contemporary Polish Theatre), (Kraków: Wydawnictwo Literackie, 1972); Małgorzata Dziewulska, 'Swinarski i Grotowski: dwa teatry, dwa bluźnierstwa' (Swinarski and Grotowski: Two Theatres, Two Blasphemies), *Dialog*, no. 12 (1990), 87–94; Joanna Walaszek, *Konrad Swinarski i jego krakowskie inscenizacje* (Konrad Swinarski and His Kraków Productions), (Warszawa: Państwowy Instytut Wydawniczy, 1991).

methods'.[153] Some members of the Reduta followed his example, obviously with quite different results.[154]

Here I would just like to point out the fact that this problem can hardly be rationalised, and examining groups as specific as laboratories depends to a large extent on the *contexts* in which a group operates, especially the cultural and political contexts (perhaps it is no accident that political systems which are regarded as totalitarian do not in principle accept laboratory groups and laboratory work). But it also depends on the personal relationships between specific people.

All the same, I do not wish to reduce arguments involving remarkable artists to the level of anecdote and personal animosity. Quite the opposite: for example, going against the dominant opinion of today, I see in Tadeusz Kantor's opposition to Jerzy Grotowski's artistic attitude one of the most important artistic debates of the second half of the twentieth century in the domain of the theatre.

When we study Grotowski's texts, our attention is drawn by formulations such as 'It was very scholarly but I could not draw any practical conclusion from it'.[155] For Grotowski, practical experience and its value were always decisive. He could have repeated after Jung: 'I am first and foremost an empiricist'.[156] Or, what is most likely, he would express this in a much stronger way: I am above all a practitioner.

[153] Cf. Juliusz Osterwa, 'List do Stefana Żeromskiego z 5 kwietnia 1924 roku' (Letter to Stefan Żeromski, 5 April 1924), in *Listy Juliusza Osterwy* (Juliusz Osterwa's Letters), (Warszawa: Państwowy Instytut Wydawniczy, 1968), pp. 60–62; Juliusz Osterwa, *Reduta i teatr. Artykuły – wywiady – wspomnienia* (The Reduta and Theatre: Articles – Interviews – Memoirs), ed. by Zbigniew Osiński and Teresa Grażyna Zabłocka (Wrocław: Wydawnictwo Wiedza o kulturze, 1991); Juliusz Osterwa, *Z zapisków*, ed. by Ireneusz Guszpit (Wrocław: Wydawnictwo Wiedza o kulturze, 1992); Mieczysław Limanowski and Juliusz Osterwa, *Listy* (Letters), ed. by Zbigniew Osiński, (Warszawa: Państwowy Instytut Wydawniczy, 1987).

[154] Cf. Zbigniew Osiński, *Pamięć Reduty. Osterwa, Limanowski, Grotowski* (The Memory of the Reduta: Osterwa, Limanowski, Grotowski), (Gdańsk: słowo/obraz terytoria, 2003), pp. 29–110.

[155] Jerzy Grotowski, 'Głos' (The Voice), *Dialog*, no. 1 (1980), 109–123 (p. 114); reprinted in Grotowski, *Teksty z lat 1965–1969*, pp. 111–144 (p. 122).

[156] Carl Gustav Jung, *Letters: Vol. I*, ed. by Gerhard Adler and Aniela Jaffé, trans. by R. F. C. Hull (London: Routledge and Kegan Paul, 1973), p. 195.

As a result there is the distinction between 'Grotowski's practice' and some kind of 'Grotowskian theory' or 'philosophy' (or how shall I put it?). After all, his whole 'philosophy' and 'world view' were always: practice, practising, research, experiencing, sometimes making discoveries, constantly on a creative adventure. And this encompasses *totality* and *completeness*, understood and treated in this case as the antithesis of all incompleteness and schizophrenia, all divisions, splits or dilemmas so characteristic of our times.[157] In his honorary degree speech delivered at Wrocław University in April 1991, Grotowski said: 'One has to devote oneself totally to make the act total. And a total act [is indispensable] to make man total, as Mickiewicz suggested'.[158]

This means precisely that it is impossible to accomplish a 'total act' if one is not a 'total human being'. Therefore the actor's 'total act' in Grotowski's practice means aspiration towards the transformation of man, always in practical experience, and through practising the craft. If this is not understood, it will lead to fundamental misunderstandings, as in the case of those theatre people (as well as critics) of a completely different artistic lineage, type and quality of work who point to Ryszard Cieślak's roles in the Teatr Laboratorium in Wrocław. For Grotowski, a laboratory was undoubtedly a central concern in the totality of his artistic output. Perhaps it was the most important thing besides the 'total act'. These two issues were interdependent: the 'total act' of Ryszard Cieślak in *The Constant Prince* would be completely impossible outside the Teatr Laboratorium and a laboratory type of work.

I agree with Eugenio Barba that 'among the fundamental aspects of the scenic profession, a theatre-laboratory concentrates mostly on those that concern the actor'. But I would like to add that in other companies as well we meet the dominant

[157] Cf., for example, Grotowski, 'He Wasn't Entirely Himself'.
[158] Jerzy Grotowski, 'Przemówienie doktora honoris causa Jerzego Grotowskiego' (Jerzy Grotowski's Speech on Receiving his Honorary Doctorate), *Notatnik Teatralny*, no. 4 (1992) 19–24 (p. 21).

position of the actor. These are companies which we would not call laboratories or which do not treat themselves as such. For example, the Stary Teatr in Kraków in performances directed by Konrad Swinarski and Jerzy Jarocki. It is telling that Grotowski valued highly these two outstanding but very different directors, despite the fact that their aesthetic was completely different from his own,and in many ways stayed at the opposite end of the scale.

I share also the conviction that: 'Despite enormous historical, morphological and contextual differences, a continuity and an essential similarity exist between certain theatres of the Great Reform in the first decades of the twentieth century and the experience of the theatre laboratories in the second half of the same century'.

But instead of a long argument, for which there is not enough space here, I recall Juliusz Osterwa, who in 1924 stated that theatre cannot be a 'business venture' but should strive to be a project where 'everything depends on a base, on a ground, on a foundation, on a notion'.[159] Over eighty years later these words have lost none of their relevance. At least, they deserve to be treated seriously. Osterwa responded to this basic, fundamental challenge which embraced the deepest sense and calling of the theatre art, by creating, together with Limanowski, the Reduta Theatre. Grotowski and Flaszen responded to the same challenge in a completely different way when they created the Teatr Laboratorium project.

Translated from Polish
by Grzegorz Ziółkowski and Paul Allain

UGO VOLLI
A biographical note on Jerzy Grotowski

Jerzy Grotowski (Rzeszów 1933 – Pontedera 1999), Polish theatre director. [...] Grotowski's independent theatre adventure began in 1959 (he had previously studied acting and directing at the thea-

---

[159] Osterwa, 'List do Stefana Żeromskiego z 5 kwietnia 1924 roku', p. 61.

tre school in Kraków and one year in Moscow, and between 1957 and 1959 had directed a few performances). In 1959, together with Ludwik Flaszen, he was assigned a theatre in the town of Opole. It was a small theatre with only 13 rows of chairs, hence the name Teatr 13 Rzędów. Grotowski put together a group of collaborators who were as young as he was, the most important of whom was the literary and theatrical critic Ludwik Flaszen who was also the theatre's literary director. After two years, Eugenio Barba, an Italian student residing in Norway, joined him, who would go on to become his right-hand man. Grotowski began working on in-depth linguistic and pedagogic experimentation, with the declared aim of creating a theatre capable of resisting the competition of the cinema and television. [...]

The performances Grotowski staged underwent a deep process of dramaturgic processing, which often sought to renew their sense, with a radical shifting of setting and psychological mood, and unprecedented experimentation of scenic space. [...] Yet work focused in particular on the actor's art. His actors quickly fell in to a daily routine of training based on technical and creative exercises, and above all made efforts to overcome physical and psychological limits and achieve a veritable 'self-penetration'. They would work on the voice, on the body, transform the face into a ductile mask, seeking above all an extreme truth of the actor's presence. [...]

In the meantime, Grotowski, as a director, was breaking all the rules: destroying the separate space of the performance, eliminating artificial elements such as external lighting and recorded music, mixing actors with spectators, manufacturing amazing performances with extremely poor materials, inventing sarcastic interpretations of the sacred texts of Polish classical drama. In 1965 the theatre moved from Opole to a much more important city, Wrocław, but remained in a very small venue and, although changing name several times, always kept the appellation Teatr Laboratorium, almost as a declaration of intents. European visitors began turning up. Three of his performances (*Akropolis*, *The Constant Prince* and *Apocalypsis cum figuris*) travelled to Europe, the USA, Australia, Mexico, drumming up enormous interest. Grotowski's book *Towards a Poor Theatre*, compiled together with Eugenio Barba, became the bible of theatrical experimentation all over the world, from South America to Japan.

When his international fame was at its height, in 1969, Grotowski again did the unexpected: he dropped out of the theatre scene, at least the traditional 'performance theatre'. In his plans to make the theatre a *space of encounter*, the creation of extremely sharp and perfect productions was not enough. He was searching for more truth, tired of accepting the principle of make-believe underpinning every performance.

He took charge of groups that worked for weeks on end in empty halls, without a script and without spectators, searching for 'organic actions'. Or he took his collaborators to places in nature, making them become aware of their bodies and the natural surroundings and substances. He invented the 'dramaturgy of the encounter', the paratheatre, interest in which peaked in the late 1970s. But not even these secret and moving ceremonies, which came to Italy via a notable Venice *Biennale* in 1975, went far enough for him. He saw in them the defect of being limited to an interpersonal meeting and of staying on the surface of the core issue, that of human nature.

Grotowski went on to explore the most diverse cultures, searching for traditions that use the body in movement as a tool for revelation and experience: Haitian vodou with its African roots, Mexican traditions, the songs of the Bauls from India. He reported these physical 'experiences of solitude' in a series of seminars that were given the title Theatre of Sources. He gradually drew up a theory of the Performer (with a capital 'P') as an individual capable of channelling in his body ancestral memories and cosmic energies and theorised 'art as a vehicle'.

This rich experience, accumulated through the 1980s and 1990s, did not remain in the private sphere, but was disseminated through meetings, seminars, exchanges, conferences, organised mainly in Pontedera, where his laboratory was based thanks to the generous help of Roberto Bacci's Centre for Theatrical Experimentation. He published a few texts about his theory of the 'Performer', while a couple of films illustrated his activity. On very few and sheltered occasions it was possible for carefully chosen people to view the ceremonies (which he no longer called performances) resulting from the final phase of his work. They consisted of a ritual event with simple physical actions and highly evocative chants, striking emotionally the 'witnesses' (no longer spectators). Grotowski was increasingly the master of generations of actors: a secret master, apparently silent, but essential.[160]

---

[160] *Dizionario dello spettacolo del '900*, ed. by Felice Cappa and Piero Gelli, (Milan: Baldini & Castoldi, 1998).

NANDO TAVIANI
Enclave

*From the Galapagos of the theatre rain down loved and
monstrous animals into the puddles and swimming pools
of our houses. Yet we pretend not to recognise ourselves*

Federico Maloyan[161]

Theatre enclaves and theatre laboratories

By 'theatre enclave' I mean those theatrical formations that
stand by themselves without adopting the conventions of the
theatrical system in which they live (artistic forms, production methods, inner organisation and ways of entering into
contact with the spectators).

The distinction between theatre enclave and theatre laboratory applies not to different phenomena, but to different
ways of looking at them. The characteristics of the theatre
enclaves, as we will try to define them in these pages, can
be found in theatre groups and troupes in Europe (mostly in
Italy, Scandinavia, Poland and France) and in Latin America.

Theatre enclaves often distinguish themselves from 'normal' theatres by their name. They proclaim their own difference of category (laboratory, workshop, *taller*, *atelier*, etc) or
hoist a word-symbol (Sun, Living, Nucleus, Continuous, An-
gel, Odin, Hidden, Cruelty, Burning, Trap, Exile, Tribangi).
These theatres – and this is something unheard of in the eyes
of tradition – are indifferent to the mother tongues of their
actors. They don't regularly produce or stage performances;
they don't adopt standard and 'reasonable' rehearsal sched-
ules; they don't engage actors for one season or one production only, and they usually keep to one director. Theatre enclaves often work on a 'project' basis. When possible, they
apply for grants destined for research, cultural innovation and
social activities. But they are not recognised as a specific theatrical category nor are there funds intended only for them.
Above all, they contradict the actors' habit of moving from

[161] From a personal letter to the author).

one theatre to another, a predominant trait in almost all theatrical systems. They tend to maintain a continuity, with many comings and goings, but also with actors remaining for many years, even decades. When an actor leaves, it is not because of the end of a contract. It is not a simple goodbye, but a true separation – consensual or traumatic.

The dimensions of a theatre enclave generally correspond to those of a small to medium-sized troupe. But from a socio-cultural point of view they have the nature of small and different 'traditions'.[162]

None of the characteristics listed above are exclusive to theatre enclaves, nor does every theatre enclave share all those characteristics with the others. As a whole, however, these traits serve to define them, even though each remains different in its own way.

In terms of political geography, we find at times miniature states encapsulated within a larger state. In terms of theatrical geography, theatre enclaves occupy similar positions. They are small places in which theatre is reinvented from top to bottom for self-study reasons, for convenience or because of extremism, reconstructing the completeness of an entire world in a small circle.

It is enough to place our point of view outside the general theatre system to realise that theatre enclaves are also outposts, enabling the theatrical imagination to be grafted onto the socially repressed sphere. By the same logic, they are also particularly suited to scientific exploration of the performance language and to building bridges with other traditions. A style of humble, disciplined life and a sense of intellectual aristocracy, concentration in peripheral places and international openness are vital contrasts for theatre enclaves.

---

[162] This is not an exaggeration. A tradition is such not because of its dimensions or antiquity, but because of a certain completeness of functions; because of the density (and not the extension) of its history; because it is aware of its difference; because of its own peculiar patrimony of ways of thinking, knowledge, habits and technical procedures.

The terms 'theatre enclave' and 'theatre laboratory' are almost synonymous. The adverb *almost*, however, must be strongly emphasised. The word 'enclave' focuses attention on borders and invites us to consider the separation from the theatrical system not only as a stratagem to protect one's own independence but also as a preliminary condition to shape a *collective mind*.

The importance of *separation through meaningful differences* for the growth of artistic and cultural life, for increasing socialisation and integration, in a word: for innovation, can never be stressed enough. Throughout the twentieth century the main sources of innovation have apparently been the theories and, more concretely, the independent theatrical territories or theatre enclaves.

Also in culture, the enclosure – the membrane (*témenos*) that isolates and yet allows processes of exchange and symbiosis like those happening at an elementary level in a cell – marks the passage from a simple coming together to an organism endowed with its own life. In the case of the theatre too, the *témenos* is a severing, not a form. It is a basic principle of individualisation: *us* distinct from *them*. The importance of the project moves on to a second plane.

The word enclave reminds us that we are not speaking of organisational structures but of territories and ecosystems: not of organisation of work but of an amalgam of different people. We can try to understand *a posteriori* how an amalgam of people works, but we cannot plan it beforehand in the hope of making it efficient with a good casting.

The common idea of management does not work for theatre enclaves. It shatters them. Instead another procedure is more useful: a particular form of common sense, which management experts call 'mirror organisation' (and which some people wrongly associate with serendipity). Here are some examples: treating casual circumstances and happenings as if they were the objectives of a previously planned project; accepting and justifying what is found without searching for it, and attributing to it a past; choosing functions on the basis of people and not vice versa; keeping the 'black sheep' instead of getting rid of them (the 'black sheep' is organic and necessary in an ensemble, Grotowski taught: if you get rid of one of them, you unintentionally oblige someone else to become a 'black sheep').

A theatre enclave can appear mighty, long-lasting, skilled in art and commerce, piracy or monasticism, but its life always depends on the relationships among its people. They stand on unrepeatable foundations. As with certain living organisms, the more they are fragile, the more they are resistant. However, theatre enclaves do not offer the convenience of bureaucratic organisations that can be stopped and reformed, or brought to a standstill in order to repair a piece or a sector, and then be set in motion once again. If the life of a theatre enclave is suspended or blocked, nobody can expect this life to return.

In addition to centripetal and centrifugal forces, another vital contrast is that between the leader and the ensemble. If this discordant harmony collapses into simple harmony or obvious discord, the enclave perishes: it has become a firm or a sect. As a rule it falls apart.

This is what I think I have understood about theatre enclaves in just over thirty-five years. It is not much. And I have understood the little I know only after I gave up limiting myself to the study of books and started to compare historical landscapes with what emerged from my field work. Historical landscapes are made up of thought, and therefore it is good that they are wide and branch off into mutable boundaries. Fieldwork, on the other hand, must be circumscribed, and requires enduring attention. It implies the experience of details and nuances that are apparently mute.

My field of work has been Odin Teatret and the theatres it frequents most.

There is no need to repeat it: Odin Teatret is the most significant theatre enclave of the twentieth century, the most long-lasting and the most complete, since it has been able to reconstruct within itself the complexity and the ramifications of an autonomous tradition: craftsmanship, artistic principles, elucidation of memory, invention of personal values, scientific investigation, territorialisation (transformation of a non-diversified space in a territory made up of channels of communication, relationships and correspondences), creation of performances, transmission of know-how and writing of books by several of its members. But to tell the truth, there is also something else: cleverness. This cleverness dislikes solemnity, and forces its members to keep their feet on the ground: a cleverness which trains itself for oceanic crossings on small lakes.

The Beginning

Odin Teatret entered the stage by the back door, so to speak, a narrow and semi-professional door. They were careful where they put their feet. A voice (like that of Don Juan to Sganarelle) reminded them that those who too often lift their eyes to the sky frequently end up with their ass on the floor.

The situation in Norway in 1964 was not enough to explain their conduct. In the early 1960s, half-amateur, half-experimental theatre groups sprang up everywhere in Europe. They were active in school gyms, in church basements, in the shadow of factories, even in the repositories of city theatres. In anger and elation, they grew in the atmosphere of uneasy warmth during the economic boom and the quake of 1968. It was an infectious, optimistic theatre, ephemeral and fanciful, which would be in existence for nine weeks or nine months and then fade away.

Odin Teatret acted instead like it wanted to set up camp and stay. It established an atmosphere of self-discipline, silence, work and anarchic moralism. At the start about a dozen were involved. Very soon they were reduced to less than the half. They were Norwegian, placid-looking, reserved and gentle, of lower middle-class extraction. They did not have a common ideology and religion, nor did they share a way of naming their secret discontent. A young, dark-skinned man led them.

This young man was European. He was born on the extreme southern tip of Italy, in the regions of Magna Grecia. But he looked like an Arab. And the Arab nations and Turkey were much closer to his Italian home than the latter was to European Norway. In Norway, in the country of Ibsen and Munch, where he had emigrated at the age of eighteen, he was completely foreign and exotic. And the North, with which he was in love, was exotic to him. He had grown up in the baroque Catholicism of the pope-kings, among the colourful ceremonies of southern saints and holy virgins, the mellifluous mortal traps of sexual taboos and under the blind discipline of a military college in the years following a war which had been lost in a tragic and humiliating way. Step by step, he made his way. He spoke Norwegian fluently, but sometimes made embarrassing blunders. For example, he used the same word to indicate both fingers and toes, as in the Romance languages. But in Norwegian, *finger* is one thing, and *tå* another. However, in the mouth of a young instructor of actors who imparted peremptory orders during their training, confusion between the two types of 'finger' could have unsettling results. The foreigner was a university student, a worker and now he also wanted to be a theatre director.

In drawing the contours of Odin Teatret, the difference between the leader and 'his' group must be stressed. This distance, which was more than just one of ethnic identity, was perhaps decisive in rendering acceptable the harshness of his command, as if it were the effect of an invincible disparity of mentality. Probably this circumstance made his way of doing and thinking, which they would never have tolerated from a native Norwegian, more bearable to the young students.

This distance did not depend only on geography.

Less than ten years separated Eugenio Barba from his Norwegian companions, who had all been rejected by the National Theatre School. But for twenty-year-olds, it was a lot. But even more, an unusual intellectual prestige distinguished him. In Norway, he belonged to the working class; he was a welder in a workshop, a socialist (in southern Europe he would have been called communist); a university student, soon to take his MA in French and Norwegian literature and history of religion. He had been a sailor and had visited India and the Far East. He had lived for months in a *kibbutz* in Israel and for years in Poland, where he had become acquainted with the normal theatre and, more closely, with that of one alchemist of the stage. There he had experienced 'real' Socialism. In Oslo, he mixed with the intellectual student elite and was a friend of famous and controversial artists. He knew ancient 'dead' languages such as Latin and Greek. He could consume an inordinate amount of alcohol. In the nights of words and cigarettes, his voice rose loudly against the claims of his socialist friends. The last word was his: among so many well-off leftists, he, the foreigner, was the only true worker.

In the beginning, his new companions, actors and neophytes, saw only one of his faces: a serious and severe expression, concentrated behind his horn-rimmed glasses. Behind his commitment shone enthusiasm. And behind the enthusiasm, something reminiscent of an incandescence hidden in a frozen cave. 'We should be careful', thought his young followers while their director explained the theatre he had experienced in that unknown Polish city of Opole, where he had studied and from where he had brought back a bundle of photos with half-naked actors doing acrobatics and assuming bizarre and untheatrical postures.

Theatre semantics of 'his/her'

In Europe, when we observe the great theatre of the twentieth century (which in actual fact is often made up of minuscule theatres), when we speak of Copeau, Grotowski, Piscator, Stanislavski, Osterwa, Meyerhold, Brecht, Vilar, Littlewood, Reinhardt, Beck and Malina, Mnouchkine, Sulerzhitski, Vakhtangov, Kantor and Brook, we might say that the core of the problem lies in establishing the sense of the possessive, the *his and her*, in relation to their theatre. And when we speak of Barba, of *his* theatre, *his* group, *his* actors, and even *his* performances, the possessive must be intended as something in-between the meaning it assumes in expressions like '*his* city', '*his* time', '*his* nation'; and in expressions like '*his* activity', '*his* ship', '*his* handwriting', '*his* car', '*his* childhood'. 'His', in short, means a great deal more than a belonging to, and much less than a possessive.

Barba and 'his' companions advanced ever further on a wider stage. First it was the Norwegian province. It soon became the Scandinavian regions. Then there were the vast lowlands of Europe's alternative theatre. Finally, a broader horizon: the Eurasian theatre. Meanwhile, they had moved their base from the Norwegian capital to the Danish provinces, to Holstebro, a small town of 18,000 inhabitants. They were to become a mixed group with people of different nationalities. They would change a lot (as is natural), but they would never become unrecognisable (and that is less obvious).

Today, almost fifty years later, let us look at them afresh. A lot of people surround them now: friends, allies, collaborators living close by and far away, admirers, curious passers-by. But the number of actors has not increased. A few are the same as at the beginning. They are, as a rule, never more than a dozen, often less. Most of them have had only one director, and this director – Eugenio Barba – has almost always had them as 'his' actors. For years. They are not 'his' as he is not 'theirs'. Barba's greatness is reduced in the absence of 'his' actors. Just as the greatness of every single actor is lessened in the absence of 'their' director. This condition, lived for decades, should be enough to make us understand how extraordinarily fertile and at the same time fierce an enclave is.

The struggle between different mentalities and opinions, translated into action instead of discussion; the loyalty to common pacts; the individual far-sighted egoism that each of them has learnt to defend – these features appear, with hindsight, to be the binding material of the Odin Teatret enclave. With variations, it is the cement of every theatre enclave. The stronger the tension, the more solid the cohesion. This means that the more a theatre enclave is stable, the more it is on the verge of splintering.

I have mentioned a few actors who have been with Odin since its Norwegian beginnings in 1964. These are Else Marie Laukvik and Torgeir Wethal. They abandoned family and mother tongue to follow their theatre to another country. Dane Iben Nagel Rasmussen saw their first performance and, shaken, joined them in 1966. From that moment she began changing Odin Teatret with the technique of the *fait accompli*. Tage Larsen has been with them since 1971, his first improvisation became one of the peaks of *My Father's House* which, between 1972 and 1974, was shown 322 times throughout Europe, spreading Odin Teatret's name and influence. Roberta Carreri saw this performance in Milan and joined the group when it was undergoing one of its internal 'earthquakes' in 1974, leaving its safe venue in Holstebro to work for five months in the village of Carpignano in the deep south of Italy. Her solo performance, *Judith*, composed with Barba in 1987, still tours all over the world. Julia Varley is English. She was admitted in 1976 after a long trial period. She made herself accepted by the group by driving the theatre's lorry. Her first performances were in *The Million* and *Ashes of Brecht*. Today she organises and leads many of the theatre's activities. In 1987 two professional musicians joined and became actors: Jan Ferslev and Frans Winther, followed in 1990 by Kai Bredholt. Over the last few years the latter has radically renewed Odin strategies of 'bartering' and intervening in different social realities. Since 2003 Augusto Omolú, dancer of classical ballet and the Afro-Brazilian tradition, has participated in some of the performances, among them *Andersen's Dream*. In 2006, Canadian Donald Kitt managed to slip in.

I could start from here, not with the leader but with his peers, in an attempt to understand what a theatrical enclave is. It would be a history as meaningful as the one written according to traditional criteria, with the 'directors' as leaders. It would correspond more to the truth, if only we knew how to make it sufficiently clear. We would need the keyboard of an author skilled in narrative multi-centrism. But if the writer was talented enough, we would see only the interweaving of different paths, nodes, bifurcations and crossroads. We would enjoy the novel, but perhaps lose sight of the real story of the theatre enclave.

Rift or rhino

If we had a historical atlas of the theatre, we would find, in the twentieth century, radical changes to geographical maps. In the two or three preceding centuries these maps marked the frontiers of the theatres and national languages crossed by troupes' itineraries. Nowadays these maps would show the various colours of many small different territories, pugnacious in their apparent isolation. In some cases, theatre enclaves would be represented not by small coloured circles but by arrows: the nomads who travel incessantly, who do not 'tour' yet are on the move all the time. The clearest example is the Living Theater, which since the 1960s has been a theatre enclave often without any fixed abode.

Odin Teatret has always had a permanent base. Yet it is stateless. Since 1966 it has resided as Nordisk Teaterlaboratorium in Holstebro, in Jutland, the wind-blown region where Theodor Dreyer filmed Kai Munk's play *Ordet*. After a few years almost all the non-Danes working at Odin think that the theatre is what most closely resembles a 'country'. They speak different languages among themselves, which means that they have to translate everything. While working, they have in common a sort of Scandinavian pidgin, so even the Danish members of the theatre end up feeling a bit like 'foreigners'. Eugenio Barba holds a Danish passport, but there is no way to make him speak Danish. He sticks to *his* Norwegian.

When they had just started working in Oslo, Eugenio Barba sent an article in English entitled *The Creation of a 'Rift Theatre'* to a Dutch 'alternative' magazine. It is his first tale about Odin Teatret. The text was not published and remained buried for years among papers.

Barba wrote: 'Apparently the circumstances and the cultural climate are not propitious to the formation and development of a "rift-theatre"'. Then followed a quotation from *Guerilla Warfare* by Ernesto 'Che' Guevara: 'one need not always wait for all conditions favorable to revolution to be present; the insurrection itself can create them'.[163] Barba stressed at once that he did not believe that theatre was able to ignite a revolution. But he believed that it was possible to provoke a revolution within the theatre: 'The tactics of such a "rift-theatre" consist in working in complete isolation, far from any official artistic circles, never content with its achievements, and obstinately fighting to overcome every professional obstacle.'

Fanaticism? Undoubtedly. But it is a fanaticism reserved only for himself and which does not seek proselytes, oscillating between audacity and timidity: 'I can well imagine the reader's cynical smile when reading these "commandments" of professional ethics.'

Then the rhythm of the discourse slowed down and Barba observed himself, his companions and his theatre from on high:

> On a quiet street in Oslo there exists, unknown to all, Odin Teatret. Here a very small group of actors is preparing itself to put into practice the 'idealistic' views expressed above. [...] The economy of the theatre is assured by weekly contributions which every member of the group pays into a common kitty [...] Another method of incrementing the economy of the theatre is to periodically enforce a week's work outside the theatre, turning the salary over to the

[163] Ernesto Che Guevara, *Guerilla Warfare*, introduction by Marc Becker (Lincoln: University of Nebraska Press, 1998), p. 143.

common kitty. We try to avoid such a method, however, in order not to interrupt the rhythm of the training. [...] Contact with the outside is limited, yet the theatre gains only valuable stimulation from this. But the fact that Jens Bjørneboe, a noted and much discussed Norwegian author, has given one of his unpublished plays – *Ornitofilene* – to us for our first production, or rather our 'launching of hostilities', constitutes a proof of confidence and a source of encouragement.[164]

They were amateurs but thought of themselves as professionals. They were well aware of not having rights or duties towards anybody, since nobody had asked their theatre to exist. They were isolated and in the dark, but not inactive. Right from the first few months, their theatrical life was founded upon the complementarity and the alternation of introverted and extroverted activities. The economic poverty was such that their desire to purchase visibility and prestige could not be considered megalomania: the publication of Scandinavian magazine *TTT* (Theories and Techniques of the Theatre) or the organisation of the first overseas tour of Grotowski's Teatr Laboratorium with the performance *The Constant Prince*. In the 1970s, as the group gradually consolidated, activities became more and more demanding, never very profitable and even loss-making: international workshops on the techniques of the actor; production of didactic and documentary films and videos; seminars on Asian classical theatres and their performances; sociological studies; 'barters' through theatre, with their songs and dances – a particular cultural and social strategy that helped to make Odin Teatret well-known. From 1980 activities increased in scope and volume, with a diversification of goals: the sessions of the International School of Theatre Anthropology (ISTA); Holstebro *Festuge* (Festive Week); *Transit*, an international women's theatre festival, the 'Odin Weeks' etc.

---

[164] Eugenio Barba, *Theatre. Solitude, Craft, Revolt*, ed. by Lluís Masgrau, trans. by Judy Barba (Aberystwyth: Black Mountain Press, 1999), pp. 27–33.

It is worth noting that none of these activities was aimed at proselytism (since it is extremely difficult to enter and work at Odin Teatret). They were not developed to enforce a method and a theoretical vision, or in the name of 'ideals' such as anarchy, pacifism, socialism or environmentalism. If we understand the word *style* in a deeper sense, we could say that all these endeavours are demonstrations of a style of life: taking a stance through the theatrical craft, without propaganda or preaching.

The massive range of 'extrovert' activities grew at the intersection of economy and anti-economy. It is evident that these activities offered the opportunity to seek funding and justify the subsidies that the Nordisk Teaterlaboratorium received from the Holstebro municipality and the Danish state. But it is also evident that these initiatives often ran the risk of precipitating the theatre into bankruptcy.

Nordisk Teaterlaboratorium / Odin Teatret is today a small Danish cultural institution, yet it is known all over the world. It enjoys a sound financial standing – solid like the budgets of all theatres, from the richest and most famous to the most marginal and wretched: always only just in the black and on the edge of the precipice. Some of Odin's members or their close collaborators and friends, when they sense another impending economic crisis, wonder: 'Why does Odin Teatret insist on undertaking initiatives that from the very start are known to be economically unfeasible? Why does Odin Teatret organise self-financed tours to places that cannot afford to host it? Why so many social and extra-theatrical activities, which bleed the theatre? Why not stay in Holstebro, concentrating on deepening and practising our craft, instead of jeopardising the money which guarantees our independence?'

Eugenio Barba meticulously carries out his role of leader, and at times explains the reasons for this kind of 'politics'. At other times he imposes his own will, throwing on the table his personal motivations: 'If I cannot work in this way, why should I still be interested in doing theatre?'

I repeat, theatre enclaves are delicate organisms. They are amalgams of people, not associations with well-regulated attributions of power. Everyone within the enclave has a huge power, stemmed only by circumstances. Theatre enclaves hold votes. But only when a problem is not very impelling and a ballot suffices to resolve it. The true struggle takes place when ultimatums are issued: I remain – I leave. If the number of people were not limited, it would be chaos, an unending brawl followed by a continuous succession of splits. Since the number is small, a sort of order-in-life is the result: the democracy of small numbers, simultaneously anarchist, monarchic and formally democratic.

As regards the 'anti-economy', at its roots is the principle that Norwegian writer Jens Bjørneboe formulated approximately this way, when Odin Teatret moved to Holstebro with a small subsidy from the municipality: 'You are an institution now, but so small that it makes everybody laugh to give you this status. But that is what you are. And an institution inevitably becomes a rhinoceros, shortsighted and armour-plated. Unless it always succeeds in living above its possibilities.'

The game of contexts

The confining nature of the border forces us to look beyond it. In this, theatre enclaves are similar to islands: they remain independent as long as they fight against isolation.

The theatres functioning within the system find a ready-made environment (buildings ready to host performances, rules for touring, connections with other institutions and funding bodies, spectator organisation, theatrical seasons, repertoires from which to choose, relationships with critics, recognition of cultural role). Theatres that have grown up as enclaves must, instead, adjust to the environment in which they live, as well as adjust this environment to their lifestyle.

The term *enclave* automatically raises the question of its context. The most interesting question, however, is another: Which new context takes shape around an enclave? The con-

III

text of a theatre is not only something previously existing, the landscape in which it grows and to which it adapts or reacts. There are also the contexts that have developed around the new organism resulting from its very presence and activity.

In the early twentieth century a few great independent theatrical micro-systems stood out as prototypes for a possible general transformation of the theatre (from the Art Theatre in Moscow to the Berliner Ensemble in Berlin). In the second half of the century – beginning with the Living Theater – artistic diversity and independence seemed to be closely associated with a small nucleus of people: theatrical minorities that did not imagine themselves as the avant-garde of a theatre to come but identified themselves with their extra-territorial right. Peter Brook's trajectory is a good example of this. Never in his career did he dream of reforming one of the theatre institutions that he had always directed successfully and innovatively. When he had the strength and the experience to try a radical and coherent development, he escaped from the 'good' theatres and founded a small enclave. He moved to Paris, picked out a core of actors of different nationalities and colours, and installed them in the suburbs, close to the rattle of an elevated open-air métro, in the empty shell of an old, dilapidated theatre.

Probably it is through an intrinsic need that the daring motivations and artistic extremism of the alchemists of the stage seek the support of the material structure of the enclave. It is impossible to say if such a structure is the cause or the effect, if it provokes or protects the existence and the density of experience of a theatre laboratory (in these cases, cause and effect relationships are reversible). It is, however, possible to ascertain that such an *enclave structure* is necessary. History teaches us this: inside 'normal' theatre institutions, including the outstanding ones, magnificent performances can be created, but there is not enough oxygen for a continuous working process and for keeping alive a micro-tradition that combines aesthetics and theatre science. There is not the freedom to take reckless and essential paths whose length one cannot predict. In other words: from the point of view of theatre innovation, 'normal' institutions are deprived of (almost) everything.

Since they did not want or were unable to understand this elementary truth, excellent talents were wasted and, after a first flowering, started to inhale contaminated air. Just think of Jean-Louis Barrault, Giorgio Strehler and many more.

The theory of places

Theatre changes within material frameworks. These transformations do not happen within a supposed dialogue between theories or with the clash of opposing aesthetics or different choices of method. In order to exist, a method needs to have opened up the way in a well-determined territory, in a materially circumscribed field of work.

Theories offer visions *towards* which we can orient ourselves. Independent territories are places *within* which we can orient ourselves. Theatre enclaves, rather than being the result of theories, have a tendency to generate them.

But even pure (in the sense of sterilised), impracticable and utopian theories acquire strength and effectiveness when they are so suggestively devised in images and words as to become a constellation of stars that steer concrete attempts to open up a new road. But these stars must really *shine brightly*. A theory is such, not when it can be turned into practice, but when it meets and vivifies a practice, translating it into concepts and visions. Then theory is shattered and besmirched in the game of misunderstandings. Otherwise a theory is a harmless fable, belonging to the literary genre of Art-fiction.

The independence of the territory is not only a necessary condition for practicing new values. It is a value in itself: but *a preliminary value*.

We should not believe that the condition of enclave is itself a positive characteristic. Just as a theatre laboratory can be the screen that conceals a busying oneself in a scholarly pursuit of the many curiosities of the craft, an enclave can also produce a squalid theatre. It can, for example, be suitable ground for small tyrannies to develop, or for the survival of a routine. It is a shelter, and the more it is rigid and proud, the more the work it is sheltering may be mediocre.

Independence in itself is neutral. It does not have the authority to feed the presumption of a political or moral superiority, a greater freedom for its inhabitants, or the commitment to an ideal. From independence, a sectarian spirit can grow (with the risk of introversion and isolation), or a strong urgency to open oneself towards the outside (with the risk of dissipation).

It is therefore understandable that Eugenio Barba constantly reminds himself and his companions that 'difference' must continually be auscultated. It cannot simply be defended. Defence, when successful, strengthens and thickens the bark. But difference is a value only if it is vulnerable.

Words that think

It is true that words think, especially when they clash with each other, twisting their meaning. Take, for instance, *laboratory*, *difference* and *superstition*. The sense of each of these, alone, is clear. The moment they enter on a collision course with the others, they become something rich and strange – less clear and truer.

Difference has always been at the centre of the reflection developed by Eugenio Barba over the years concerning his personal story and that of his theatre. He has coloured this reflection in many ways. Recently, the word has put the bow where the stern was, and sails towards the future. Barba explains *difference* not as a disinherited condition of departure but as a destination, a decisive goal to be conquered. It is not something to which we have to remain faithful, or from which we learn and draw inspiration, but rather an aspiration.

In relation to *difference*, we meet other terms in Barba's writings: *dissidence*, *group*, *interculturalism*, *laboratory*, *re-*

volt, meaning, subterranean history of the theatre, superstition, vulnerability, vocation, wound. Theoretically, there is no connection between them. But in practice things are otherwise. And the term *laboratory*, in their company, seems to jar.

Equally, the term *superstition* jars. Barba uses it in an etymological and paradoxical way: something that 'is above', poised over the practice in order to give it a name and a value. It is a mute value that does not demand to be shared but that each one formulates in a personal way out of the blows he or she has given and that he or she has received, that is, their own biography. This is different for everyone and marks whatever transcends the horizontal dimension of the work and its results.

Through tangential paths, *laboratory* and *superstition* plot together a thought. Do they mean to say that the laboratory is a superstition (or *the* superstition) of the theatre? Is the laboratory, then, the emblem of a potential *magnitude* of theatre work?

Besides measuring earthquakes, we can use magnitude *to think* of the theatre.

This word was chosen by Charles Richter in the 1930s to establish a measure for classifying the power of earthquakes. It is therefore appropriate to apply it to the theatre, whose effectiveness coincides, in the end, with the tremors it is able to produce within the spectator. Richter used a Latin word to say that the power of an earthquake is measured not only by observing the extent of its destruction, but also by assessing the energy generated in its epicentre, its source.

For theatres, the energy of the epicentre should be measured by the work taking place behind and before the performance: in the furnace of the laboratory.

A natural history

It always stirs emotion to rediscover in the narrow field of my own investigation, in new and unexpected forms, the rise of dynamics analogous to those regulating the structure of vast parts of the past. This has been one of the pleasures in re-searching theatre enclaves.

If we observe the big theatrical eco-systems through the eyes of a naturalist, some recurrent vital tensions emerge with clarity. These are infra-cultural tensions, between the micro-cultures of the actors and the dominant cultures of the spectators, between the 'novelty' that upsets the repertoire and the repertoire of consolidated performances, between the discontinuity of the different *mises-en-scène* and the con-tinuity of techniques and specialisations of the actors (for ex-ample, stock roles, in the sense of *emplois*, or training and exercises), between artistic creation and theoretical explana-tion, between people of the stage and those of the written word, between organisational and commercial forms and po-litical and ideal standpoints, between 'successes' and memory lingering in the heads and the senses of spectators.

We find the equivalent of all these tensions in the enclave. It is not always easy to recognise it, because the equivalent is very different from a mirror image.

The mirroring, on a lesser scale, of the strong tensions typi-cal of the normal theatre system makes enclaves *analogous* theatres. They are like the Galapagos islands, where – be-cause of their isolation – certain evolutionary processes tak-ing place in nature are present in odd forms compared with the continents.

In what sense, for example, is it justifiable to speak of Eu-genio Barba as a 'director'? A detailed answer to this question would make us see that *difference* is not a trait or a character-istic but a continuous motion between the dissimilar and the equivalent.

Eugenio Barba's work as 'director' is very dissimilar from the work characterising the director both in the theatre sys-tem and in many theatre enclaves and laboratories. Of course I am not speaking of that which distinguishes one artist from another. I am speaking of a difference in the nature of the work itself developed by Barba. This work is somewhat similar to that of an author whose pen is three-dimensional. In reality he is a *commutator of meaning*. It is as if the inventive and ravaging burden of a poet were plunged into the actors' work. This poet is rooted in the troupe like Wilhelm Meister, for example. But Eugenio Barba is not Wilhelm Meister, since he was the first teacher of 'his' actors. Now, when these are autonomous, and some of them also excel by themselves, not only does he make a montage of the materials proposed by them, entwining these into coherent sequences, but he also stirs them up, pushes them in other directions, sets them on fire, projecting them into contexts and stories which neither he nor the actors had foreseen.

In best-case scenarios, there is no longer either director or actor. The spectator is immersed in a field of forces where the people involved are able to drop the distinctions of their specialisations, roles and functions. The spectator senses the dynamics of a *collective body-mind* thanks to deeply incorporated techniques, professional expertise acquired over time and, above all, relationships strengthened by the ups and downs of shared experiences.

In less fortunate cases, there is a struggle between individuals who can clash with one another without being hurt too badly because of their familiarity.

In the early years, when Barba was also the teacher of 'his' actors and often the co-author of their scores, his role of 'commutator of meaning' was concealed behind the dense and multiple relationship of the daily *corps-à-corps* between 'director' and 'actor'. Today, the relationship between Barba and the actors recreates, on a small scale, something rarely discernable in the vaster fields of the history of the theatre: a series of tremors that certain writers inflicted on the repertoire, forcing actors to expand or to abandon their professional skills. It is enough to think of Ibsen and Chekhov, Strindberg and Brecht, who demolished the foundations of the theatre they knew so well from the inside. Or to recall what Goldoni tried to accomplish, realising it in his writing rather than in the theatre practice of his time.

This dynamic of destruction-and-innovation occurs over decades and centuries in the broad expanses of European theatre. However it becomes unique when we find it again – with similar functions but very different features – in the restricted space and time of a theatre enclave such as Odin Teatret, whose handful of artists are almost always the same over the years and in a state of constant 'confrontation' with 'their' commutator of meaning. This unique situation is also an eloquent example of what can be born in the climate and under the pressure of a long-lasting enclave.

There are plenty of micro-societies. Why should a theatre enclave attract us or become a relief for our discontent, if it is just a small artistic milieu able to defend itself? It could only claim our respect and admiration, and we would find confirmation of the many and free identities of the theatre. But would our *identity as individuals* be challenged?

If what happens in a theatre enclave attracts and moves us it is because we are confronted with firm foundations, protracted periods of formation and complex architectures of rules and traditions. But their function is just to hold up the precariousness of the peaks, the deep voids of the inner caverns, the sudden lesions of the crevasses from which arise echoes that actors pretend not to hear and spectators pretend to appreciate as art. All this has to do not merely with a set of new relationships and artistic rules, albeit intelligent, original and alternative.

The word *enclave* on its own says little. But does the word *laboratory* not risk saying too much? Does it not suggest something progressive, hopeful and comforting?

The Odin enclave often dissimulates its own harsh and quaked ground behind a busy pedagogic availability. It seems to nurture the hope that there are useful teachings for those who, in turn, set out on the road of new transgressions and earthquakes – without which theatre itself is of little use from the point of view of quality, benefits and personal sense.

The illusion that the strength of artistic and pedagogic principles can prevail over entropy is denied by the quality of Odin performances (quality as a symptom of tremors, not as a perfection of technique and forms). They are enigmatic performances. These enigmas have nothing to do with puzzles and simple answers to obscure questions. Quite the opposite: the knots are clear, while their consequences are dark. These knots invent a way to retie themselves each time the spectator unties them. So it seems that they – the knots of the enigma – loosen that part of us with which we are not familiar. Like a compassionate act, born out of rigour, constantly renewing itself.

This phenomenon, which is exceptional among theatres, is evident and concrete but also difficult to dissect. Therefore no one pays it due attention, as if it were an anecdote and not the summit of the micro-history of a different theatre.

At the very moment in which we face an artistic reality endowed with an objective power, then the paradox of the individual who writes the history of the theatre comes into play. Among the objects of his or her history, a spectator must necessarily be present, together with the geography of his or her inner landscapes. Here it is not a question of a collective 'audience' but of an objective 'individual spectator'. What I write seems to be the expression of a personal way of feeling and the autobiography of a passionate spectator. Instead, it is the contrary: a clash, neither searched for nor wanted, with the ambiguities of the poetry of the stage.

In still rarer cases (which we lightly call 'masterpieces'), the eyes of the spectator see with a gaze that is no longer his own. It is an impersonal gaze, freed from its jail: the bars and paradigms of his brain. The experience of such a gaze has been thought of, imagined and described by poets and scientists. On the final pages of *Tristes Tropiques*, Claude Lévi-Strauss saw with such a gaze.[165] But it is one thing to speak

---

[165] Cf. Claude Lévi-Strauss, *Tristes Tropiques*, trans. by John and Doreen Weightman (New York and London: Penguin, 1973 pp. 414–15.

of it and point it out, and another to be immersed in it, even if only for a brief moment, thus experiencing this impossible experience. Once again we have a *témenos*, a cut, a separation that engenders clairvoyance and fear.

Like the hiss of a blade, this sharp gaze was something this spectator who writes these pages was able to feel in the last scenes of *Talabot* and *Mythos*, two performances composed in 1988 and 1998 by Odin Teatret.

It takes separation, the foundations of a micro-tradition, the invention of a technique, the superstitions of a laboratory with no indulgence and no finality to forge this thin blade, which is sharp and sometimes even sharper. And when it reaches this absolute sharpness, it becomes a ray, a laser, thrust into the depths of the theatre, extinguishing it.

Translated from Italian by Judy Barba

NANDO TAVIANI
Information on Odin Teatret

The life of Odin Teatret as a theatrical enclave (or theatre laboratory) can be depicted schematically through the complementarity and alternation of introvert and extrovert activities. Among the introvert ones we find Barba's work with the actors, the actors' work on themselves (training, autonomous elaboration of materials for a production, working demonstrations) and rehearsals – which can last up to two or three years.

The extrovert activities include Odin's own productions presented on site and on tour in Denmark and abroad; 'barters' with various milieus in Holstebro and elsewhere; the organisation of encounters for theatre groups; hosting other theatre groups and ensembles; seminars in Denmark and in the countries where the Odin brings its productions; the publication of magazines and books; the production of didactic films and videos; sessions of the International School of Theatre Anthropology (ISTA); the Centre for Theatre Laboratory Studies (CTLS) in collaboration with the University of Aarhus; the annual Odin Week; the triennial *Festuge* (Festive Week) in Holstebro; the triennial festival *Transit* devoted to women in theatre; children's performances, exhibitions, concerts, round tables, film clubs and other cultural initiatives in Holstebro and the surrounding area.

There is no rigid separation between the above two spheres of activity. They are planned and realised by the same people and often overlap, transferring energies and stimuli from one field to another. The life of the Odin enclave depends on the precarious equilibrium between these two different dynamic dimensions.

In reality there are three dimensions: the third one consists of the many books and essays written by Eugenio Barba and by the actors Roberta Carreri, Iben Nagel Rasmussen, Julia Varley and Torgeir Wethal, translated into many languages.

1964–65: Odin Teatret was established on 1 October 1964 in Oslo, Norway. Three of its five founders – Eugenio Barba and the actors Else Marie Laukvik and Torgeir Wethal – are still a part of it today (2009). While concentrating on its professional apprenticeship as autodidacts, the Odin published *Teatrets Teori og Teknikk*, a quarterly magazine which until 1974 appeared with twenty three monographic issues and books. Odin Teatret's first production, and Eugenio Barba's first direction, was *Ornitofilene* (The Birdlovers, November 1965), an unpublished text by Jens Bjørneboe.

1966–68: In June 1966 Odin Teatret found its permanent home in Holstebro, Denmark. Its innovative workshops initiative transformed this small town into a meeting centre through practical confrontation with artists of the new theatre wave in Western as well as Asian theatre and dance. From June 1966 to 1977 Odin pioneered practical seminars twice a year. Among the teachers were Jerzy Grotowski, Ryszard Cieślak, Dario Fo, Étienne Decroux, Jacques Lecoq, the Colombaioni brothers, Charles Marowitz, Otomar Krejča, Joseph Chaikin, Julian Beck and Judith Malina, Jean-Louis Barrault and Madeleine Renaud, the Javanese choreographer Sardono, the Balinese masters I Made Pasek Tempo, I Made Djimat and I Made Bandem, the Japanese Noh masters Hisao and Hideo Kanze, Butoh artists Kazuo Ohno and Natsu Nakajima, the masters from Indian classical forms Shanta Rao, Krishna Namboodiri, Uma Sharma, Ragunath Panigrahi and Sanjukta Panigrahi. The latter is among the co-founders of ISTA in 1979. Eugenio Barba edited *Towards a Poor Theatre* by Jerzy Grotowski (*Teatrets Teori og Teknikk* no. 7, 1968).

1969–73: Barba's third production, *Ferai* (1969), with a text specially written for Odin by Peter Seeberg, brought the theatre international recognition. The following production, *Min Fars Hus* (My Father's House, 1972) which, like *Ferai*, was for only 60 spectators, confirmed its prestige and at the same time put it in contact with a young theatre milieu in Europe and abroad which was extraneous to the official theatre and to the elitarian avant-garde.

1974–75: After playing *Min Fars Hus* 322 times all over Europe's festivals and main towns, Odin Teatret moved to Carpignano, a village in southern Italy, where it worked for five months between spring and autumn 1974. The following year, Odin went once again to Carpignano for three months, and then to Ollolai, a village in the mountains of Sardinia. Odin branched out into a new field of activity with open-air performances for many spectators, itinerant shows and parades. These performances were put together by assembling material belonging to the repertoire of the individual actors or of the whole group (theatricalised exercises from training, clown gags, etc).

The practice of the 'barter', based on active reciprocity, began while in Carpignano in 1974. Instead of selling its own performances, the Odin enclave exchanged – bartered – them with cultural events by the hosting milieu (political and religious associations, villages, neighbourhoods, schools, psychiatric hospitals, prisons, etc). The barter offers not only an insight into the other's forms of expression but is equally a social interaction which defies prejudices, linguistic difficulties and differences in thinking, judging and behaving. The practice of bartering through theatre was to characterise Odin's social action until the present day.

The Odin enclave now introduced itself to the outside with a double face: performances for few spectators in sheltered environments; and crowded, colourful and grotesque open air performances. The first required long periods of preparation, with the director and actors starting afresh each time; the others derived from a rapid structuring of existing material.

1976–80: During April and May 1976, Odin Teatret participated in the Festival of Caracas with *Come! And the Day will be Ours*. Outside the Festival's framework, it was active with encounters with other groups, barters, parades and open air performances. The Odin bartered with a Yanomami tribe after a lengthy journey to their territory in Amazonia. It was the beginning of lasting ties between the Odin enclave and numerous Latin American theatre enclaves. Some of these were invited by Barba the following autumn to Belgrade to the International Encounter of Group Theatre within the BITEF Festival/Theatre of the Nations. On this occasion, Barba published the manifesto on the Third Theatre.

New independent activities emerged within Odin involving individual actors or Barba with only one of the actors. This also applied to ISTA (International School of Theatre Anthropology) in its first years.

ISTA is not a rigid institution, but a milieu, an interlacing of changing relationships. It assumes a defined form only during its public sessions. Then it becomes a *performers' village*, where actors and dancers from many traditions and genres meet with scholars to compare and analyse the technical foundation of their scenic presence. What makes the meeting possible is a discordant way of thinking and a common desire to question the actor-dancer's stage behaviour. It is within this milieu that Barba has compared the Odin enclave's experiences with other theatre and dance genres, circumscribing a new field of study: theatre anthropology, the study of scenic behaviour in an organised situation of representation.

An ISTA session centers on a theme or a question that is placed under investigation (improvisation, organic effect, founders of traditions, form and information, etc.). It includes several masters from different traditions and their ensembles, thirty to eighty participants and a group of about ten scholars/researchers. It usually lasts between fifteen and twenty days although the longest session, Volterra 1981, went on for two months. In addition to the international public sessions, always accompanied by a two-day symposium with practical demonstrations and performances with the masters' ensembles, ISTA has developed another recurrent activity: The University of Eurasian Theatre.

Session after session, since 1990, an ensemble going by the name of *Theatrum Mundi* has grown out of the collaboration between Odin actors and ISTA masters. The *Theatrum Mundi* productions are events involving between forty-five and fifty performers and musicians from diverse traditions, with Eugenio Barba as director. Staged performances include: *Ego Faust* (2000), *Ur-Hamlet* (2006 and 2009), *Don Giovanni all'inferno* (2006) and *The Marriage of Medea* (2008).

1980–90: New productions: *Brecht's Ashes* (1980), *The Gospel According to Oxyrhincus* (1985), *Talabot* (1988). In this period the dynamics within Odin Teatret assumed two further dimensions. Individual lines of research sprang up in addition to collective work.

In tandem with her presence in Odin Teatret, Iben Nagel Rasmussen founded the group Farfa. Then, in 1989, she started The Bridge of Winds, an international assembly of actors and directors usually active in their own countries and periodically joining her for a few weeks to concentrate on personal research. The actor Toni Cots – Barba's closest collaborator in planning the first ISTA sessions – developed with Basho a self-directed activity of pedagogy and performances in conjunction with his tasks inside Odin. Julia Varley helped to found the Magdalena Project in 1986, a network of women in contemporary theatre, co-editing its annual journal *The*

Open Page and organising since 1992 the triennial festival *Transit*. Torgeir Wethal filmed and edited films about training (Grotowski's, Decroux's and Odin Teatret's) as well as Odin performances and barters. Every Odin actor, in a more continuous and formalised way, has developed autonomous fields of action.

At times it is difficult to strike the right balance between extrovert and introvert activities, as well as between activities involving the whole group and those of individual actors. The Odin compactness, which appears unassailable from the outside, is experienced internally as a problem that needs to be constantly monitored. One of the consequences of these inner dynamics has been the flourishing of 'small' performances, often with an intensity equal to that of the whole group's productions.

It is in this context that a new genre has developed: working demonstrations. These are structured like a performance, with one or two actors presenting and expounding the fundamental principles of their theatrical craft. Although the original purpose was a pedagogical one, the working demonstrations soon become a way to interrogate the nature of the actor's technique and to investigate the dialectic between 'cold' and 'warm'. Quoting Barba, technique manifests itself as a 'dance of algebra and flames', the raw material of a theatre-in-life. Seen as a whole, the working demonstrations indicate clearly that the Odin enclave is not characterised by a uniform vision but by a mosaic of methods and individual perspectives that make up a 'small tradition' with a manifold face.

The Odin enclave alternates in an increasingly evident way periods of concentration with periods of opening up to the outside.

Since 1989 Odin Teatret has organised an intense *Festuge* (Festive Week) every three years in Holstebro, hosting foreign theatre groups and artists but above all collaborating with over a hundred local associations and institutions. Theatre, music, dance, figurative art, lectures and debates are interwoven with the daily activities of schools, churches, military barracks, the police station, old people's homes, the train station, buses, shops, the hospital, cultural institutions and run-down spaces. The *Festuge* pervades the whole town, day and night for a whole week with a grotesque and disturbing spectacularity, from impressive intercultural performances for large crowds and barters to actors' visits to private birthday parties and incursions to administrative offices.

Since the 1980s another recurrent annual activity is *Odin Week*. It provides an opportunity for from thirty to fifty people from theatre and academic circles in different countries to be introduced to the multi-faceted structure and life of the Odin enclave. They train with the actors, get acquainted with their personal working methods, with the management and organisation of the theatre, with their community activities and international projects, watch many performances and working demonstrations and have a daily theoretical/practical meeting with Eugenio Barba.

1990–2009: New productions: *Kaosmos* (1992), *Within the Skeleton of the Whale* (1997), *Mythos* (1998), *Ode to Progress* (2003), *Cities under the Moon* (2003) and *Andersen's Dream* (2004). Since 2008 Barba and his actors have been working on a new production which for the moment has only a provisional title. Barba speaks about it as a performance with a happy end.

Tours have the tendency to turn into long artistic, pedagogical and cultural residences in foreign countries in close collaboration with local theatre groups, universities and associations, mostly in Europe and Latin America. The initiatives and projects of single actors have multiplied, projecting them towards new contexts and experimentation. The tension between centrifugal and centripetal forces within Odin reaches its climax. The visitor's eyes, however, will perceive this tension as an effervescent milieu which blends actors, directors, dancers and scholars of different generations and nationalities in a ceaseless, at times frenetic, swarm of initiatives.

At the same time, Odin Teatret persists in strengthening its roots in Holstebro and its territory. In the first three months of 2009, a dense programme of 'Interferences' has been developed: through previously agreed projects, the world of the theatre intrudes into the daily life and activities of the community in the town centre and nearby villages. Yet again an effort to find a new use and meaning for theatrical practice in civil life.

The house of Odin is growing: in 2004, the fortieth anniversary of its foundation, a new space was inaugurated: the Centre for Theatre Laboratory Studies (CTLS). It comprises a library, an archive for the documents of Odin and other theatre laboratories, an area for the digitalisation and production of audiovisual materials on the theatrical craft and for the editing and arranging of materials accumulated during almost fifty years of activity. The CTLS has a stable relationship with the University of Aarhus and with the Grotowski Institute in Wrocław, Poland.

In 2008 Odin Teatret, the Grotowski Institute and the Theatre Arts Researching the Foundations (TARF) in Malta created Icarus Publishing Enterprise, whose purpose is to present texts in English by artists and specialists on the practice and vision of theatre as a laboratory.

Is the small theatre group born forty-five years ago in Oslo now at risk of contracting elephantiasis? Well, the risk is mitigated by one essential factor: the number of actors has remained the same, and most of them have been together for decades.

In 2009, Odin Teatret's permanent staff consists of twenty-two persons, eleven of whom are actors. Its turnover is about 15 million Danish kroner (2 million Euros). The earnings from the various activities of the Odin enclave fluctuate between 40 per cent and 50 per cent of the grants received from the Danish Ministry of Culture and the municipality of Holstebro.

When today Eugenio Barba is asked about the future of his theatre, his answer is uncompromising: 'Odin Teatret will exist as long as one of its present actors wishes to continue its activity. After that it must disappear. The Odin *is* its actors. Our name will not be transferred to an empty shell – to a building or an institution.'

Translated from Italian by Judy Barba

IV

*The relationship between Studios
in the first half of the twentieth century
and theatre laboratories in the second.
The appearance of the Red Queen and her race.*

M any years of both practical work and discussion had highlighted, among the group I have called the 'collective mind', constantly emerging aspects of theatre laboratories. It was soon clear, however, that every theatre laboratory had different characteristics, and that the traits common to all (a much longer rehearsal time, a different production rhythm compared to 'normal' theatres, an interest in teaching and the tendency to collaborate with a permanent core or at least with a stable network of actors) were shared by many experimental theatres.

Moreover, the longest surviving laboratory theatres have undergone changes so radical that it sometimes seems difficult to identify, in their old age, the laboratorial characteristics of the early years. Do they stop being laboratories after the first seven years?

The 'collective mind' began to look at the problem of the relationship between theatre laboratories (i.e., small theatres of the second half of the twentieth century, the most recognised examples of which are the Teatr Laboratorium and Odin Teatret) and the theatres of the Great Theatre Reform at the turn of the twentieth century. The term 'The Great Reform', Osiński explained, was in all likelihood coined by the significant Polish director Leon Schiller, who worked between the two world wars.[166] Schiller was adept at coming up with ready yet lasting definitions. He also coined the expressions Monumental Polish Theatre and Immense Theatre, the latter inspired by a definition by Wyspiański.

While some of us were still trying to put together a set of characteristics that would make it possible to define which theatre might legitimately be considered a laboratory, and to gauge the influence of the protagonists of the Great Reform at the turn of the twentieth century, Raquel Carrió, a theatre scholar and playwright, had her say. In Cuba she has trained

---

[166] Here I am paraphrasing Osiński's personal letter to Barba, dated 22 December 2007. One of Schiller's first programmatic texts is the long essay 'The New Theatre in Poland: Stanisław Wyspiański', published in Edward Gordon Craig's journal *The Mask*, vol. II, nos. 1–3 (1909), 11–27, and nos. 4–6 (1909), 59–71.

entire generations of theatre artists and intellectuals at the Instituto Superior de Artes. She explained to us:

> It would be very difficult to delimit what is and what is not a theatre laboratory in Latin America. Not just because the term 'laboratory' is taken up by other theatre practices, since it is not a concept originating from Latin American groups or theatres. But also because, once adopted, it extends to a wide variety of practices. Those in Mexico, for example, have been called campesino (peasant) theatre laboratories since they occurred in rural zones and with peasants as actors and spectators. At the other extreme, there are the closed experiences of scenic research conducted in groups connected with Universities or Study Centres.
>
> But what exactly defines the nature of a laboratory in Latin America? Is it necessarily a closed space, isolated from any sort of contamination, dedicated entirely to the study of techniques of the actor and of performance? And might one talk of a methodology or of a united Model of methods and techniques characterising theatre research in our continent?
>
> If we were to identify laboratories on this basis, most of the leading theatres in Latin America, the most controversial, innovative, those capable of having an impact on the social life of our countries, would not be covered by such a definition. Teatro Galpón in Uruguay, Teatro Experimental of Cali and La Candelaria in Colombia, Arena, Officina or Macunaíma in Brazil, Cuatrotablas and Yuyachkani in Peru, Teatro Estudio, El Escambray and Teatro Buendía in Cuba, Ictus or El Gran Circo in Chile, and many others, have certainly not been places devoid of intense contamination, with internal and external experiences, inside and outside the theatre. These experiences have undoubtedly contributed most to the particular nature of their performances.
>
> It would therefore appear that diversity (of techniques, methods and languages) is the distinctive trait of the theatre in Latin America. But it is not the only one. There is also the sense of rebellion, of opposition to all proposed models.[167]

Having ruled out the possibility of putting forward a prototype, Raquel Carrió spent some time on the difficult relation-

[167] The quote is from the transcription of Raquel Carrió's address 'Irradiations in Latin America' at the conference *Why a Theatre Laboratory?*, Aarhus, 5 October 2004.

ship between theatres in the late twentieth century and the great models of the turn of the century. She spoke about how in the theatres of Latin America the desire to take advantage of the teachings and inheritance of the masters of the European Great Reform had been at odds with the desire, the need even, for originality and independence. And about how this impasse had been overcome, if only in the form of recognition and dialogue, and never as a simple application of systems and principles. It is a problem that crops up again in the relationship between Latin American actors and Grotowski's example.

One of the listeners, Ana Woolf, an actress and director from Argentina, took part in the discussion by conducting a quick survey among theatre-makers in her country on Grotowski's influence. Beatriz Seibel, a prominent scholar who has been writing about various aspects of Argentinian theatre, defined him a 'mystery'. She spoke about his books being circulated underground, the multiple interpretations regarding training, the meaning of exercises and his ideas. She described the 'Grotowski entity', consisting of baffling photocopies, the latest developments from Europe, documents held onto tightly by the lucky few. Theatre critic Susanna Freire pointed out that Grotowski had demonstrated that the theatre is, or can be, a space for spiritual communication. Antonio Célico, the director of El Baldio Teatro, spoke, again regarding Grotowski, about a 'theory of misunderstanding'. Then Bianca Rizzo (who comes from a parallel world, that of dance, being a choreographer and ballerina) spoke about what had been deduced from writings by or on Grotowski, about what has remained over time: the belief in the existence of a collective group intelligence; the importance of a 'negative way'; the image of a naked actor in a pose of offering, appearing as a source of light. The young Gabriela Bianco, creator of the Teatro de Lengua de Señas in Argentina, recalled that Grotowski had conferred upon the theatre the role of a space for gaining knowledge about reality. Ana Woolf herself recalled the strength of watchwords, sometimes obscure, but loaded with meaning, with which some of Grotowski's utterances had been repeated. She quoted some of them, which she had taken from the transcription of Grotowski's seminars at Odin Teatret in the late 1960s[168]: '*Ne pas jouer; cherchez; ne pas exister pour soi; exister pour qualqu'un d'autre; il n'y a pas de création sans douleur; on paye toujours et beaucoup; payer avec tout notre être; sans payer il n'y a rien; il faut brûler jusqu'à la fin*'.[169] She concluded with a personal memory:

It was on television back in 1981: black and white. 'There's nothing on this evening', my mother said, and she went off to read a book. I stayed to watch, and lay down on the sofa to watch a popular comedy programme, *No toca botón*. The entire programme was based around a comic, Alberto Olmedo, and his sidekick, another comedy actor, Javier Portales. There were *double entendres*, *soubrettes* and all the usual stuff. There were a lot of quickfire sketches. One was set in the waiting room of a fashionable psychoanalyst. Portales, dressed very elegantly, is sitting in an armchair, waiting. He is reading a thick book. Olmedo comes in, he too very elegant and also holding a big book. He sits down and begins to read. After a long television minute he looks at the book being read by the other, and asks him in a serious fashion:
'Stanislavski?'
'No. Grotowski,' Portales answers gravely. Then Portales looks at Olmedo's book, and asks:
'Grotowski?'
'No. Stanislavski.'

A parody about Argentina's intellectual classes.

The story so far

It may be useful at this point to outline the main points of the discussion thus far, before going on to explore the new

---

[168] Since the original transcription of audio recordings of the seminars had become illegible, Ana Woolf took it upon herself to copy the Ahrne typewritten version. See the following chapter.

[169] 'Don't play; search; don't exist for yourself; exist for someone else; there is no creation without pain; one always pays and dearly; pay with all your being; without paying, there is nothing; you must burn right to the end'.

problem that was emerging: the possible continuity or fili-
ation link between theatre laboratories of the second half
of twentieth century and the Studios of the first half of the
century.

Firstly, one should recall the point of view that favoured, in
laboratorial work, the status of the theatre as a non-religious
abode. This position had emphasised the new, profound and
spiritual value that emerged in particular with Grotowski but
had been latent even before then. This totally new, fascinating
value, which allowed the actor to work on himself, emerged
in the periods spent rehearsing and training. By virtue of its
very nature, it was unconcerned with the need to produce
performances.

Secondly, there is the opposite point of view, according to
which the performance gains in depth the more one moves
away from the point of departure, creating an unfilled or hol-
low space, a *detour* in the creative process between the start
of the work and the end product. It is a dangerous space,
which may cause arbitrariness and dispersion. But it is fundamental in allowing body language – which due to its very
nature can only be mysterious or tiresomely mimetical – to
begin to talk.

A *byt* change

Byt is a Russian word which indicates a complete change in
mentality, habits, theatre standards, even in the everyday life
of the theatre. The memory of the great directors of the early
twentieth century has remained alive. It would have been impossible to forget the importance and influence of artists such
as Meyerhold or Tairov. Even so, some things did get lost.

The 1940s – with World War 2, Nazism and Stalinism, plus
the death of some of the early protagonists – was a cut-off
point. What was lost was not the memory of the single artists
and their single works but rather the *byt* change.

The essence of the *Wielka Reforma*, the Great Reform, was
quickly buried, for obvious and dramatic historical reasons.

The birth of theatre laboratories midway through the century, starting with the movement led by the Grotowski-Barba pairing, managed to retrieve a part of the memory of that *byt* and laid a claim to the thread of direct continuity *vis-à-vis* the laboratorial experiences of the great early directors. Grotowski had naturally referred to Stanislavski, also on account of the political situation in Poland, which had caused him to study theatre in Russia. Perhaps also to protect his work behind the broad shoulders of a master of the theatre accepted by the socialist authorities. Barba had started in the theatre as an amateur and an avid reader. As a substitute for conventional study, he had read widely, particularly books about Poland's theatre culture and was aware of the importance of devoted amateurs in the early years of Meyerhold and for the whole activity of Vakhtangov and his many Studios.

Now the time had come to question the reality of this continuity: it might have been a process that had never been interrupted, only momentarily concealed; or it might have been continuity recognised only *a posteriori*. The difference was significant, even though it may have been difficult to appreciate the impact of this difference in relation to the obviousness of the continuity. As far as I was concerned, the question was beginning to appear illusory. We discussed the matter above all at the Aarhus conference.

Richard Schechner

At the Aarhus conference, Richard Schechner, director and founder in 1967 of the New York-based Performance Group, editor of *TDR: The Drama Review*, university lecturer and the only man of the theatre, apart from Barba, to attend the conference, took the floor on day two. The Performance Group was inspired by Grotowski, and Schechner had been in charge until the end of the 1970s.[170] The group had been

---

[170] In 1980 the group changed its name to the Wooster Group.

influential for the new theatre in America. But the director
– with his round face, greying hair, braces evident over a pink
shirt, displaying a sense of great superiority *vis-à-vis* petty social inhibitions, such as sitting tidily on a chair – did not speak
about this experience of many years previously. He came as a
witness, to talk to us about America.

Was there really a half smile, while he was talking, in
response to the heated discussions and meticulousness in
specifying dates? I thought so then. Now, re-reading his address, I am not so sure. He was the first theatre-maker to
speak, after a host of scholars. Perhaps I had a guilty conscience. Perhaps something inside me said that it was not so
wrong to have some doubts about this much obstinacy regarding what might be trivial details (are Studios and theatre laboratories really the same thing? Are they different? Is
it correct to talk of theatre laboratory from 1898 and Stanislavski onwards, or from 1959 and Grotowski's and Flaszen's
Teatr Laboratorium, or from 1923 and the American Theatre
Laboratory?).

I had to admit that in my eyes a form of partial continuity was evident. Perhaps I needed someone to object and
to repeat: of course it's necessary, this obstinacy reveals the
shadows, the reality beyond the declarations of intent. In any
case, the American director embodied the first point of view
regarding the problem 'continuity or discontinuity' between
the first and the second halves of the twentieth century: that
of total indifference to the question.

Schechner spoke on the second day of the conference,
6 October, in a bizarre pocket of silence. He told us that the
future would appear with the beautiful and alien face of a bar-
barian prince, someone who has come to destroy. He sought
to focus on connections between the past and the present,
between the present and the future.

RICHARD SCHECHNER
Why a Theatre Laboratory
in a Third Millenium

The theatre as the central focus of public debate is long gone. What movies and television began, the Internet has finished. Theatre is still intensely important to its devotees – witness this room. And if theatre itself is disappearing, not so theatre laboratories. All that's left of the non-commercial theatre is a collection of laboratories from Barba's floating islands to the many acting studios and schools of New York; from the far-flung work of those engaged in social theatre in stressed locations like Sri Lanka or Afghanistan to those working in the prisons of Brazil or the United States. While Stanislavski fled his own Moscow Art Theatre seeking a creative refuge in his Studios, and while Grotowski formed his laboratory at least partly to avoid the strangling strictures of a totalitarian regime, we meet triumphantly at large public universities under official auspices to listen to 'masters', eat well, and fan the sparks, Hasidic possibly, or maybe just academic. When exactly did theatre, as a genre, 'really' transform itself into something it was not in the epoch 1890 to… you pick a date – 1927, the first sound movie, 1945, the end of World War 2 heralding the explosion of television, 1985, the arrival of the Internet, etc. […]

We have argued about what a laboratory is. We could perhaps better inquire what theatre is. The wildly expanding genre is 'performance', and theatre is just a sub-genre; and the kind of theatre we are discussing a still more limited phenomenon. I think we in this room mean theatre to be the kind of artists, groups, works and concerns of the Great Reform at the turn of the twentieth century to the work of Brook, Mnouchkine, Odin and like-minded individuals and groups at the turn of the twenty-first century.

If there is time, I would like to discuss with you certain activities that are 'like' but not exactly the same as the theatre we have been discussing: performance art emerging from the intersections of the visual arts, Happenings, and various rituals; neo- or invented rituals; social, political, and therapeutic theatres that employ theatrical means for non-artistic ends; Internet and virtual performances using sophisticated technologies and codes. These kinds of performances overlap with each other and, to some degree, with the work we have been considering; and yet each is distinct. At the theoretical as well as at the historical and practical levels, we need to identify similarities and differences among these activities. Each of these performance activities – I resist calling them all 'theatres' – have their own laboratory traditions, their own more or less private arenas where adherents investigate what they are doing, how and why.

But before going further, I will take a detour, because sometimes the long route is the shortest way home.

In the American theatre at least, we have many great actors who do not employ an 'extra-daily' body in the sense that the masters of corporeal mime, jingju or kathakali do. I mean, of course, actors such as Marlon Brando, Meryl Streep, Al Pacino, Dustin Hoffman, and many more reaching back to at least the 1930s. Mostly we know these artists through the movies, though they often also or first worked on the stage.

Let me trace, in brief, the history of this kind of acting, even while admitting that I have often myself opposed the kind of theatre that brought it into existence and which continues to mark it. This history is replete with ironies that are not yet fully understood.

The American Laboratory Theatre was founded in 1923, six months after the Moscow Art Theatre's visit to the USA. The principal acting teachers were Maria Ouspenskaya and Richard Boleslavski, himself a Polish member of the Moscow Art Theatre. Boleslavski's *Acting, The First Six Lessons* was, and even today remains, an important book in the transmission of a certain phase of the Stanislavski technique to America. After the Lab disbanded in 1933, Boleslavski went to Hollywood where, along with Ouspenskaya and Michael Chekhov, he had a big impact on film.

Enrolled in the American Laboratory Theatre as students were Stella Adler, Harold Clurman and Lee Strasberg. In 1931, Strasberg, Clurman and Cheryl Crawford founded the Group Theatre. One year after its founding, Elia Kazan joined the Group. I can't detail the Group Theatre's history here. Suffice it to say that the Group brought together the most extraordinary collection of individuals – actors, writers, directors, designers, ideologues, teachers – ever to work as an ensemble in the American theatre. What came from the Group Theatre influenced – and continues to largely determine – the kind of American acting and American theatre we see in movies, on many stages and in television.

The link between the Group, which dissolved in 1941, and the future American theatre included, but was not limited to, The Actors Studio. The Studio was founded in 1947 by Kazan, Crawford, and Robert Lewis. Within a year, Lewis was gone, continuing on his own to be a very influential teacher. In 1949, Strasberg joined the Studio, becoming its artistic director in 1951, a position he held until his death in 1982. Stella Adler, Lewis, Sandford Meisner and others – all claiming a direct link to Stanislavski – left the Actors Studio but opened studios of their own. In fact, several of these studios are still very active in New York. Ought we to consider them, and the Actors Studio, as acting schools, workshops or laboratories? My own Tisch School of the Arts at New York University has an acting department of more than 1,300 students. These study at the Strasberg Institute, the Stella Adler Studio and other professional schools in New York. There is an in-house studio, The Experimental Theatre Wing, which has counted as its teachers and guest directors many leading lights of the American and even world experimental theatre. For several years before his death, Ryszard Cieślak was a teacher in the Experimental Theatre Wing. Graduates of Tisch-New York University populate the American theatre and film in all its varieties, from off-off-Broadway and experimental theatre to television and Hollywood. At the 'ground floor', that is, the level of working actors, designers and directors, the lines between these different kinds of theatre are blurry.

I am not eager to exclude the New York or Los Angeles acting schools from consideration here. Many of the teachers work in what we here would call a laboratory situation. They not only transmit what they know, but some develop new methods, such as Mary Overlie's Viewpoints, through continuous investigation and revision. Does the fact that some of the teachers are incompetent or that several studios not only exploit their students – accepting anyone who can pay – but also pander to commercial interests make a difference? Wasn't the Odin formed from actor school and theatre 'rejects'? Do we want to consider only 'good' laboratories? To what degree do we wish to be scholars and to what degree do we want to be advocates?

And where do the universities come in? It was not until well into the twentieth century in the USA, and later still in Europe, that theatre – not dramatic literature – became an accepted object of study. At the time of the Moscow Art Theatre, and for decades following, the universities were not the major players they are now. As we all know, most serious scientific research in both the hard and social sciences takes place under university auspices (and thereby under the indirect control of the states funding those universities). At present, as this room gives evidence of, most theatre research is also taking place at universities. Don't the acting classes, the PhD dissertation researches, the productions and so on constitute most of the laboratories of our day? Don't the activities of DasArts in Amsterdam or in the Theaterwissenschaft at Giessen belong to the tradition of the theatre laboratory?

But what kind of experimental or laboratory work is actually being done at universities? The facilities are there, the money though not unlimited is certainly there, but mostly, in the USA at least, professors see their role as teachers of theatre history or trainers of persons for places in today's theatre. Very little is being done to advance the kind of experimental laboratory work comparable either to what goes on in the sciences or what was done by Stanislavski, Meyerhold or Grotowski. The universities host or control enormous material and human resources. Why have we not critically examined their work and the possibilities, or failures, of the universities as sites of theatre laboratories?

Let me return to Lee Strasberg and company. It should be noted that Clurman, Strasberg and Adler 'got' Stanislavski not only through Boleslavski and Ouspenskaya but, briefly, from Stanislavski himself. While in Europe in 1934, Adler worked with Stanislavski on a daily basis for several months. Two years later, Strasberg and Clurman visited Stanislavski. They did not work with him on a daily basis, but discussed acting and directing with him. Each person developed her/his own particular view of Stanislavski's system. Adler's reaction against Strasberg was particularly vehement. As presented today on her school's website, Adler objected to his [Strasberg's] relentless emphasis on affective memory exercises that made acting increasingly painful for her. 'The emphasis was a sick one. [...] You couldn't be on the stage thinking of your own personal life. It was just schizophrenic.'

Adler's tradition was not only Stanislavski's Art Theatre but also the Yiddish theatre, where her father was a star. Between 1880 and 1940 a dozen Yiddish theatres were active in New York performing a repertory ranging from *Der Yeshiva Bokher* (The Yeshiva Student), an adaptation of *Hamlet*, to *Hedda Gabler* and new Yiddish plays. If Grotowski was later influenced by Hasidism, the American theatre and film was, at its most creative moment, strongly inflected by Jewish and Yiddish culture streaming to the New World from Germany and even more from Russia, Poland and other Eastern European countries. This immigration was a flood long before the Nazis came to power.

Strasberg was one of those European Jews, born in Budanov, the Ukraine, in 1901 and arriving in New York with his parents in 1908.

Whatever Adler's opinion, Strasberg had the last laugh. Having met Stanislavski, Strasberg could also claim to base his method on the master's practice. And as is frequently the case, the teachings of a master are open to widely divergent interpretations. Of course, we all know that Strasberg's interpretation became known as The Method. The Method is based on delving into the actor's personal life and experiences at a very deep level. Strasberg also returned from Moscow with information about Meyerhold and biomechanics. But biomechanics never figured prominently in Strasberg's own teaching of acting. In Strasberg's words, also taken from the internet this morning: 'Acting is the most personal of our crafts. The make-up of a human being – his physical, mental and emotional habits – influences his acting to a much greater extent than commonly recognized.'[171] Again, there is no time to delve into these matters in any detail here. I note only that researching the 'most personal' might also, in its own way, be said to be a key method of Grotowski during his poor theatre phase. Of course, Grotowski hated exactly what many consider The Method leads to: sentimentality and self-indulgence. Furthermore, Grotowski emphasized a most rigorous corporal and vocal training. But, granting that, I suggest also we look a little deeper.

The Strasberg laboratory, or Actors Studio, featured exercises in emotional memory. Strasberg was famous for developing an exercise he called the 'private moment', where an actor was asked to lay bare to the assembled Studio members her most intimate experiences. Strasberg never intended that these memories and associations be performed before an anonymous group in a public theatre. He did want, in his own way, as Grotowski argued, for the actor to use his own self as a 'scalpel' to cut to the deepest level of his being. The great difference is that Grotowski connected the intimate to the archetype and insisted that all personal associations be channeled through a very strict, codified training later to be integrated into an equally strict performance score that was closer to dance than ordinary theatre. At least this was Grotowski's practice during his poor theatre phase. Things changed drastically during paratheatre but then returned to a highly disciplined work in Objective Drama and Art as Vehicle phases. Grotowski also explored the performance practices of Asian and Caribbean-African cultures. Strasberg stuck to Euro-America. And Grotowski, unlike Strasberg, saw his actors

---

[171] Lee Strasberg, http://www.leestrasberg.com/about/quotes.html [accessed 6 October 2004] (para 5 of 9).

through from training into performance. Strasberg rarely directed; when he did, the results were catastrophic.

But Strasberg's importance is not to be found in his directing or even his teaching as such. His importance is in how The Method crystallized and legitimized an already-present American tendency toward shameless self-display. We can see this as far back as the nineteenth-century poetry of Walt Whitman ('Song of Myself' or 'I Sing the Body Electric') on through Madison Avenue's pseudo-personalized sloganeering to today's many television talk shows. Strasberg-trained actors enable Americans to enjoy the public display of private emotions and memories, glossing these as the highest kind of theatrical art. In acting before Strasberg, the performer developed means to show the character's emotions, to tell the story of the character effectively. Strasberg argued that his Method would give actors a better tool to accomplish this classical aim.

Several experimenters – me among them – went further. We deconstructed characterization. Working with The Performance Group from 1967 through 1980, I developed exercises that put onstage the actual experiences and feelings of the actors not masked by characterization but 'as yourself'. It was this practice that Grotowski so strenuously objected to in my work. Nevertheless, I did it. In *Dionysus in 69* (1968–69), sometimes the actors used their real names and acted out their immediate feelings during the performance. In *Commune* (1971–74), I took more steps in directly performing the personal. The play began with each actor singing a 'Song of First Encounter' in which he or she told the audience how they had come to join The Performance Group. In *Commune*, actors were free to invent character names for themselves or use their own names. Spalding Gray used his own name, 'Spalding', as his character's name. The actors also helped select the texts that we used in constructing the *Commune* montage – those texts combined known works with the actors' and my own writings. [...]

Let me now conclude by asking a few fundamental questions. We assume here that a laboratory is a good thing. It is, ideally, a sequestered time-space where actions can be researched in an effort to find truth, to train people, to make lasting contact with other human beings, and so on. But in the larger world outside of theatre, outside the arts, there also are laboratories. Most of these have to do with military, medical, business, or pharmaceutical research. The results streaming from these laboratories profoundly affect all our lives.

Mary Wollstonecraft Shelley's *Frankenstein* tells the story of a laboratory gone mad. Dr. F. does not know what he is creating in his laboratory. And the results of his research are twofold: the monster of the tale and our aesthetic enjoyment in reading Mary Shelley's writing – and seeing the myriad films deriving from it, including whole legions of monsters other than Frankenstein but like him in theory, ranging from Godzilla to god knows what. The underlying cautionary tale of Frankenstein is that our collective reach has exceeded our grasp. That is, to put it in other terms, our knowledge and power are far in excess of our ethics. Or, in terms of still another old tale, we have eaten the fruit of knowledge without knowing finally how to digest it.

At the start of the last phase of modernism, the final turn of the Enlightenment, that is, from the midpoint of the nineteenth century to the first world war, great advances of knowledge promised boundless hope. From Darwin to Marx to Einstein to Freud, the basis for a grand future was at hand. And yet what these profound thinkers imagined has not helped the rest of humankind enjoy even a tiny plot of utopia. Instead we are faced with ecological catastrophe, genetic engineering, global capital run amok and space-borne atomic weaponry of incalculable destruction.

What's to do?

Can we, ought we, isolate ourselves in our theatrical monasteries or floating islands, our laboratories? Is doing social theatre to ameliorate the pain good enough? Is there any way that we can reverse the action of a Greek tragedy that we as a species, as a group of religions and cultures, are collectively in the next to last scene of? We have had our peripeteia – our programs tell us so. But I don't see any reversal at hand. Nor can I, being a child of the Enlightenment, a believer in progress if not in a *deus ex machina*, call for a limit on scientific, no less artistic research. I am even an alchemist like Faust willing to negotiate an extension of my contract with Mephistopheles. At the same time, I really feel that my children are going to have all hell to pay for the ethical failures of my generation. I know most of the good arguments for continuing to do our work as best we can; for celebrating the artistic giants who have preceded us and the geniuses still Hassidically among us. But I also fear that we happy few are whistling in the dusk at the fire while great darkness slouches towards us.

Sincerely, I ask your help in thinking through these questions.

Studios and laboratories

It is interesting to see that the spectre of Frankenstein, which was evoked by Schechner, often hovers over the discussion on theatre laboratories. I imagine it comes from the fear of having too much influence, of creating different human beings. All laboratories form actors that have not only physical abilities but also a 'different' mentality. A difference that has been given a variety of new names: ethics, spirituality, a love for art. But which is the necessary consequence of a body that is not only gymnastic and well-trained but also accustomed to reacting and speaking in its own disturbing language, ever changing, mysterious and unexpectedly profound, which some great theatres have shown us.

But this is the black face of laboratoriality, the particular smell that surrounds it. It is evidently an odour of blasphemy, almost of scandal. Which however is not backed up by any scandal.

The time has finally come to tackle the problem of the relationship between what we might call – to facilitate the distinction – the Studios of the first decades of the century and those that we can call the theatre laboratories of the second half. Halfway through the century there had been a fracture. For many reasons – probably more of a historical-political nature than artistic – the living example of the theatre of the great masters had disappeared. Many of their needs, their questions and much of their know-how, had become buried. Suddenly, after about thirty years, their traces returned in 'anomalous' theatres, such as those forming part of the 'new theatre' in the 1960s.

My address at the Aarhus conference focused on casting doubt on the wisdom of considering Studios and theatre laboratories as a single, homogeneous phenomenon, despite the obvious affinities connecting them.

Continuity-discontinuity

Theatre laboratory, I argued, is a banner, or a pointer, that has been very useful for quickly indicating 'anomalous' theatres. As such it has been perceived, quite rightly, by theatremakers. But as a historical problem, it implies the existence of various problems, phenomena, solutions and questions to which we must still give a face. It proves above all the necessity of beginning to unravel the diversity of these problems and phenomena. In short, it does not simply indicate a *theme* but opens up a *problem*. A muddled, multi-layered and intriguing problem. One which requires, among other things, a little bit of tidying up and a rediscovery of the differences.

The conference had been organised with this continuity in mind, as could be seen by the introductory address made by Janne Risum, professor at the University of Aarhus:

Some twenty years ago the Italian theatre scholar Fabrizio Cruciani proposed the theory that this spreading trend in the twentieth century of opening schools, ateliers, laboratories, centres and the like, rather than simply staging performances, is an exodus from the existing conditions of the theatre, and from the theatre institutions, not so much in order to create new theatres as to create new theatre cultures. These new theatre cultures reject the more uniform demands of the past as regards the art of the theatre. They replace theology and teleology with the dialectics of searching and learning. They start cultivating a field of creative diversity here and now in the hope of finding a way to a more motley, dynamic and humanly necessary theatre of the future.[172] Inspired by Cruciani, Barba has called this cultural dynamic 'the drift of the exercises' toward a theatre operating in 'the territory of potentialities'.[173]

Cruciani's theory holds a beautiful vision. It has rather the quality of being a romantic rationalization from the point of view of the antiauthoritarian youth revolt of the 1960s. This vision is also its limit as a tool for understanding history. For instance, Stanislavski and Mey-

---

[172] Cf. Fabrizio Cruciani, *Registi pedagoghi e comunità teatrali nel Novecento* (Pedagogical Directors and Theatre Communities in the Twentieth Century), (Rome: Editori & Associati, 1995).

[173] Cf. Eugenio Barba, *The Paper Canoe. A Guide to Theatre Anthropology*, (London and New York: Routledge, 1995), pp. 108–113.

erhold were more authoritarian than that, and they also hoped for more, when they hoped that the social role of the theatre might be compatible with the role of the state, and interact with it in a positive way. Today we are rather at the other end of this process.

The notion of theatre has indeed changed. Grotowski had his doubts and stayed in his barn in Tuscany. Odin Teatret, for instance, may still call itself a theatre laboratory, and be justified in doing so, but it was always also a producing theatre, and by way of habit, also among its audience, its 'territory of potentialities' has moved closer to Shakespeare's wooden O.

With this symposium, the Centre for Theatre Laboratory Studies[174] invites you to examine some of the aspects of this entire development. It is obvious, however, that it has so many simultaneous, paradoxical and widely ramified aspects that even though some family patterns are evident it would be ridiculously reductive to look for a simple genealogical tree. The danger the other way round is not to be able to see the wood for the trees.

To say it with a paradox, it is the convention of the modern theatre that it has no convention in common. Or so it is assumed. Here we are facing a very broad, heterogenous, and scattered environment of Studios, ateliers, laboratories, schools, centres or as some prefer to call themselves: simply theatres. This calls forth some general questions to have in mind: If they have nothing in common, why are they not just called theatres? If they have something in common, why are they not called the same thing? When are those names used more or less as synonyms? And when do they stand for different approaches? And does the recurrent choice of a name reflect an actual tradition based on a special approach? For instance, to what degree do theatres using a laboratory approach or defining themselves as laboratories actually share activities or values? That is, what is the technical-artistic meaning of the term laboratory, and does a theatre laboratory tradition exist which could be defined objectively? And so on. Evidently such existing patterns would be found to interact more or less.

The theatres of the Great Reform at the turn of the century and the small theatre laboratories in the second half are too

---

[174] The Centre for Theatre Laboratory Studies (CTLS) is the branch of Odin Teatret devoted to research, library studies and the creation and management of its archives. CTLS functions in collaboration with the Dramaturgy Institute of the University of Aarhus and was the organiser of the conference.

different, in terms of size, function, audience and status to be able to talk about similarities. This is obvious. But together with many theatres of the Great Reform, there were also Studios, ateliers and schools: tiny, isolated theatre communities, often inclined more to study and research than to attracting an audience. In more than one case these communities even appeared to *contradict* the theatres from whose shadows they emerged, and to be more important, more interesting for the great directors who had created them. These Studios, schools or laboratories have often appeared, *a posteriori*, as the first cases, or prototypes, of what in the second half of the twentieth century were called theatre laboratories.

All of these Studios and schools that had grown up *next to* the art theatres sought to build the foundations of the actor's art. Fabrizio Cruciani argued that the vast and many-faceted activity developed in these separate zones – pedagogic work or pure research on movement and on rhythm, on connections between the physical and the mental, attempts to lay the foundations for a theatre science – should be considered as a veritable theatrical *opus*, with its own autonomous value, in the same way as a performance or a book. This activity had revealed a vital aspect for the theatre: the need for 'lengthy time frames' detached from rehearsal and performance times. It was necessary to seek the place of the 'lengthy time frames'. In the 1970s Cruciani had identified it as being in the separate zones of the schools and Studios. Studies on twentieth-century theatre drew strength from this idea: that the history of the theatre is not just a history of performances.

Among the constants that can be seen when looking at twentieth-century theatre, one of the most significant is the will and the need to move away from the theatre, from its ideology, from its milieu and from its production methods. The existing theatre is perceived as being unsatisfactory and inadequate. There is constant talk of the 'death of the theatre', motivating a search for new theatre forms and realities. The 'loss of the centre' causes theatre-makers to confusedly look for a meaning in a society which questions the 'need for theatre'. [...]

Behind the art theatres that isolate themselves in micro-groups in order to restore a fulness of value to the human being-actor, and behind the radical groups that use the theatre to provoke a different social reality – behind both of these attempts, theatre people seek a place for new values and relations. The history of the great directors of the twentieth century (the director-pedagogues and the masters, not the director-interpreters of a text) may be seen in this sense. The theories of the great directors may be viewed as an acute expression of the crisis of values that twentieth century theatre assumes as self-awareness. These theories are utopias planning not only techniques and particular ways of doing theatre but also restoring a meaning for the theatre in society. They were, in short, plans for a society that demands a theatre or a theatre project lived as an embodiment of the future and of the possible. [...]

The history of theatre in the twentieth century has certainly not only been the history of performances. One only needs to compare the contents of any history book with what the reviews of the period say in order to see how large a part of the theatre iceberg has been submerged by historians. Appia, Craig, Fuchs, Stanislavski, Reinhardt, Meyerhold, Copeau: the artists who are the history of twentieth century theatre established practices and poetics that cannot be confined to one or more performances. The lines of tension have been their utopias, the continually restructured foundations of the theatre of the future, the cultural nuclei which were created around and through the theatre. It is the rise of a theatre culture where it is meaningful to begin and endure but not necessarily to reach a conclusion and perpetuate itself. This culture settles like a lasting and penetrating halo around the theatre surrounding those fragile and temporal entities – the performances – in which, nevertheless, the passion and work of theatre practitioners were manifest. Schools, ateliers, laboratories, centres: these are the places where theatrical creativity has been expressed with the greatest degree of determination.

The practices and poetics of the great masters led to a different kind of theatre whose essential element was pedagogy: the search for the formation of a new human being in a different and renewed theatre and society. It was a search for a way of working which may keep an original quality and whose values are not measured by the success of performances but rather by the cultural repercussions which the theatre provokes and defines. In such a situation, it was no longer possible to teach theatre; one had to begin to educate, as Vakhtangov emphasised. [...]

Educating in creativity, transmitting experiences, setting up schools, establishing a teaching process: all these many fertile initiatives were necessarily ambiguous. They had to do both with the search for 'rules' that could concretise an efficient form of training and with expressive experimentation in order to give form and substance to an idea and a cultural project. Schools are born and continue to exist not for immediate and personal reasons but in order to last and to achieve objective goals. These theatre schools have teachers and courses (and thus a plan, an ideology and rules) as was the case with Meyerhold's and the Proletkult schools, with Copeau's Vieux Colombier and Les Copiaus, with Dullin's Atelier as well as the many different schools which sprang up in the effervescent and heretical German culture.

If on the one hand a school (like the theatre) is a compromise with what already exists, on the other hand it is a place where utopias become realities, where the tensions which sustain the theatrical act take form and are put to the test. In an age in which the theatre of the present lives as a forecast of the possible theatre of the future, change and mutation have become institutionalised in theatrical micro-societies. New types of schools are started in order to renew the theatre, to lay the foundations of the theatre of the future and to broaden the perspectives of the future of the theatre.

'Out of the need for a new organism,' Copeau said in an interview on schools with Anton Giulio Bragaglia (appearing in the *Impero* on 23 December 1926), 'arises the need for a school, something which is no longer simply a group of students directed by a teacher, but a real community capable of being self-sufficient and of meeting its own needs.' But Bragaglia goes on to explain, with evident and polemical partiality, 'not schools but the Theatre-School', agreeing with Copeau that 'school and theatre are one and the same thing'.

So the question of what to learn is thus replaced by the more dynamic, artistic and hazardous problem of who teaches and how.[175]

Five questions

I believe it useful to raise a few questions before such a historical vision becomes too one-sided.

---

[175] Cruciani, *Registi pedagoghi e comunità teatrali nel Novecento*, pp. 55–56. The book gathers various writings starting from 1973.

1. Is there really anything that might allow for a *thread of continuity* that unites in a single chain the laboratories of the entire twentieth century? In short, what justification is there for treating the phenomenon as a historically unified one, apart from an *a posteriori* sense of belonging?

2. What needs in the early decades of the twentieth century led to the creation of places set aside solely for research work? What are the characteristics of zones dedicated to research within large theatre organisations associated with the Great Reform and directing?

3. Is it possible to define in general terms, valid for both the first and second halves of the twentieth century, the type of research and experimentation on the work of the actor conducted in theatre spaces that in one way or another can be related to the idea of theatre laboratory?

4. In what way and for what reasons did theatre laboratories of the late twentieth century recognise their own past in a context that was considerably different from their own, such as that of the early twentieth century?

5. When we think of the Studios, workshops, schools and ateliers of the early twentieth century, how much do the problems that we have experienced directly in theatre laboratories at the end of the century weigh on our views of the past?

These are questions that seek to highlight the differences and the lack of historical continuity between the first and second halves of the last century, well aware that historical events clearly interrupted theatrical research.

Studios and theatre laboratories

What has often been underlined, referring to the protagonists of the Great Reform, is the internal split between the institutions of the art theatres at the turn of the century and their Studios. Schechner too spoke of the Studios as 'creative refuges' in relation to the theatres of the principal directors at the start of the last century. Stanislavski and Copeau were emblematical in this sense. It was this isolation of the Studios, their characteristics and their 'diversity' that caused people to see a continuity between them and the small experimental theatres of the latter half of the century, of which Grotowski's and Barba's theatres are prime examples.

The art theatres, even when they become powerful institutions, embody a necessary *façade* but are no longer an object of desire for the more radical protagonists of the Great Reform. Deemed to be no longer essential, in many cases the institution would seem to be limited to the production of performances and maintenance of the repertoire. Studios, on the other hand, appear to have become the place for real research, freed from production needs and from the need to perform on stage. As I have already said, this is certainly a justified point of view, whose roots lie in the testimonies of some of the leading directors of the early twentieth century.

This standpoint has, perhaps, been excessively swayed by the example of Grotowski and others from quite a different period. In other words, we have viewed the activities of the small Studios of the turn of the century through a filter, consisting of the tiny enclaves of the second half of the century.

For this very reason it is interesting to underline again what would otherwise be a futile and pedantic comment: the fact that early-twentieth-century Studios, schools and ateliers were conceived and created in a completely different way than the later theatre laboratories. They were established as *satellites*, separate bodies revolving around the central and institutional body of a large theatre.[176]

---

[176] Cf., for instance, what is noted by Fabio Mollica in his important afterword to *Il teatro possibile. Stanislavskij e il Primo Studio del Teatro d'Arte di Mosca* (The Possible Theatre: Stanislavski and the First Studio of the Moscow Art Theatre), ed. by Fabio Mollica (Florence: La casa Usher, 1989), pp. 144–220. Mollica writes of the creation of the First Studio at the Art Theatre: 'The impression of Stanislavski's gradual distancing himself from the Art Theatre is a false one if perceived with excessive rigidity. He continues to view the Art Theatre as his home, taking part in its organisation, the choice of repertoire, the assignment of parts; he never lost the pleasure of working creatively within it. [...] On 5 January 1912 Nemirovich-Danchenko informs the Art Theatre members of Stanislavski's wish to create a Studio in which

This was certainly the model for Moscow's Art Theatre. Other Studios, Meyerhold's for example, were basically places detached from their theatre. Béatrice Picon-Vallin has spoken about this at length. Meyerhold, however, appears to consider his Studios as places in which to navigate in the theatre ocean in search of practices and techniques that would then flow into the overall work for his performances and in his theatre.

Studios often became guiding satellites, going to some extent against their original nature or against their original reason for existing. Studios, workshops, special projects, such as Les Copiaus in Burgundy, were built (or imagined) as peripheral places. This detached, satellite dimension made them particularly appropriate for experimentation, pedagogy and forms of training: all activities that had become the main area of interest for directors and that had been hampered by the needs and dimensions of their own theatres.

It does not appear that Studios were built or conceived as new bodies that were to have taken the place of the old institutions. They were projects designed to acquire temporary independence, or rather a substantial *interdependence*. Or to *transform themselves* from Studio to theatre.

Unlike theatre schools, where aspiring actors would train with experienced actors, the Studios were conceived as reservoirs not of the acting art but of the *essence* of the acting art. From there, directors would have been able to fish out ideas, working methods, new propositions to be developed and deepened for performances. However, they were also places in which to start the theatre afresh and cultivate among youngsters a mentality differing considerably from that considered normal for the actor; in which to lay down strict living rules; in which to inflame and keep alight the passion for the theatre (all conditions which, for the actor, were as necessary as technique, physical agility and knowledge of the various 'systems'). It was a zone detached from normal everyday life.

"he can develop his system and, prepare actors and entire productions, decided by the Art Theatre, but without specific deadlines'".

At times, perhaps, there was something more. But they were always *complementary* places to the great institutions. Created not to replace them but to keep them *alive*.[177]

The very idea of being able to create, for one's own theatre, an ecosystem that is so vast and complex that it includes great central institutions, fervent complementary Studios, schools and forms of continuous learning, is one of the most interesting and disconcerting examples of a grandiose, boundless way of thinking, typical of the early theatre directors. Yet it was made possible by the availability of considerable resources.

A luxurious equilibrium

The well-known stories of struggles, misunderstandings, difficulties and crises often hide the fact that the rebel theatres of the early twentieth century – those of Stanislavski, Meyerhold, Copeau and so on – were *rich* theatres, compared with the independent and laboratorial theatres of the late twentieth century. If they often went through periods of economic crisis, or if – after having been planned – they did not become reality, it was because they required considerable resources and had been designed with excess.

It was not just economic wealth. Theatres were planned on a monumental scale and thus needed patrons. But they also had enormous resources. In addition to financial resources, they could also draw from a vast theatrical know-how, almost unimaginable for today's theatre-makers. This know-how was

---

[177] It may be interesting, at least to give a clue as to the mentalities involved, to recall the way in which Craig had once described his future school as a place for bringing together three different lines, each of which, when alone and going beyond its limits, is a boomerang that ends up suffocating creativity: study of the past (a historical, serious study, which would have been purely arid on its own); research on the present (practical, which alone would inevitably veer towards commercial aspects) and research on the future (what we might call 'pure research': which alone, in his opinion, would have been simply crazy). Cf. 'The Fit and the Unfit: A Note on Training', *The Mask*, vol. 6, no. 1 (January 1914), 230–233. Craig's views are significant, expressing a way of reasoning about one's own experiments, viewed as being crucial phenomena, destined to change the way people go about doing theatre, and certainly not as secondary, avant-garde initiatives. Indeed, reasoning on a large scale.

within easy reach: from actors embodying the pinnacle of Europe's theatre tradition of the previous century, from an almost daily contact with the theatre practice and performances of all types and from the existence of a compact intellectual network, with solid yet informal structures and contradictory but dynamic connections (secret meetings, arguments, complicity, solidarity, long-term relationships and contacts creating a common history).

Finally, these theatres were 'rich' because they were complex structures, vast microcosms, inside which there was room for different spaces and times. They were thus able to support the incredibly multifaceted ecosystem that some great directors at the turn of the century had invented: a luxurious equilibrium between the know-how gained through maturity and the extremism of youth.

As soon as this luxurious equilibrium was disturbed, new satellite-institutions were created to restore it.

Studios as compensation chambers

For all new theatres of the first years of the twentieth century, the laboratory zone was invented as *complementary opposition*, like a compensation chamber in relation to the central body. The protagonists of the Great Reform appear to have invented a complex organisational system to counterbalance an essential need for order (even a re-invented and revolutionary order) with a categorical imperative for change. The result was the creation of a special balance, the product of constant conflicts, but effective, quite close to the edge of chaos, without falling off the edge.

This ecosystem, not the Studios, was the real rebellious invention of the early directors.

At a given level of development, the most important strategic alliances and the most radical stimuli do not come from forms of collaboration or cooperation. They come from contrasts, almost as if it were necessary to single out or invent 'opponents', counterparts or representatives of the alternative. This leads us to a fundamental principle: every success contains the seeds of one's downfall, just as every invention must bring about the creation of a countermeasure. The great directors of the early twentieth century seem to have instinctively realised this.

We can also see this in our everyday experience: no theatre laboratory can preserve its original characteristics for a lifetime. Otherwise they would face the risk of turning into an ideology. If it perseveres, any utopian community turns into its opposite. Grotowski chose to close down his theatre laboratory. The 2009 version of Odin Teatret is a far cry from the early Odin of 1964. This fact may concern or upset us, it may even cause some to express regrets. But in order to understand this situation – the necessity of change, in any direction – it may be useful to reflect on the 'luxurious equilibrium' brought about by the existence of the Studios.

Any genuinely new theatrical form, be it a performance, a production method, a training model or a global attitude to the profession, has brought about a feeling of a downfall, sooner or later. Not so much ageing as rigidity and the fear of being incapable of fresh change.

This is how one should look at the invention of the Studios and of the schools, in the first years of the twentieth century: like the creation of a countermeasure, of an internal adversary. Not so much the creation of a new theatre built in the form of a place of study or of passion, but as a necessary counterbalance, cleverly and carefully developed in order to keep intact that luxurious balance that made it possible to maintain the life of a small art theatre within a large-sized institution.

It is perhaps for this reason that Studios appear to have had more extreme characteristics than those of the great theatres, even at the time of their birth. Not because Studios were avant-garde and places devoted to study, but because of their specific role: to stimulate the central body, already inured to the changes that had provoked its birth. To make them feel someone breathing down their neck. Although they appear to be independent, their main goal is to establish a state of interdependence. Seldom do they take the place of the central body, even more rarely do they do so successfully or while remaining true to their original goals.

Whatever the 'central body' that must be stimulated – whether it be a stable ensemble of actors, a semi-permanent group or even the director – each case must be considered individually.

It is useful to observe the differences of the great theatres of the past: the ecosystem comprising the central body and the Studios, the creation of a luxurious equilibrium in life and not only in art. This teaches us something about inevitable problems, such as ageing, change and regression. It transmits to us the discovery made by master directors: that every success contains the seeds of one's demise, and every invention must consequently bring about the creation of a countermeasure, which must always be extreme, tiring, upsetting, even painful. It shows us that if left to its own devices, the theatre tends towards normality. Without a really extreme invention, like that of the luxurious equilibrium of the Studios, after a certain number of years the only possibilities are to 'abandon ship' or to move towards the norm.

Laboratoriality and research

We naturally believe they *have an affinity* with the small theatre laboratories of the late twentieth century that considered themselves as their heirs. They are not just experimental theatres. Their research covers a broad expanse, making it possible to develop parallel lines of value – ethical, existential and so on. But the reason for this affinity should not be seen as a tendency to develop an independent theatre culture, opposed even to the performance-based theatre. The resemblance is to be seen in the way they worked on creating performances and on influencing the actor. And in the fact that in both cases work is based on a mixture of art and life, on a slow merging of habits and clichés.

Preparation times were long of course. But it was a necessity that came from a long way back, when the early-twentieth-century masters rediscovered it. It came from the oldest professional acting traditions in Europe: a life rooted on separateness, a difference that heightens the actor's presence on stage.

The early-twentieth-century directors devised methods and systems to facilitate the slow merging of art and life. So they invented very long rehearsal times, communes, schools, Studios. They built zones that were separate, not from the performance but from everyday life. By establishing separate theatre zones, they created the equivalent of the actor's marginality in past times: extra-daily life. Did they sense that the culture of the body and its language arises and is developed from *difference*?

The Red Queen's race

The Studios were to have served to create a rivalry (Studios *versus* central body) that sought not the victory of one of the two forces but what in biology circles is known as the *Red Queen principle*. It indicates the existence of forms of continuous change but not necessarily progress or the victory of one solution over another. It refers, for instance, to a race for change between two species, genders or entities that are rivals or connected in some way. But it is a race that does not move and does not open up a gap between the contestants, because at the same time the second 'pole' is changing and moving: like the race of the Red Queen in Lewis Carroll's *Through the Looking-Glass*, in which the contestants are running while staying in the same spot. The Red Queen's race points out the importance of evolutionary changes in a species that appears to want to win, as if driven by the goal of acquiring superiority, but that is constantly caught up by parallel changes of the species it is competing against. This is a race whose deep meaning seems to be one of equilibrium.

At the end of the road

A laboratorial situation could be defined as one that implies not only paths of artistic production but also varying existential processes: paths of knowledge, transmission of knowledge, research and study of the deepest structures of the theatre. To progress along these paths, this type of theatre is concerned not only with the impact a performance can have but *also* with the theatrical sphere that starts from the actor's everyday life and arrives at his work: that zone, in other words, that concerns only those who do theatre. It is a zone that has always existed, of course, and that has always had an impact on how theatre work is performed. But no one *worried about it* until the twentieth century.

The time devoted to preparing a performance proved to be insufficient to deal with this zone and to create paths that were not just productive but also existential and dedicated to technical research. A laboratory requires longer and uninterrupted times. Even though continuity can have many different faces.

The existence of a zone in which there are *also* existential paths, and research conducted into more profound structures than just production, changed midway through the twentieth century due to a number of concomitant causes, not the least of which was the birth of two laboratorial realities, Grotowski's and Flaszen's Teatr Laboratorium and Barba's Odin Teatret. These two theatres, 'twins' for many years, united yet very different from each other, have been a joint and bivalent frame of reference. They were able to represent in an *explicit* form some paths and some directions.

It may accordingly be said that a new form of laboratoriality came into being midway through the century. Its characteristics are very different from those of the earlier Studios. Within our discussion this new form was called 'theatre laboratory', first because it was the most common formula of the second half of the century, secondly to distinguish it from laboratorial forms that were partially similar to it but actually very different, born in the first half of the century.

Finally, processes dealing with existential aspects and those concerned with research into and creation of new performances do not follow parallel, independent paths. It may be said that the former serve to make an impact on the depth of the performance but are not indispensable in terms of aesthetic quality. The reason is that the continuous nature of laboratorial situations, and the lengthy times involved, make it possible to perfect, with reference to the actor's art, a *body language*, which is the only autonomous language of the theatre. It is the most important and most complex of languages, the only one activating, in the spectator, the sphere of both aesthetic pleasure and inner life.

More than a final summary of the discussion, this is a summary of the ideas I had formed during the course of the discussion.

A discussion like this cannot have conclusions. It would make no sense to restrict the reality of theatre laboratories and Studios and make them fit into a single model. Our discussion did not serve to achieve a purpose, a result or to set up a formula. There was no culmination and no victory. Things went differently. It opened up one mental space after another, leading us towards the discovery of a reality made up of one layer inside another. Like an onion, this reality, with a thousand layers to peel off, mocks us and pretends to be reduced to nothing as you approach its core.

V

Five pieces from different mosaics,
with views of vanished landscapes.

As you will see from the small number of remaining pages, we have arrived at the end of the road, or rather of the discussion. I am sorry not to be able to offer the reader more definite conclusions. Our discussion ends with a divergence of voices, each of which founds its discordance on a sounder common base.

In this final chapter we will take a look at some finds, coloured tiles and miscellaneous images that are nevertheless related, like fragments of different mosaics coming from various strata of the same archaeological site. The great thing about excavations is that the saved fragments are not dust-covered memories. They are intact pieces of stories, shinier than *real* objects and more *present*.

Working on this book, I came across many vivid testimonies. I have chosen five descriptions, both direct and indirect, of the work of a theatre laboratory. I have attempted to place around them some pieces of information from the original context. Here they are, in sequence, documents that are difficult to decipher and difficult to forget. They have no definite purpose, they are disturbing and lingering. When preparing the book they were the first I thought of discarding. In the end, they are the last to stay on the table.

First fragment: home. A spectator speaks

The first testimony is also the simplest. It is a description of theatre laboratories as they appear to a traveller, a recent arrival. The speaker is Nicola Savarese, whom we have already met in this book. What follows is the transcription of a tale he told at Scilla, looking towards the sea during one of the sessions of the University of Eurasian Theatre. Savarese was explaining that a laboratory is first and foremost a 'home'.

> I was lucky enough to visit the two theatre laboratories that created such a category in the history of the theatre, Jerzy Grotowski's Teatr Laboratorium in Wrocław and Eugenio Barba's Odin Teatret in Holstebro.

I visited them both in the 1970s, at different periods. At the time I was not a field researcher, although I would go to the theatre to see performances. I had been present at rehearsals, and I had a more than abstract idea of what a theatre was with its inhabitants. But when I visited these two theatre laboratories, my idea of theatre changed from my initial impressions. Some images, like snapshots, stayed with me and took root over time. What at the time I thought to be oddities, anomalies of the theatre, became the fundamental characteristics with which I am now able to distinguish a theatre laboratory.

The first point: theatre laboratories are unusual and eccentric places, located in towns (that I reached after a long journey) indicated in the guidebook as not being capitals, either political or cultural. Wrocław in Poland and Holstebro in Denmark are two such towns. They are not villages. Wrocław indeed is quite a big city, and compared with Holstebro it might even be called a metropolis. But they are not capitals, and I am undoubtedly well off the route of the cultural *grand tours*. Two towns that are too large to be anonymous but too small to be able to afford waste. In other words, they would never agree to or finance a purposeless activity, as sometimes happens in the big cities.

Entering their buildings, not large, a little isolated or out of the way – in Wrocław the theatre was situated in a side street of the town centre, in Holstebro it was an old farmhouse on the outskirts – I was welcomed in a small sitting room with a cup of tea. They sat me down and I met some people, while others continued to pass by, with things to do. I had the impression of entering not a theatre but a home. This impression was confirmed by the fact that neighbouring rooms, shown to me before the workrooms, were a library, a kitchen, actors' rooms more similar to those of a house than to the dressing rooms of a theatre. As regards the theatre, there was no traditional stage as such. The workrooms were occupied at the time. I would see them later on in the evening or one or two days later on the occasion of a performance, a rehearsal or a training session.

It seemed to me to be the actors 'home', their fixed abode. There wasn't a lot of time to live outside the theatre, and when they finally did go home it was to sleep. It was almost as if they had no other home, where they could spend as many hours as in the theatre. One might say they had holiday homes. Otherwise their home was the theatre. This was the first real reflection: a theatre as a home.

Second point: in this house they performed activities that stayed secret for a long time. I remember having asked to attend their meetings and being refused permission. In the workrooms they were doing something that was called *training*, a physical activity, as I would discover later.

Third point: this house was inhabited not by 'actors' but by a group of individuals who had their own stories, identities and personalities, and who were working in a group. I prefer the term 'group', because at the time the Odin was a small group, not a large company.

As well as these group activities in the training room, there were others decided by one person – a leader. At Odin I remember being struck by the fact that this person would give instructions about the most basic of matters. There was a board with instructions regarding various tasks and the names of those responsible, which changed from day to day. These chores were: cleaning the toilets, kitchens, hallways and workrooms. Rather odd tasks, it would appear, for actors. But I saw these people, whom I had known for years, do all of these things: cleaning the bathrooms and corridors, vacuum-cleaning the library room, washing the workroom floors. They did not seem like theatre activities to me.

Years later, during the two months of the lengthy ISTA session at Volterra, in 1981, in the early morning when the participants had gone out for a run, I was surprised to hear Barba say to me: 'Nicola, let's empty the ashtrays.' And we did. So the theatre director would do what his actors did: the cleaning. It was not beneath this leader to perform such tasks. That surprised me a lot, because back then, in Italy, the idea of a collective was bound to other types of association, mostly of a political nature.

Another thing that I believe is related to what I have said above, is that these people had something that was never mentioned, but that could be clearly perceived: they had a great respect for their colleagues. I got to know Odin better, but I remember having met Cieślak, I had to take him to edit the film of *The Constant Prince* together with other Teatr Laboratorium actors, in Rome. They all showed great mutual respect, waiting for their companions to finish speaking before voicing their opinion. This for me personally was something unattainable: we scholars, after years spent working together, are still incapable of observing this elementary form of respect.

This respect was not just formal, it went deeper, was something I have seldom seen. I would call it respect for the work. There was never any other instruction, apart from what I had always heard repeated: do not trivialise work. They are principles underpinning the theatre laboratories that I visited.

Having had time to think, I would add another main characteristic, since I believe that what marks out a theatre laboratory from all other theatres is training. And what is training? An activity not aimed primarily at preparing for the performance. It may seem odd to you, but in Asian theatres, for example, there is no training in the sense of an abstract form of education of the body and the voice. Training, in the theatre laboratories of Wrocław and Holstebro, was called an island of freedom for the actor.

The place, the actor's home, the group, training, respect for one's work and one's fellow actors. This is what I found in my meetings with theatre laboratories.[178]

Savarese's voice betrays that particular nostalgia felt by some for the image of an out-of-the-ordinary home.

But perhaps the dream of an out-of-the-ordinary home, so important for the theatre, may be appreciated more fully if for one moment we take our gaze off the theatre and look at a context allowing for estrangement. As in the words of Henry Thoreau:

I sometimes dream of a larger and more populous house, standing in a golden age, of enduring materials, and without gingerbread work, which shall still consist of only one room, a vast, rude, substantial, primitive hall, without ceiling or plastering, with bare rafters and purlins supporting a sort of lower heaven over one's head – useful to keep off rain and snow ... a cavernous house, wherein you must reach up a torch upon a pole to see the roof ... a house which you have got into when you have opened the outside door, and the ceremony is over; where the weary traveller may wash, and eat, and converse, and sleep, without further journey; such a shelter as you would be glad to reach in a tempestuous night, containing all the essentials of a house, and nothing for house-keeping; where you can see all the treasures of the house at one view, and everything hangs upon its peg, that a man should use. [...] A house whose inside is as open and manifest as a bird's nest, and you cannot go in at the

---

[178] Scilla, University of Eurasian Theatre, 2003. Savarese's address was transcribed by Teatro Proskenion.

front door and out at the back without seeing some of its inhabitants; where to be a guest is to be presented with the freedom of the house.[179]

Second fragment: an actor speaks on improvisation

This is the voice of Torgeir Wethal, an Odin Teatret actor since its foundation in 1964. He talked about his first meeting with Barba and his first steps at Odin Teatret in a book of which only one chapter has so far been published.[180] Here he shows the meeting of the two cells from which his theatre laboratory would grow – an actor and a director, both equally inexpert.

Barba's hand trembled as he lit a cigarette. We were seated around a large table, fourteen or fifteen youngsters, boys and girls. I was the youngest, at 17. Participants had been chosen in a rather random manner. Barba knew some of them already, others he had merely spoken to. He was meeting many of them for the first time. The only thing they had in common was some form of familiarity with the theatre. On that day he let us peep through the keyhole on a sort of work and a life that were alien to us. Who wanted to go with him inside that room? What was behind that door?

Were these the questions? Was this what he was trying to explain to us? I don't remember. Indeed I remember nothing of what was said that day, apart from the fact that the well-known writer Jens Bjørneboe had agreed to write the script for the group's first performance, and that Barba wanted to find a venue where we could work. We had no idea what awaited us after this meeting. But he had managed to arouse some curiosity in most of us. Curiosity, and a desire for adventure. [...]

Almost a month passed and we had heard nothing. Finally one day he found a place and told us. We could start working in Halling school. The classroom was small, less than fifty square metres, in the attic of the old building. The stairs were very long. Over the next few months we came to hate and curse them. It was the great obstacle that had to be overcome before being able to start our evening work.

---

[179] Henry D. Thoreau, *Walden, or Life in the Woods*, ed. by Walter Harding (New York: Houghton Mifflin Company Books, 1995), pp. 237–38.
[180] Torgeir Wethal, 'Frammenti del mondo di un attore', *Teatro e Storia*, no. 6 (1989), 107–144. The meeting took place in September 1964, Barba was not yet 28 years old.

Our bodies ached, full of twinges, and we couldn't move after such physical activity. The road to the attic was long and steep. [...]

I spent much of my childhood and all of my youth in the theatre. At the age of ten I was already acting on Oslo stages and, as an amateur, in school theatres. When I began to work with Eugenio Barba and what was to become Odin Teatret, I was seventeen years old.

Over the years many people have asked me whether I have missed anything, if I have missed what many people experience during their childhood and youth.

No, I don't miss anything; in any case nothing of what my questioners are thinking. Indeed I am so bold as to believe that I have lived more intensely in the theatre than would ever have been possible on the outside.

As a child I was able to prolong my stay in the world of fantasy. This is usually interrupted when school begins. And later I had a precise setting – the theatre – through which I could relate to the world. An inherently changeable setting. In this changing framework there have been situations in which I have experienced and learned more about myself and about the world around me than I would have been able to do 'outside' the theatre.

Everything you feel and the experiences you have when you are seeking a foundation and an expression for a performance has an influence on you as a person. In the same way as all profound experiences.

In the traditional sense of the term, I have never *acted* a part in an Odin Teatret performance. Most of our performances did *not* arise from the interpretation of written texts, but were the result of long and particular working processes. The starting points for these processes were concrete and exacting themes. Themes that had emotional and historical parallels with us and with our time.

Both the 'characters' and the story of the performance grow slowly during the course of our meeting/dialogue with the theme. A world is slowly constructed. I live in this world. Everything I do as an actor certainly has a connection with the chosen theme, but at the same time it has a starting point within me.

The end result, the performance, is an image of our opinions. A full set of images with different meanings, kept together by respect for what the theme demands, and that becomes the story.

In the meeting with each new performance, I have always needed to try and discover sides of myself and models of behaviour that are more concealed than those I usually show in everyday life. One must discover them and, together with the director, give them a form that has a meaning in the story of the performance.

Improvisation has been *one* of the paths towards this knowledge and towards a mastery of these unknown sides of myself. When I talk about improvisation, I mean concrete working techniques.

The term *improvising* – doing the unexpected – has led to countless interpretations and ways of implementing it. I believe that in Odin Teatret there are as many ways of handling an improvisation as there are actors. The importance of improvisation as part of the working process also varies. And in Odin Teatret some actors have had more numerous and deeper experiences than others in this field.

Personally I rarely use any longer the technique I am about to describe, but it is in any case one of the foundations for what I do today. It is a professional experience that is an important base for me as an actor.

My personal take on improvisation began in the attic of Halling School in Oslo, Odin Teatret's first workroom. Right from the start we worked on *études*. An *étude* was a form of explanatory improvisation: go through a wood – push your way through the branches, one strikes your face – you reach a river, you jump from stone to stone, halfway across you stumble – you get to the other side and walk through a swamp – etc.

After improvising, the order of actions was fixed, and each action was polished and refined. This required a concrete internal visualisation. The setting and all details had to be seen with the inner eyes. In my first work diary, in the autumn of 1964, I wrote:

'With regard to *études*:

1. Feel before expressing something.
2. Observe and see in detail before describing what you have seen.
3. Listen before replying.
4. Sight – hearing – taste – smell – touch: these senses must be taken into consideration and be constantly active'.

Later I removed the word 'feel' from my working terminology. *Feeling* is the result of the meeting between you and the world around you. If you begin with wanting to *feel* something, you can only obtain an expression that is strained. You can't force yourself to feel something, this being the end result of many factors; you and...? But apart from that, the words of 1964 are still valid. And they've been at the core of my way of improvising for years, even though their content gradually came from bigger and more complex worlds than at the beginning. I have thus often been confronted by the unknown and the unconscious. My reaction to these meetings caused me to perform actions in a way that previously I would not have been able to identify as being mine.

If I remember well, one of us stayed alone with Eugenio after the day's normal work had ended. A calm, sweet seriousness surrounded the first meeting with what I had first conceived as the most important part of the work where Eugenio wanted to take us: *psychotechnics*, improvisation.

Some years later, when people began to become familiar with our working method, we changed terminology. 'Psychotechnics' created a false sense of mysticism. When working with new people, the word often generated reactions similar to the mechanisms of a psychodrama. That was certainly not our intention.

Eugenio attempted to explain to me what I had to do:

> There are people who are more important to you than others. There are situations you have experienced, dreamed and desired which are more important to you than others. There are places you have actually been to, or visited in your imagination, that are more important to you than others. Begin with a situation that is a combination of a known face and a precise action in a precise place. Let that world come to life. Follow it. Live it. There are no rules. Everything can change along the way. Perhaps it all seems like a daydream, or a deep dream. Perhaps it's something you remember. Take all the time you want. Place yourself in a comfortable position.

Eugenio's explanation was probably not exactly like that. But that is the essence of what I remember from those years. But I clearly recall the particular situation.

I lay down on the floor and closed my eyes. Everything was hushed.

I was relatively inexpert in many fields of life. Nevertheless, or perhaps for that very reason, I had a fervid imagination and a great ability to dream. I often lived with intensity without doing anything. (That may still be so today. And it's one of my handicaps professionally speaking. It may be difficult for me to find something more attractive than my dream world.)

To begin with I was in the dark: dense and pleasant. Slowly I allowed space, people and actions to emerge within me. I saw friends, relatives, people and faces that passed me by or were taking part in what was happening. Old, interrupted situations were lived out in full.

Withheld reactions actually occurred. From time to time there was chaos. Different actions and faces flitted to and fro and mingled confusingly. This happened above all when the thought that something had to happen soon permeated the other awareness, the awareness I was experiencing. It could not be by chance that I had to simply stay there, on the floor with my eyes closed. I don't remember how long it lasted. My notion of time disappeared – as still happens now during my improvisations.

In the end I opened my eyes and got up from the floor, where I had been lying still all the time.

It may seem absurd if one thinks about it now. Most directors would have interrupted the actor after a while and say they probably hadn't explained themselves very well.

During that hour or hour and a half that I think my improvisation lasted, while lying down still on the floor, Eugenio sat there watching; he did not interrupt me and afterwards he did not comment on what I had done. Only a few days later, when we resumed this work, did he give some explanations. Now, years later, I believe that the hour he spent watching me was the time he became my second *master*. The hour in which no physical action took place contained an immense treasure trove that took me years to express in a theatre space.

I should point out that it was the first time. No one had given me an example of what an improvisation might be, and Eugenio had never previously attempted to express, during the course of our practical work, the words that could have helped the actor. Help him not only to start on his secret journey but also to show and share it, first with the director and then with the spectator.

My first improvisation was like a film that is projected with a bulbless projector. All the images are there, and pass in front of the lens, but the room remains in the dark. For some actors it is correct to say that the improvisation has to be projected in space. For others, having reached another stage, it is simpler: the body lives and plays its part in what is happening. Everything and everyone around him, that do something with him or with whom he does something, are of course invisible for the spectator. Simply, the actor has to react in full to what is happening, through his actions. His improvisation *is* in space. The actor that uses 'the screen', on the other hand, will usually see his images first in his head, then he will show them to the outside world. In both cases the improvisation should not be recounted to the spectator as a narrative.[181]

---

[181] Wethal, unpublished manuscript.

Third fragment: letters between directors

In 1998 Eugenio Barba spoke about his Polish apprentice-ship. He described it in a bold, astonishing book, combin-ing autobiography with an analysis of the historical changes brought about by the Teatr Laboratorium, in which the face of the theatre is one of adventure, and the prevailing sentiment of the memory is gratitude. *Land of Ashes and Diamonds* nar-rates Barba's arrival in January 1961 at Jerzy Grotowski's and Ludwik Flaszen's (then) unknown Teatr 13 Rzędów, where he would remain for almost three years. A year later the name changed to Teatr Laboratorium 13 Rzędów. At the end of the book are twenty-six of Grotowski's letters to Barba from the period 1963–69.

Almost ten years later, in 2007, Grotowski's brother Kazi-mierz, the physicist mentioned earlier on, found some card-board boxes that the director had stored away before leaving Poland in the early 1980s after Jaruzelski's coup d'état. In one of these boxes were Barba's replies to Grotowski's let-ters. These letters were consigned to Zbigniew Osiński, who copied them and sent them on to Barba. The first of Barba's letters, in chronological order, was from 1963, and may almost have been of symbolic value, since it had been sent from India. As soon as it saw the light of day, it practically disintegrated, due to humidity and the ravages of time. It might have been a symbol of their relationship, Osiński wrote, because India was a physical, mental and professional place that Barba and Grotowski had in common, right from the outset.

Subsequent letters from Barba had mostly been written after 1964. There are not many, but they are long and de-tailed: a young director, certainly self-confident and certainly alone and inexperienced, writes to a fellow adventurer who has been half brother, half master, only a couple of years older then himself. He informs Grotowski that he has founded his own theatre in Norway. The Polish master is his only frame of reference, albeit a distant one. Barba writes in French, calling Grotowski 'Monsieur le Directeur', while Grotowski, replying in Polish, fondly addresses him as 'Drogi Panie Eugeniu-szu' (Dear Mr Eugenio).[182]

Having returned to Oslo after his four-year Polish stay, Barba had gone to a number of Norwegian theatres asking, with a mixture of arrogance and naivety, to be hired as a director. Then he brought together a group of very young aspiring actors, who had been rejected by the national theatre school, and founded Odin Teatret. As he worked with them full time, unsalaried (like the actors), but unlike the actors without the aid of family support in Norway, the personal 'economic difficulties' he tells Grotowski about were considerable.

Oslo, 20 November 1965

Dear Mr Director,

I did not reply to your last letter for a number of reasons. First of all, due to a lack of time. I will describe to you below my work schedule, and you will be able to see how little time I have for correspondence. Secondly, I no longer have a typewriter (I sold mine due to economic difficulties), so I have to use the typewriter of the Institute of Indology at the University, where I go every Saturday. Finally, your penultimate letter had irked me somewhat. If you remember, you wrote that the book was not ready due to my negligence.[183] According to Bozzolato, I had not sent the photos and drawings. I've no idea how Bozzolato follows the publisher's activity. In any case, everything was ready well before Christmas, I had sent the photos, drawings and even the clichés that I had bought from *Vindrosen* (the Danish magazine). So everything is ready, and the book will come out by the end of the week.[184]

It is not easy to answer the questions you asked yourself and me in your last letter. All I can do is to describe to you how I am trying to resolve the problems with my group.

[182] The originals are kept in the Archives of the Grotowski Institute in Wrocław. Photocopies thereof, plus Osiński's accompanying letter, are kept in the Odin Teatret Archives, Fonds Barba, Series Grotowski, Binder 5.

[183] Barba refers to his first book, *Alla ricerca del teatro perduto*, which would be published by Marsilio (in the collection 'Biblioteca Sarmatica', directed by Giampiero Bozzolato) in December 1965. The book was devoted to the work of Jerzy Grotowski and his Teatr Laboratorium 13 Rzędów.

[184] The letter mentioned by Barba has obviously been lost, as it is not among those published or kept in the Odin Teatret Archives.

I contacted the people in October, based on a list of youngsters rejected by the theatre school. We work from 6 pm to 10 pm. Right from the start I put the pupils under pressure as regards the work schedule: I wanted to select them on the basis of their patience and endurance in work. Six of them left after just a few days. There remained three girls and two boys. Their age varies from 18 to 21. I immediately used training to form them ethically and not only technically in order to shape these youngsters in terms of personal Morals, of which professional morals will be a part. To form youngsters that can find in the work itself both a goal and a result of their work: *karma yoga.* For me too the theatre has become a *darshana,* a standpoint from which to explain myself and the phenomena surrounding me. I have tried to develop in my actors a sense of identity between their private personality and the theatre (our group as a whole). After a few months of work, I must say I have managed to fuse these five people together in a very unselfish collective. First the group, then our private person: that is the password. It is quite an extraordinary result, because these five people did not know each other before I contacted them, and because they have very different characters and psychic traits.

Right from the outset I made each of the pupils act as the instructor. Now they all lead one or more sets of exercises. I have avoided using the jargon of Opole, and I have sought to create a new vocabulary deriving from the working circumstances with my pupils. Now we have a venue that we rented at the start of January. The rent is covered by a sum that each of us pays weekly to the theatre.

Our working day begins at 9 o'clock in the morning. We work without a break for three hours. At midday we take a half-hour break, we eat and drink a coffee. I take advantage of this break to talk about work-related problems. Then we resume, working uninterruptedly from 12.30 to 4 o'clock. That is our normal working day. Afterwards, from 5 to 8 o'clock, there are always one or two actors who carry on working, with me or with an instructor. In actual fact, we work from 9 o'clock in the morning to 8 o'clock at night, with a break of one and a half hours.

Now let me move on to exercises. I had to solve a number of problems, because these five youngsters do not come from a theatre school, they are just people who wanted to be actors. My job is chiefly to form them, so mine is a pedagogical task. And I came up against a series of difficulties that I had not foreseen. These youngsters did not have prepared bodies, they were not plastic, their vocal apparatus had many organic problems. But during my stay in India I learned a fundamental truth: anyone can become an actor[185]. The only condition being that you work obstinately for ten hours a day. So I had to create a set of new exercises to solve the problem of body preparation.

Here is the list of subjects taught:

sport (tennis, swimming, fencing)
gymnastics
acrobatics
plastics
ballet
jumping (I will explain this later)
pantomime
face exercises
leg exercises
hand exercises
voice training
play-improvisation (improvisation like a child playing)
naturalistic studies (Stanislavski)
psychotechnics.

Acrobatics: we developed a set of rather dangerous acrobatic exercises performed on the bare floor, i.e. without rubber mats. Now my actors can fall on the floor as if they were made of rubber, they have overcome fear and the instinct of preservation. They have also acquired good body control.

Jumping. Having to solve the problem of corporal education for these pupils, I asked myself: is it possible to find a dynamic unit of measure that is at the base of every movement? I decided that the basic unit of movement was the jump. Now we have about 50 ways of jumping that are in fact artificial[186] gaits. Each one is performed at a different rhythm and in different scenarios.

---

[185] Barba had travelled throughout India from July to December 1963 where he came across kathakali in Kerala. He was the first to write a technical description of it, which was published in France, Italy, Denmark and by Richard Schechner in the USA: Eugenio Barba, 'The Kathakali Theatre', ed. and trans. by Simonne Sanzenbach, *Tulane Drama Review*, 11. 4 (1967), 37–50. When he returned to Poland, some of the Kathakali exercises were adapted and practised for a short time in the training of Grotowski's actors.

[186] Artificiality (*sztuczność* in Polish) was a very important term at that time in the terminology of Grotowski. It corresponded to a non-natural and composed movement, and had a dialectical relationship with *żywiołowość* (vital core, organic essence) in the actions of the actor.

Each exercise is performed according to a scenario[187] created by the individual actor. Exercises are not repeated mechanically, but are performed like an *étude*, with a new motivation every day. All exercises are performed with face 'masks' obtained by means of muscular contractions, which vary from day to day and for each set of exercises.

I am now studying a whole new chapter of exercises, which I call 'the muscular memory of the actor'. This means that the actor must be aware of every muscle in his body, and be able to control relaxation and contraction. I am reading books on vegeto-therapy and on autogenous training, and in a couple of weeks I will try it all out. To start with, it is necessary to do relaxation exercises by means of autosuggestion to facilitate the relaxation of muscles. I do half an hour of relaxation before a performance and before beginning our working day.

During work there is absolute discipline. I can safely leave the room without the fear of the actors taking advantage and doing nothing. Personal relations with the actors are cordial, except when I think there has been a lapse in their professional Morals. In such cases a set of disciplinary measures is in place; for instance, I do not speak to them for a few days. But you are well aware of these things, having read Machiavelli's *The Prince.*

All the problems that crop up during the course of the working day are discussed by the group as a whole. As well as personal problems related to work (shortage of money, bad moods, annoyance with colleagues). I try and get all problems out into the open, in order to avoid grudges and the formation of cliques. Absolute unity is required, if we want to succeed.

I have also set some 'moral standards'. No one for instance can accept a job on television, in a film or in another theatre without the group's consent. This is because work in another artistic area affects not only the actor doing it, but also the whole group, with one of its members expending his or her energies for a job that is not for our theatre and that does not produce technical benefits to improve the actor. An actor can work on television only if the whole group allows it. But he must give half of the money he earns to the group's general fund, and must agree to work after hours with instructors to recoup the hours of training he has missed. It is a problem that has

---

[187] A scenario could be anything from a plot in *Anna Karenina* or *Hamlet* to the story of the discovery of a treasure. It was used by the actors to give a different meaning and logic to training exercises every day.

cropped up, and was solved in this way when one of my actors got a role in a film. I did not want to influence the actor, who turned to me and asked me to decide what he was to do. I got the whole group to discuss the problem. At first it did not give its permission – on the grounds that he would not have learned anything, and so he would not have been able to give or teach anything to the group. But then it gave its approval subject to the conditions I have described above.

I believe it would take at least three nights of conversation to explain everything to you. Let us hope that my financial situation improves, as I am weighed down by debts. I have no photos of our training, all our money goes on the rent (a hundred dollars a month). It is very expensive, especially for us, who are jobless. That is all for now. I am tired, as always, now that the day's work at the theatre is over. I will write to you again very soon. I have not answered your questions, but it is really difficult in a letter. I *am* unable to put everything down in writing, I have no patience. Writing exhausts me. Well, all the best with your work, may the God of the prophets assist us…

Eugenio Barba

Fourth fragment: a seminar. A participant speaks

When Odin Teatret moved to Holstebro, a tradition was immediately born: each year Grotowski would go there to take part in a two-week training workshop.

For four years, from 1966 to 1969, Grotowski's workshops were a fixed appointment. Although they were limited to thirty participants, and although they continued for only four years, they were crucial for creating a new way of conceiving the theatre, as well as for cementing the Odin Teatret – Teatr Laboratorium bond, so important for determining the breakthrough of theatre laboratories.

Odin had moved from Norway, its native country, to Denmark (where it still lives) in June 1966. For the first time it had its own house. And in July, just one month later, the first workshop with Grotowski was organised. In subsequent years Odin Teatret got into the habit of arranging two seminars a year, one lasting a week, on a specific theme, which might have been commedia dell'arte or the political theatre, with the hosting of different groups of actors and directors.

The other yearly workshop, lasting two weeks, was on actor training, attended by Grotowski, and run by him and other artists.

It is probably difficult to appreciate the innovative effect that these workshops had, since nowadays they have become a relatively familiar and widespread phenomenon. But back then, this practice did not exist. It was an invention or reinvention by Odin. Within a relatively small circle these workshops had an explosive effect.

The first person to listen to is the Danish critic Stig Krabbe Barfoed, who had come across Odin Teatret when it was still a Norwegian 'avant-garde' theatre:

> Before the 1960s got their historical identity during May 1968, in Denmark we had an intense debate on culture. In 1961 cultural matters were transferred from the Ministry of Education to the newly established Ministry of Culture. State support for culture and artists became more transparent, resulting in doubts and discussions. The guardians and propagators of culture became busy explaining themselves. In the disagreements that ensued, wide-ranging political, social, and geographical differences were revealed.
>
> In 1961, I arrived directly from the University of Copenhagen to a daily newspaper in a northwestern province as a critic and editor of cultural matters. In order to display some of the avant-garde artistic expressions that were circulating at that time, otherwise than in print, some friends and I established a modest organisation, which took care of experimental theatre groups on the road. Groups that would not otherwise have visited our town: for example, African groups, La Mama from New York – and one day in 1965 a small Norwegian group, Odin Teatret, founded and directed by an Italian, Eugenio Barba. They performed *Ornitofilene* by Jens Bjørneboe.
>
> The following year this theatre group settled next to us – in Holstebro, a municipality with about 18,000 inhabitants, a small town, surrounded by potato fields and spruce plantations. The town council and some public officials had the idea that the answer to solving the problem of unemployment lay in attracting investors from the rest of the country by offering not only cheap sites but also a high level of education and cultural life. To this end the town council invested in a high school, a conservatory of music; the local Museum of Arts

was developed and quite a fortune was spent buying a bronze sculpture by Giacometti. And then they 'bought' the hardly known Odin Teatret by offering an empty farm on the outskirts and a modest contribution. In return Barba and Odin Teatret promised nothing, no specified number of performances, only to start work in the place on the first of June 1966. At the same time the theatre added: 'Nordic Theatre Laboratory' to its name, partly to have more evident access to funds from the Nordic Council, supporting cultural cooperation among Scandinavian countries.

From the very beginning one got an idea of the 29-year-old Eugenio Barba's strategic gifts. He managed to define the enterprise in a proper way and use the artistic and tactical experiences that he had acquired as a student in communist Poland and through personal contacts in France, Italy and Hungary. He established contacts in order to promote the Polish director Jerzy Grotowski's theatre for a worldwide audience.

In Holstebro, Barba immediately proved his ability to choose the right people for the different jobs in his organisation, on stage, in administration, and on the board. He offered equal salaries to all employees, himself included, and no limits on working hours or tasks; on the other hand, all employees took part in the decision-making process.

Besides the work on performances – designed for sixty to one hundred spectators, a new one every two years – Odin Teatret started up training seminars for actors and all-round seminars for authors, actors, academics and journalists from all over the world, twice a year. They were intensive seminars, where we spent one or two weeks in Holstebro as guests of the theatre and were invited to stay in the homes of residents of the town. From early in the morning to late at night we were filled to the brim with impressions and experiences. We met some of the most important European actors and directors – among them Grotowski, of course – dancers from India and Bali, Noh and Kabuki actors from Japan – you name it![188]

This was 1966. Participants of Odin seminars were unfamiliar not only with the type of practical work but, above all, with

---

[188] Stig Krabbe Barfoed recalls the early years of Odin Teatret in a review of Elsa Kvamme's book, *Kjaere Jens, Kjaere Eugenio: Om Jens Bjørneboe, Eugenio Barba og opprørernes teater* (Dear Jens, Dear Eugenio. On Jens Bjørneboe, Eugenio Barba and the Theatre of the Rebels) (Oslo: Pax Forlag A/S, 2004) Cf. Barfoed, 'Dear Jens, Dear Eugenio. On Jens Bjørneboe, Eugenio Barba and the Theatre of the Rebels by Elsa Kvammme' *Nordic Theatre Studies*, vol. 17 (2005), 97–99 (p. 97).

the mentality, the rigour and the passion with which these seminars were run. They were weeks of very hard physical and mental effort. They were a break, not only from everyday activity but also from any other form of theatrical passion.

The best testimony comes from a Swedish novel: *Katarina Horowitz drömmar.*[189] The author, Marianne Ahrne, is now a film director and writer. In her novel she described her meeting with Grotowski – the start of a longstanding friendship – replacing her own name with that of 'Katarina', and talked about Grotowski's Odin workshops.

When, later on, we read the transcriptions of Grotowski's talks, or lectures, in Holstebro, we will see that Ahrne's description of his workshops, despite being placed in a carefully crafted work of fiction, is by no means a romanticised account, but a veritable *reportage:*

> The man in her dream was a Pole by the name of Jerzy Grotowski. The first time she met him was in the summer of 1967 during a workshop at the Odin Teatret in Denmark, and since then all over the world. They had a pact. He whistled, she came. Once she had received a telegram with no more than the place, Belgrade, and date, September 23rd. She had gone and found him as easily as if all the details had been written down. He joked about her being a witch, but she knew that he in fact was the great magician. He illuminated life itself. And she thought that if she, at the age of ninety, were to be known as nothing other than an old lady who had met Grotowski, then that was fine by her.
>
> That first workshop was a kind of homecoming. When Katarina Horowitz worked with Grotowski and later on heard him speak, she knew that this was what she had longed for since the day she was born.
>
> He sat behind a rickety table in the gym, dressed in a black suit and tie and with dark sunglasses on his then melon-shaped face. Rumour had it that he could hardly see, but if so he must have had a third eye, for there was nothing in the room that escaped him. He watched the actors working on violent physical exercises and he saw into the depth of their souls. No one got away with cheating.

---

[189] Marianne Ahrne, *Katarina Horowitz drömmar* (Katarina Horowitz's Dreams) (Stockholm: Norstedts, 1990).

[…] He wanted everyone to go beyond his/her limits, as he himself always did. Watching him work with an actor was like being caught up in a hot current, in something that, amidst the contradictions and the hardships and the tearing pain, always resulted in the release of divine sparks. They were liberated in the actor, in Grotowski and in everyone watching. Katarina Horowitz thought that he was able to love even with whip in hand. He lashed people's masks and their false defenses, their sluggishness and stupidity and cowardice, but never their naked hearts.

'The human being, he once said, is a suffering creature that does not deserve to be scorned.' […]

The following summer she returned to attend yet another workshop […] That year Grotowski wasn't supposed to show up until the end of the workshop. Until then they all worked with exercises and a small scene. They also studied acrobatics with Italian clowns – the Colombaioni brothers – mime with Stanisław Brzozowski from Poland and song and speech techniques with Jolanda Rodio, a Swiss opera singer.

When Grotowski arrived they played out their scenes, each of which was a disaster.

'It seems to me that we meet again with a blend of pleasure and discomfort,' said Grotowski. 'You will always find people who are too faithful to a method. That leads to the greatest failures. A tree must grow in order to live. It has to grow away from its roots. The method is the root, but creation is the crown'.

He said that he was not interested in a school with good or bad pupils but in people able to break free and be true to their own lives.

Katarina Horowitz remembered from the previous year that he had asked them not to expect ready-made recipes from him. No one would become a good actor because he could stand on his head or learn certain exercises. In this case, though, they had all fallen into the trap.

The run-through of the scenes and exercises took all day and most of the night. His criticism was extremely sharp. Some of the participants left.

'That's good,' said Grotowski. 'This way we will know who wants to work and who wants nothing but amusement.'

At three o'clock in the morning he invited those still present to train together with Ryszard Cieślak, the actor from his own company who had played the part of the *Constant Prince*. What followed were the most intensive physical exercises Katarina had ever experienced.

The work went on for hours, and afterwards they all felt a kind of inner peace, vitality and joy. The sun had risen. Grotowski continued to speak.

'Why,' he wondered, 'is the atmosphere in here better now, after this work? Because, at length, no one can bear living a lie. What you did earlier was boring, because no one went beyond his limits. That's why everybody felt irritated.'

He then analysed their work in detail. Katarina listened and knew she had found someone who really wanted to use her powers in full, the one who shouted MORE instead of LESS, but whose capacity was so superior to her own that she would need all her life to reach the goal. Not to become Grotowski. That was not the point. But to become Katarina in the same way that Grotowski was Grotowski. Just as in the story of Rabbi Zussya, who said:

'When I stand before the Eternal One, he will not ask: Why haven't you been Abraham, Isaac or Jacob? He will ask: Why haven't you been Zussya?'

After a few hours of sleep, the physical training continued. Anyone wishing to rest or back out could do so, but thenwas not permitted to return to work. As the hours passed the rows of bodies shining with sweat thinned drastically.

'I'd rather die than give up!' thought Katarina.

Days and nights blended together until early one morning Ryszard picked a few participants, Katarina among them, to continue and try to work on live impulses together with him.

'I want you to surprise me,' he said with a smile that could stir the dead.

'Hold the details until it hurts. Pain is nothing. The limits of the possible are nothing. Cross the limits of the possible.'

He himself crossed them constantly, and without a word he revealed the secret of the great actor: when you forget yourself and give everything to your partner, that is the point when a miracle can happen.

Later on Grotowski said that the ones chosen for this training were not the ones who had worked well, since no one had, but those who were least lukewarm.

'He who is not willing to pay with his whole being will never achieve creation, only infantilism. To mobilise your assets you have to conquer fatigue. It is when you have overcome all resistance that the deep wells start flowing. To cross the boundaries with your whole being, with honesty, discipline and precision – that is the method, nothing else. To give yourself as in love. If you avoid the challenge, you can neither create nor live.'

The following evening Grotowski asked those who wanted to work to stand up. Only twelve out of fifty remained, and four of those were from Odin Teatret. [...] Before the next work session started, someone came to fetch Katarina. Grotowski wanted to talk to her in private. She went to him, her heart fluttering.

He was sitting behind his usual table in the empty gym. She stopped a short distance from him. He pointed to a chair next to his. [...] 'It is as if nothing you ever do could be enough. In that way you will end up working only to be accepted by the person you see as your judge – not working to realize the unknown within you. It could be a Jewish characteristic. But it is also specific to you. [...] When I saw you work yesterday, I understood why you wanted to write.'

Katarina held her breath. It was incredible he could remember that.

'Why?' she asked, fearing the answer.

'For those without defense, writing is a way to explain oneself to the world.'

She shivered, and her eyes filled with tears. It was clear that he knew all the secrets.[190]

Fifth fragment.
Grotowski in Marianne Ahrne's transcription

Does it make any sense to study only the time of youth? The harshness, the rules, the punishments, the Morals, the physical strength, the ability to work twenty hours a day? The workshops of fifty participants, of whom only eight make it to the end? It is probably impossible to recognise anything that resembles Odin Teatret today, not only in the words of Marianne Ahrne, but also in those of Barba when writing to

---

[190] The chapter on Grotowski's workshops in Marianne Ahrne's novel was published as 'Da *I sogni di Katarina Horovitz*' (From *Katarina Horovitz's Dreams*) in *Teatro e Storia* nos. 20–21 (1998–99), 447–54 (pp. 447–53). This text will be published in a revised version in *Grotowski's Empty Room: A Challenge to the Theatre*, ed. by Paul Allain (Seagull Books, forthcoming 2009).

Grotowski in 1965, and even in most of the picture painted by Savarese, or in Torgeir Wethal's account.

And yet… the time of youth is the time when fatigue is possible. I do not know what would happen if we remained the same for ever. But what matters is the imprinting.

The final testimony relates again to the workshops given by Grotowski at Odin Teatret from 1966 to 1969.

A workshop is not a theatre laboratory; in a way it is the very opposite. For a start, it does not last long. Then, in its purpose, in its mental horizon, there is no performance at the end of it. Yet a workshop can be (and Grotowski's workshops certainly were) a *simulation* of a theatre laboratory: a theatre reconstructed in the lab, so to speak. But inevitably this means that many of the essential characteristics of a theatre laboratory (a form of silence, for instance, or not judging the work of one's colleagues) are worse than absent here: they are turned upside down. In these workshops Grotowski, after having seen an *étude*, sometimes asked for comments from participants about what they had seen. The answers were sincere and ruthless, and pupils were slaughtered. The opposite of the rules of a theatre laboratory. So the rules had been *overturned*: perhaps so that, given the limited time of the workshop, participants might attain the concrete experience of the *fracture*. Who knows.

For many participants, meeting Grotowski may still have meant meeting a relatively unknown director, or rather a maverick celebrity. He was usually accompanied by his actor Ryszard Cieślak. In 1965, when Barba was writing from Oslo, they were an unknown director and actor of an ignored group, who lived in a small town in Poland. Now, after the triumph of their Teatr Laboratorium at the Théâtre des Nations in Paris in June 1966, they were a key element for experimental theatre people all over the world. Cieślak followed Grotowski to Holstebro in 1966, 1967 and 1968. At the last workshop on training, in 1969, Grotowski went on his own.

At the first seminar in 1966, Grotowski was a bulky, round-faced director, wearing sunglasses and a dark suit over a black shirt and tie, who could say terrible things in a French betraying a heavy Polish accent. In following years Roald Pay's photographs show him to be much thinner, with an open shirt, long hair, a determined manner, a sparse beard. Always fearsome. He never allowed notes to be taken.

Right from the first year, however, Barba secretly placed a microphone in order to record the whole workshop, in agreement with his actors and unbeknown to Grotowski. Then, hidden from his actors, he told Grotowski. The two directors agreed to 'secretly' record everything, without anybody knowing about it. Officially, not even Grotowski. Then Marianne Ahrne, when she arrived, was given the task of transcribing, in absolute secrecy, these 'non-existent' recordings.

So today we have available Grotowski's words during the three workshops in 1967, 1968 and 1969. They are transcriptions of recordings. There are no references to actions, and there is no description at all of what is happening. There are no clues as to the *way* in which Grotowski or the others speak, the warmth of some tones, the coolness of others. They were kept in a locked cupboard in Barba's office, among other materials regarding Grotowski: typewritten sheets, in French, that have faded and become almost invisible over time. And now they are on my table.

The participants train, guided by Ryszard Cieślak. Grotowski interrupts them and comments:

I want to analyse a problem, the problem of the awareness of what one is doing. You are now doing with all of yourselves what you had been doing by halves. It is necessary to do what you do with determination, without reserve. We have seen narcissism, exhibitionism, impropriety. When concentration becomes an end in itself, a bit of narcissism always comes out. When breathing is used to find a mood, the result is always falseness. It is never necessary to seek particular emotions: sadness, fear, etc. It is never necessary to use breathing. It is never necessary to have concentration as an end.

Now begin again, with a bit of common sense, and find a certain strength, perhaps a bit of lightness. You need to know what you are looking for. Like when you want to work for or against someone else. *For* someone who is delighted about all the possibilities you have. Do not work in relation to yourselves. Work with a rhythm that wakes you up, do something concrete, decisive. Avoid movements on the ground.

The participants carry on doing the exercises, still guided by Ryszard Cieślak. After a while Grotowski intervenes again:

Now the situation is more concrete. But you still do not have concrete details. The sense of the exercises is to give up oneself and to act in relation to someone else. Give up fear, and you will find courage. Give up the temptation of fatigue. Do not pretend to be a partner. But really do it for someone.[191]

The participants continue until the next interruption by Grotowski. He explains that they should never stir up emotions through their breathing, but only through the voice and the body. He gets up and sits on the ground to lead an exercise. They begin with silent breathing. Everybody follows his rhythm, which varies. At the beginning the others imitate, then they respond.

Marianne Ahrne says that Grotowski was never on first-name terms with participants. Including Eugenio Barba, Odin Teatret actors and Teatr Laboratorium actors. The *légèreté* – the lightness – that Grotowski asked participants to rediscover, together with 'a certain strength', is a word that stands out, not only in this workshop but also in the very early Odin period, where the working context seems to take place only in a heavy and hard atmosphere. Where is the lightness?

I have often heard it asked: Isn't there any *pleasure* in Barba's or in Grotowski's theatre? Because from what they say,

---

[191] Marianne Ahrne's typewritten transcriptions are kept in the Odin Teatret Archives, Fonds Barba, Series Grotowski, Binder 12. As mentioned, they relate to three years of workshops: 1967, 1968 and 1969. My thanks go to Ana Woolf for her patient transcription of the now almost invisible pages typewritten by Marianne Ahrne.

there never appears to be any enjoyment, any fun in theatre-making. It has always seemed to me, and it is also evident from Marianne Ahrne's novel, that there is an answer to this: it is a rather unusual fun, a strange lightness. But undoubtedly it is there.

Then, rummaging through the Odin papers, I found another coloured file, this time a letter written by Marc Fumaroli, now a member of the French Academy, to Eugenio Barba back in 1968:

Dear friend, in Sweden I have found no trace of Milady, nor of any luxury, but only tranquillity and voluptuousness. At the airport I bumped into Dario Fo with his family. He asked me to pass on his regards, which I am doing now.[192]

Your workshop was really interesting, Holstebro is one of the last places where you can really enjoy yourself and I, being a snob as you know, am pleased to be one of the happy few that have access to this hyper-elitist clique. When I think of that poor Jacqueline Kennedy, who knows nothing of Holstebro and its delights, I feel really sorry for her, and at the same time I am filled with the most intense of egotistical satisfaction... I wouldn't miss next year's workshop for the world. Providing the famous magician Professor Godowski is among you. In a couple of years I look forward to meeting at your place not only Jackie, who is always behind the times (she converted to the old boys ten years after Sagan had advised the young ladies of high society to do so), but also Callas, Pasolini, Peggy Guggenheim, and so on... Then my patience will be rewarded, and I'll be able to spend the winter at Beverly Hills.

Indeed why not invite Pasolini, next year, and organise a projection of his films, including the most recent one, *Medea*, with Callas? You could also invite Carmelo Bene, author of an amazing film, *Nostra Dama dei turchi* [sic], who is about to do something else, the title of which escapes me, but apparently will be even more outlandish. You could call the workshop 'Cinema and theatre', or something like that. I think his role would be to take virulent Mediterranean microbes to Scandinavia: Dario Fo is fine, but we need to go further.

---

[192] Dario Fo visited Odin Teatret several times and participated in two ISTA sessions. The first was with the performance *La signora è da buttare* in March 1968. 'Milady' may refer to the French theatre critic Madame Temkine.

I have *rewritten* the interview with Mr Godowski, and have sent it to those concerned. It has become a wonder of clarity and irony. I have ensured that the translation does not lessen the blows inflicted on American stupidity...[193]

Fumaroli recounted the other face of the Holstebro workshops: pleasure. Albeit described in terms that are apparently frivolous, referring to the jet set.

The conditions under which Fumaroli (and the others) experienced this working pleasure were harsh: work led relentlessly by Grotowski for hours on end, and always at night. Accommodation that was clean but not overly comfortable (Fumaroli slept in a small room, shared with others, in the Holstebro school of agriculture).

GROTOWSKI: We meet again, I believe, with a mix of pleasure and discomfort. There are always serious risks of misunderstandings. Being too loyal to a method inevitably leads to failure. In order to live, a tree must grow. It must move away from its roots. The method is the root. The tree's crown is the creation. The great victories are those that move away from the roots. Some want to cut them. And they lose everything...
We are fewer in number. That's a good thing. Now we shall see who wants to work, and who is seeking entertainment. To be entertained one should invite a magician. Often working principles are discovered over a long, wearisome time. But to find the cause one needs to listen. It is necessary to discover what is blocking the way.[194]

This intense way of working, especially from a physical point of view, was not only a novelty, it was a provocation in those years – 1967, 1968 and 1969 – the years of political struggles and the student revolt. History appeared to indicate contrasting priorities. Marianne Ahrne's transcription shows

[193] Marc Fumaroli personal correspondence with Eugenio Barba, 9 September 1969. My thanks to Eugenio Barba for allowing me to read the letter. Barba's correspondence is kept in the Odin Teatret archives. It is possible to consult the letters prior to 1978 with Barba's consent. Fumaroli's letters and some copies of Barba's replies are kept in the Fonds Barba, Series Letters (Barba-LETT), Binder 4.
[194] Odin Teatret Archives, Fonds Barba, Series Grotowski, Binder 12 (1968).

two sorts of reaction on the part of participants: those who, rather than protest, took a bit of a backseat, sleeping during the long hours of night-time work, asking why they have to work at night, or asking timid questions about the *engagé* actor or the clown. Then there were those who exclaimed, with unexpectedly bright countenances, that they have never worked *this way* before. Which way exactly?

In addition to the actual participants, there was a core of deeply interested people that attended more than one workshop. Firstly those from Odin, i.e., not only Eugenio Barba but also (among the actors still today at Odin Teatret) Else Marie Laukvik and Torgeir Wethal, who had been founder members, and Iben Nagel Rasmussen, who had joined them in 1966. They were to become unexpectedly and suddenly famous in the very near future, in 1969, with the performance *Ferai*. In 1968, it was a small unknown theatre, even though it had a certain notoriety as an avant-garde theatre in Scandinavia and was a beacon for a handful of intellectuals and theatre experts in Europe.

Then, as we have already seen, there was Marc Fumaroli, a French scholar of the Baroque period and of Jesuitic rhetoric with a promising career before him. He would become professor at the Collège de France, and a member of the Académie Française in 1995, taking over from Ionesco. In that period he had close ties with Denmark, collaborating as theatre correspondent from Paris for the Danish newspaper *Jyllands Posten*, thanks to Jens Kruuse, literary and theatre critic for the same newspaper, he too a regular attendee of Grotowski's workshops, together with Stig Krabbe Barfoed, whom we have quoted above.

Among the Scandinavian actors, directors and leaders of national theatre schools, a returning participant was influential Danish poet Ole Sarvig, who had written the text of *Kaspariana* in 1966, Odin's first performance in Denmark, and radical experimental poet and film-maker Jørgen Leth. And of course, Christian Ludvigsen, who from the very start was Barba's literary advisor and played a fundamental role in helping to establish and guide Odin Teatret in the Danish theatre milieu and in relations with the Ministry of Culture. Ludvigsen enjoyed great prestige and was acquainted with the most active and experimental art milieu. He was a lecturer at Aarhus University, Danish translator of both Ionesco and Beckett and one of the founders of the important avant-garde theatre, Fiolteatret, in Copenhagen.

Among the 'foreigners', there were the first Americans: Harry Carlson, an expert in Strindberg and professor at Queens College of the City University of New York, who distributed in the US the first copies of *Towards a Poor Theatre*, and Margaret Croyden, who contributed to the 'Grotowski legend' writing in *The Drama Review* and later with her book *Lunatics, Lovers and Poets: The Contemporary Experimental Theatre*.[195] But the most faithful were the Temkines, namely Raymonde Temkine, French theatre critic, and her husband Valentin, old friends of Grotowski since 1963, who had visited his Teatr Laboratorium in Opole and Wrocław and whose home was Grotowski's refuge in Paris. More occasionally, as guest of honour, came Renée Saurel, theatre critic of *Les Temps Modernes*, with whom Barba had been in touch from years before, when he was travelling through Europe spreading information and seeking new contacts for Grotowski's theatre. Saurel went on to write a long article on these workshops in Jean-Paul Sartre's prestigious journal.[196]

---

[195] Cf. Margaret Croyden, 'Notes from the Temple: A Grotowski Seminar', interview by Erika Munk and Bill Coco, *The Drama Review*, 14. 1 (1969), 178–83; and Croyden, *Lunatics, Lovers and Poets: The Contemporary Experimental Theatre* (New York: McGraw-Hill, 1974).

[196] Renée Saurel, 'Séminaire nordique à Holstebro', *Les Temps Modernes*, no. 256 (September 1967). Rénée Saurel supported from the very start Grotowski's theatre and later Barba's. Already in 1965, in the same journal, Rénée Saurel published a ten-page review of Barba's *Alla ricerca del teatro perduto*, which had recently been published in Italy; cf. Saurel, 'À la recherche du théâtre perdu', *Les Temps Modernes*, no. 233 (October 1965) 754–63. She had read the French typenwritten text that Barba had given her. She published for the first time Grotowski's article on Artaud, 'Il n'était pas entièrement lui-même' (He Wasn't Entirely Himself), *Les Temps Modernes*, no. 251 (April 1967).

Thus the image of these workshops, of the Odin's and Teatr Laboratorium's infringing activity, began to filter through to a slightly wider, yet select, audience. The two laboratories appeared to be on a completely different planet from that of the conventional theatre, an unusual incubator for performances such as *Akropolis* and *Kaspariana*. A planet that had something in common only with the great 'actor teachers' of the past, Stanislavski in particular.

It was also possible to meet personalities from the sphere of international research, such as Charles Marowitz and Joseph Chaikin, or artists from different fields of theatrical know-how, such as the Colombaioni brothers, well-known Italian clowns who had worked with Dario Fo and Fellini, Stanisław Brzozowski, the main actor of Henryk Tomaszewski pantomime theatre from Wrocław, and Jolanda Rodio, an experimental opera singer from Switzerland. Participants would work with all of these in the morning and the afternoon. At about 4 pm work would resume with Grotowski, and could go on until late at night. On a couple of memorable occasions, all night long.

It was not just a question of practising or observing a method of work that was hard and effective. This was a process to construct a theatre science: the study of principles, research into the profound territories behind the performance, territories that theatre laboratories seek to exploit when they work, turning their backs to the direct creation of a new performance.

What happened at the Holstebro workshops served not only to eliminate the bad habits of a handful of actors coming from the traditional theatre, both expert and inexperienced, to rub out their narcissism, about which Grotowski often spoke, or even to help the young Odin actors to stand, defenceless, in front of spectators. What was being done was not simply work on the inner life of the actor or on his body. It was a study to penetrate the underground, underlying spheres of theatre art. They were workshops on training, but not to teach a 'Grotowski method'.

'Don't take me for a recipe,' Grotowski would regularly repeat.

> GROTOWSKI: I observed you while you were working with the Colombaioni brothers. It was extremely tedious. As soon as you grew tired you stopped working. No efforts, no risk. You want to save yourselves for later. You agreed to make a little effort, and that was enough for you to feel fully satisfied. Colombaioni observed: 'If I had worked like that, my father would have beaten me.' You must not stop halfway.

These were fundamental moments. But also moments of pleasure: rigour and seriousness combined (sometimes) with joking. Once, in the middle of the night Barba and Grotowski went to the school where Fumaroli was sleeping, presumably packed with others into a classroom temporarily turned into a dormitory, and whispered in his ear 'Police!', and he woke up, inevitably terrorised. Perhaps he was even more upset when he found out that this was Grotowski's way of having a laugh[197].

The photos too show people having fun, joking, wanting to return the next year, convinced they are at the centre of the deepest theatre science, and with its most refined aristocracy. Fumaroli's joke about Jacqueline Kennedy, the widow of the assassinated American president, part of the jet set and new wife of old millionaire Onassis, demonstrates this more than any testimony, as do Fumaroli's suggestions to Barba for future workshops: Pasolini, Callas, Carmelo Bene. The most disturbing, refined, famed, but not simply famous or new, names that the 'Mediterranean' culture has produced were suggested as a plausible 'side dish' for Grotowski.

> GROTOWSKI: This workshop has been a battle to acquire a working atmosphere; we have had some success only over the past two days.

[197] Eugenio Barba recounts the episode in *Land of Ashes and Diamonds*, p. 93.

Cieślak managed it on the second day of work, but he did not receive any response.

It is very significant that you believed that yesterday's programme was different from that of the first days. It is not so. It is only that the attitude of those who worked during the last two days was an honest one. An experience is proposed: one must respond. You have in you a switch: success or defeat, cheating or dialogue.

I pray to you – in the religious sense of the word: something pouring out of the heart – I pray that you have no illusions. The illusions one has about oneself are the most dangerous.

And if you cannot give up on illusions in your work, I pray that you do not do this work in my name.

Roald Pay, Odin photographer in its first years in Denmark, has left surprising photographic evidence of Grotowski's presence at Odin, especially the moments of rest and semi-official meetings. In 1971 Grotowski and his Teatr Laboratorium came to Odin not for a workshop, but for twelve performances of *Apocalypsis cum figuris*. Odin Teatret organised charters from Copenhagen for spectators who could spend the night in Holstebro and meet Grotowski the next day. In Roald Pay's snaps, we can see Grotowski or Cieślak drinking, laughing, talking to people around them, spraying each other with beer. There are photos of Barba and Grotowski sitting together at a table confabulating like two accomplices or plotters, strategists at work, and also like master and pupil. And there are photos, taken furtively, from somewhere inside, blurred, showing Grotowski sunbathing in a bathing costume.

A series of photos show Grotowski – the Grotowski from 1971, thin, unbuttoned dark shirt, longish hair – talking outdoors: it is sunny, and participants with cushions and blankets are sitting on the lawn listening to him. Seated among them, Barba is listening to him with full attention, his wife Judy, who had translated into English *Towards a Poor Theatre*, at his side.

There was a climate of palpable euphoria, of awareness. They were times of conquests, of discovery. The importance of the moment for those in the photo is clear. A consciousness that is felt all the more because they realised that the importance of that moment was real, but was understood by few people. The *happy few*, as Fumaroli had said.

Fumaroli's letter is a pointer, but without these photos it would be more difficult to decipher this atmosphere. Perhaps because in this case too the language with which the importance of the moment is noted is the paradoxical language of high society. Five photographers were taking photos at the same time, capturing Barba and Grotowski while they were talking together as if they were President Kennedy and Premier Khrushchev. Perhaps it was the only known language then to attest to the importance of an event, a meeting or a situation. Perhaps it was just self-irony. Perhaps it was a knowing overturning of values.

A PARTICIPANT: I believe it is simply irresponsible to begin such a hard training session at this time of night.
GROTOWSKI: Why?

The participant, obviously frustrated, tries to reply: because this is how to ruin a body.

During the workshop, despite the apparently dictatorial working conditions, participants had the possibility of asking Grotowski whatever they wanted. And so they did, posing the broadest range of questions. Grotowski gave answers about clowns, costumes, the problem of opposing someone or something, the possibility of working alone, the relationship between training and performance, his tendency to stage the classics, the grotesque, humour, mainstream theatre, the text, political theatre, the impact of television and the 'committed' actor (this was back in 1967).[198] He was asked whether there was room for a clown in his theatre. And what he thought about a sceptical attitude within creative work.

[198] Odin Teatret Archives, Folder Barba, File Grotowski, Binder 12, 1967.

In Marianne Ahrne's transcribed notes we can find Grotowski's answers to all these questions. When he replied to the question of scepticism, he spoke about the problem of democracy in art. 'There is no democracy in art,' he said, adding that the major creators are in any case in disagreement with those who came before. It may be immoral, he remarked, but it was so. 'Because the really great theatres have always been run by enlightened tyrants: Stanislavski, Dullin, Brecht, Copeau, Meyerhold, Piscator.' He explained that great theatre can exist only if there is a core of particular human traits. Perhaps it is unfair, he added, but that's the way things are. He advised his listeners to work with expert people, and that it was essential to be able to have confidence, since the actor can be free only if he can trust a competent director who knows his job. A director who knows he can renew himself only through others, giving them freedom, stimulating them with proposals to open up personal paths forward. 'The real director,' he said, 'is one who loses himself in the actor, who exists only as a tool to liberate him,' cancelling himself in a sort of non-existence. 'Someone who does not know his job,' he concluded, 'talks as an intellectual, because he cannot liberate the actor. He will hide behind words, he will talk of new possibilities. But there will not be new art.'[199]

He was also asked to comment on the problem of theatre venues. He replied that large halls had always seemed to him very suitable for music hall-type shows. He was of the opinion that the theatre, compared with media such as television or cinema, has one added possibility: that of offering the spectator an 'intimate' contact with a disarmed actor.

A defenceless, unarmed actor.

During the workshops Grotowski's words were always severe, and sometimes harsh. In her novel Marianne Ahrne said they were whiplashes, but they had the power to strike only the mask, never the human being behind the mask.

[199] Odin Teatret Archives, Folder Barba, File Grotowski, Binder 12, 1967.

To understand this severity, and to allow us to overcome such a trait, we should at least add to their literal, almost contemptuous meanings, the long hours of intense and painstaking work behind them. And the fatigue, which weighed on the shoulders of the director as much as on the participants, ever alert, never letting any flaw go by.

Grotowski seems to be saying that disarming the actor is no simple task. When the language which the theatre speaks is *expressly* that of the body, if the actor does not attempt to reach his limits, the spectator's body reacts not only with boredom but with irritation and even contempt.

This is the only clear indication that can be gained by reading this invaluable, 'confidential' and rich document.

From the above fragments – Savarese's account, Torgeir Wethal's testimony, Barba's letter, the memories of Stig Krabbe Barfoed, Marianne Ahrne's novel and the transcriptions of Grotowski's comments – we are unable to extract any clear picture, formulate the methods and recipes of the theatre laboratory or find definite answers to our questions.

First conclusion

So the discussion did not reach a conclusion.

'But a book must have a conclusion,' one of my university students delicately suggests to me. I think she might be making fun of me.

What is a conclusion? If my students asked me what we had obtained from this long torment, what would I answer? That the various phases of our discussion had enabled us to explore unforeseeable problems and territories. But I also believe that this discussion raised, with or without explicit conclusions, five fundamental points.

1. The relationship between the production of performances and 'theatre life'. It should now be clear what is meant by 'theatre life': the part of an actor's life conditioned by the theatre but relatively or apparently independent in relation to production. This area may include individual preparatory

activities such as training and workshops, although not related to the performance. But it may also include theatre initiatives that lie outside the most conventional logic – a visit to a prison, for instance, or to a psychiatric hospital. Or full-blown experimentation of new theatre genres. Abnormally long rehearsal times are a part of this area, as are the organisation of workshops and festivals, the daily management of the theatre and publishing activities. In fact it might include anything, but certainly it includes the specific rules governing each single theatre, especially when these rules are new: the work schedule, the way of welcoming spectators, the various ways of accepting applause or declining it. It is an area that undoubtedly regards the life of the individual, but only when it is affected by decisions and rhythms of collective relevance.

When this area is particularly rich, unforeseeable and, above all, when it is very invasive, it takes on such importance in the lives of the people involved that it seeps out into their everyday life, conditioning it perhaps more than the actual work of creation. If moreover this area is strong and interesting, it takes on, or appears to take on, an apparently autonomous role and function.

The novelty highlighted during our discussion was the unusual relationship between theatre laboratories and the 'performance zone'. Namely, the existence, within a single, small organisation, of both a performance producing zone and a well-developed research area (as the name itself implies: theatre laboratory). The difference *vis-à-vis* an experimental theatre is that the theatre research zone, in the case of laboratories, includes activities that are of equal relevance to those involved in the performance creation process. But the real peculiarity of theatre laboratories is not this, it is the existence of a permanent connection and tension between the two areas: theatre research and performance, theatre and laboratory. Between the two halves of an oxymoron.

The years of our discussion did, however, lead to a discovery: theatre serves a need and has a value for the individual who does it. But this need and this value do not necessarily co-incide with work done with a performance in mind. This value is emphasised and developed in the activity of a theatre labora-tory. We can thus state that it is possible to study the theatre from a point of view that is not purely artistic, i.e., referring not only to performances but also to the culture of the theatre.

But I also believe another important discovery was made: the theatre research zone, so strong and independent, has shown itself to have an evident and vital, albeit not fully clear, role in the creation of performances. What is certain is that it cannot be observed without taking into due consideration its very close ties with and impact on stage production. This research area is like a second working layer, influencing the depth of the end result rather than its artistic quality, thus determining the density of the performance.

Strasberg says that the physical, mental and emotive hab-its of the actor influence his way of acting a lot more than is commonly acknowledged. I believe there is a core of truth that one needs to bear in mind. But I do not believe one can speak about private habits or experiences. I believe it *is not* everyday, individual life that plays a role in the construction of performances, rather it is 'artificial' life: rendering the ac-tor's mentality different through the 'theatre research zone' and its devastating needs.

At any rate, the discussion on theatre laboratories brought to light the importance of the area of theatre research, a hol-low space between everyday reality and work devoted to per-formances, worming its way into both areas. It is the place where an inner value of the theatre can be developed for the person who does it, making a *difference*, not just physically, for him or her. It is the zone that, by lengthening rehearsal time, provides performances with shadows and meanings rooted in a group autobiography, going beyond the planned and the expected. It gives a particular depth to performances, rendering them an act of discomposure and bewilderment for both the viewer and the doer.

In a way it is the oldest zone of the theatre and is redis-covered during every theatre revolution. It is the only part in which one can seek the essence of theatre when it has den-sity: that is, life, but a rather unusual one. An upside-down life, so to speak, to be proffered to the spectator.

2. The second point is the importance of the 'laboratory di-mension', the new mental horizon set in place by laboratories. Even though it is often embodied in small-scale, unknown theatres, the laboratory dimension is the reason why the the-atre is still going in the twenty-first century when it might otherwise be considered as a genre fighting against time. This 'laboratory dimension' has given the theatre a new use and purpose, enabling it to be seen as a place for inner or political growth, a place of transcendence or simply an expression of ethnic or gender dignity and a value for the individual who does it.

This also means that the tension between the two parts – performance and activity not directly related to the per-formance – takes on a dramatic turn in theatre laboratories: as if theatre-making were made up of two inseparable com-ponents that (apparently) move in different directions. This had never happened before. In short, there are performances, and there is transcendence. In the best-case scenario they are two tendencies that are intertwined, in the worst they split into two.

This situation, a blend of values, divergences and contra-dictions, a little pompous, a little impudent, should be called an act of blasphemy. It certainly has this flavour and this de-sire.

This point is not a nuance. It is crucial.

Both the smack of blasphemy and the fertile, contradictory oxymoron-union between laboratory and theatre are perhaps the characteristics that most distinguish theatre laboratories.

3. Third point: theatre laboratories, the places where re-search into the art of the actor is carried out, have histori-cally been the places for studying the principles of the art of

making the actor's body speak, and for arousing a response, through empathy, in the body of the spectator. This I have called 'body language'. I do not wish to argue that only theatre laboratories are capable of using such a language. But in theatre laboratories this language has been able to speak even too freely, without being hidden or disguised. It has been able to raise issues – abstract or archetypal – has shaken spectators and transformed the theatre into a value for spectators too.

4. The fourth product of the discussion, and this too seems significant to me, was the realisation that there could be no definable model that might enable us to decide what is and what is not a 'theatre laboratory'. This happy shortcoming derives chiefly from the fact that in the latter half of the twentieth century this 'laboratory dimension' had a two-headed model, or at least a foundation consisting of two allied but diverging theatres: Teatr Laboratorium and Odin Teatret. With all the interesting consequences this combination entailed.

5. Finally, there is the relationship with the past, with the early twentieth century. First Grotowski's performances, then Barba's, being major performances that were, in a sense, formed on the other side of the Iron Curtain, made it possible for Western Europe to rediscover the basic tenor of performances created by the early-twentieth-century masters, and deposited mainly in Eastern Europe. Experience acquired through familiarity with these two theatres, and with a more widespread laboratorial reality, also made it possible to study the great theatre of the turn of the century in a different way and to see beyond the creation of performances, to observe the importance of other activities and projects, such as pedagogical work, experimentation and research into the actor's art, which went a long way beyond their apparent function. Nevertheless, familiarity with late-twentieth-century laboratorial activity also created a filter. Sometimes the activities of the past were observed through this filter, and many differences were neglected.

The historical view that unites in a single movement the Studios of the turn of the century and the theatre laboratories of the second half of the same century has proved to be a weak position. Not because there is not an evident similarity between the activities of the Studios and part of the activity of theatre laboratories, but because focusing on this affinity restricts the ability to explore the deep-lying usefulness of the Studios, limiting them to the status of pre-theatre laboratories. Once these Studios are observed through more dispassionate eyes, it will be possible to observe many specific aspects – such as the conflict between youth and old age, between originality and decay. One can also analyse interesting solutions: for instance, what we have called here the Red Queen's race.

Second conclusion

The functioning of a theatre is a complicated affair. The number of facets to be borne in mind is completely disproportionate to its dimensions. Complex mechanisms are set in motion, such as study on oneself and sociology, requiring long-term strategies, while they also have the rhythm, contradictory nature and violence of artistic strategies. Perhaps because it is not individual art, perhaps because it is chiefly (but not only) physical art, perhaps because it is ephemeral art. But certainly the functioning of the theatre throws up big problems, incommensurate words and elaborate strategies. And all this to produce something as small as a performance.

Perhaps this apparent imbalance between the way the theatre works and its product is what makes it so interesting to study. For this reason too, inevitably, scholars conditioned by a specific environment have moved on to bigger problems than this.

Theatre performance and life: the two feet on which the theatre walks. But they are also the two feet on which, more strangely, the history of the theatre walks and trips up. They are different and require completely different tools of analysis. The former requires the intervention of art and biology experts, the latter the tools of the anthropologist, historian and sociologist.

What our discussion gave us is the evidence that, for the historian, all types of tools have proved to be unusable, because he is unable to find, in the theatre, enough room for manoeuvre. The tools are too unwieldy, too monolithic, ineffective, and soon they will even prove harmful, since they cut the theatre to pieces, giving a view of performances while neglecting the zone that is behind the performance. And vice versa.

The main thing is not to learn to use more methodological instruments, or to use different tools together, or to learn to move quickly from one discipline to another, but rather to accept the theatre for what it is: a place full of contradictions. As we have seen in Zbigniew Osiński's text, this belief comes too from Grotowski. It is important to accept the theatre as a place of contradictions. Also as far as methodologies are concerned.

Third conclusion

'Do you remember *Art et Action*?' Nicola Savarese asked me.[200]

I might have said no to him, with the danger of making a serious blunder, since although the *Art et Action* laboratory was not so well-known as others, it was still important and a long-lasting experience. Luckily, I had recently read a book

---

[200] Art et Action was founded in 1912 by Louise Lara (who had been an important actor, member of the Comédie Française) and her husband, architect Édouard Autant (their son was film director Autant-Lara), first under the name Théâtre et Liberté, then Art et Action. The laboratory was split into five sections, each of which worked on experimentation of a new scenic form. It produced a total of 112 performances, and organised exhibitions and conferences. The laboratory also published a regular pamphlet (edited mainly by Louise Lara's niece, Akakia Viala, a pseudonym of Antoinette Allévy). Viala, who also edited the theatre's 'catalogue', was also a dramatist in her own right and assisted with theatre direction. In 1950 she directed, together with Nicolas Bataille, Dostoievski's *The Possessed*, at the Théâtre de l'Oeuvre, an important avant-garde performance, with Ionesco as one of the actors (Bataille had earlier staged *The Bald Prima Donna*).

that I had come across thanks to my being in charge of the new Odin Teatret Archives.[201] It had been given to Barba by the editor, Akakia Viala, with a nice dedication: proof of the existence of a small laboratorial thread already in the early 1960s.

Art et Action, a theatre laboratory, operated in Paris from 1912 to 1952, well before the foundation of Teatr Laboratorium and Odin Teatret. It was a small Paris theatre: refined and with high-level cultural ramifications. They had published reports on their activities throughout their life, and when the experiment had ended, with the death of Louise Lara, who had founded the theatre with her husband Édouard Autant, one of their nieces, Akakia Viala, had edited the *Catalogue*.

'Do you remember *Art et Action*?', Nicola asked, having just returned from the Biblioteque de l'Arsenal. 'Attached to the catalogue cover is a second booklet, a few pages long. It contains a description of the laboratory as if it were a home. Just as I, in Scilla, had spoken about Teatr Laboratorium and Odin Teatret'.

This is what was written:

A small house, at the upper end of rue Lepic... A narrow staircase leads to the hall – more a granary or a workshop than a theatre, in which an audience not interested in the *Tout-Paris* elite is packed in. You enter. Here, the obligatory accoutrements – white tie, blue liner, honorific purple sash – are unknown. Here there is simplicity. Affability and a warm welcome. And the still-youthful smile beneath the greying hair of a great actress who has had a glorious career on the official scene, at the Comédie (she probably remembers nothing of it; equally certainly she regrets nothing, having always accorded a preference to the underprivileged over all others). She will shortly be on stage, with the pupils and fellow actors. In the meantime she is a 'common worker', like her husband, who is an usher, as well as stagehand, prompter, costume designer, electrician, decorator. And

---

[201] Edouard Autant and Louise Lara, *Art et Action, Laboratoire du theatre: Cinq conceptions de structures dramatiques modernes*, ed. by Akakia Viala (Paris: Corti 1952).

author. And founder. And above all, *inventor*, in the broadest sense
of the term [...]
Art et Action is a collective work, that seeks neither congratulations
nor thanks. It is a *commune*, and the reward is in the day-to-day
joy in its work. One might say that Louise Lara and Édouard Autant are the organisers of a group in which, surrounded by fondness
and admiration, the most experienced help the younger members
to discover themselves, without the discipline becoming anything
other than a search for harmony. An embryo for a better society in
which, as a certain Manifesto of the Communist party proclaimed:
*the free development of each is the condition of the free development
of all.*[202]

'*Art et Action,*' I replied, 'was a laboratory that experiment-
ed chiefly with theatre genres, especially with performances.
They put on more than a hundred productions during their
lifetime.'
'Their life spanned forty years,' Savarese replied. 'Of course
they did a hundred performances, a hundred demonstrations.
Yet this description here – the laboratory like a home, where
the actors *welcome* spectators – is enlightening. With its quoting of Karl Marx's *Manifesto:* the free development of each is
the condition of the free development of all.'
Then Nicola began to fill me in on the details of the grandiose Rimbaud hoax perpetrated by Akakia and Bataille, *La
chasse spirituelle* (The Spiritual Hunt). Then I found myself
thinking about this hunt.
I have often heard it said that the scholar is a cleric closed in
the library, bowed over books, overshadowed by a law greater
than herself. I, on the other hand, have always thought of her

[202] Francis Jourdain, famed painter, cabinet maker and art merchant, recalled the atmosphere of Art et Action in four small-format pages presented as a *Préface* and interleaved between the front cover and the first page of the publication *Art & Action,
Laboratoire de Théâtre*, presented to the Bibliothèque de l'Arsenal by Mr and Mrs Autant-Lara and Akakia Viala. These few interleaved pages appear to have been written
and printed earlier, when Art et Action was still operative, like a presentation booklet,
perhaps published to be distributed to the Laboratoire's audience. They may have
been retrieved at the time the Catalogue was published and added to the various copies, even though they were of a different format.

as a hunter: unable to let the prey go, big or small, once she is on the tracks. Unable, due to her very nature, to *let go*. Unable to call off the pursuit until she has clasped the prey with her hands and her brain, and has sucked out the *meaning* right down to the marrow, until she can hang up the bare bones on the study walls.

Art et Action makes me think – I told my friend and colleague Nicola – about the rubbish Clive Barker was talking about. Rubbish is simply what remains when, after developing activities in the full range of their possibilities without relating them directly to production, the process does not end in a performance, and sometimes does not even attempt to. Then, the thread connecting the two parts is broken. With the result that normal performances fall to the ground on one side, and rubbish on the other.

Nicola Savarese nodded, adding: 'It's all grist for your mill.'

INDEX OF NAMES AND PLACES

Kruuse, Jens 250
Kurbas, Les 119
Kusumo, Sardono 184
Kvamme, Elsa 240

L
Laborit, Henri 62
Lambdin, Thomas O. 47
Lampedusa (Italy) 71
Lara, Louise 263–265
Larsen, Tage 169
Latin America 19–20, 49, 96, 161, 185, 188, 193–194
Laukvik, Else Marie 169, 184, 250
Lausanne (Switzerland) 126, 133
Law, Alma 119
Leiden (Netherlands) 47
Leth, Jørgen 250
Lewis, Robert 200–201
Lévi-Strauss, Claude 182
Limanowski, Mieczysław 149, 152, 156, 158
Lincoln (USA) 171
Littlewood, Joan 9, 14–17, 28, 167
London (England) 16–17, 36, 39, 43, 46, 58, 61, 101, 105, 107–108, 112, 119, 156, 182, 207
Ludvigsen, Christian 250–251
Lupa, Krystian 155

M
Machiavelli, Niccolo 237
Malevich, Kazimir 152
Malina, Judith 167, 184
Malinovskaya, Elena 110
Malle, Louis 52
Maloyan, Federico 161
Malta 3, 188
Mantova (Italy) 67
Marek, Magdalena 155
Marx, Karl 205, 265
Marlowe, Christopher 36
Marowitz, Charles 84, 184, 252
Martinson, Sergei 138
Masgrau, Lluís 172
Mei Lanfang 136
Meisner, Sandford 201
Meister, Wilhelm 180
Métraux, Alfred 43
Mexico 159, 193

Meyerhold, Vsevolod 5, 8, 10, 18, 20–21, 25–26, 31, 62–63, 65, 70, 72, 76, 80, 83–85, 92, 95–96, 98–99, 119–139, 150, 152, 167, 196–197, 202–203, 210–211, 214–215, 256
Miami (USA) 64
Milan (Italy) 160, 169
Mirecka, Rena 36
Mnouchkine, Ariane 9, 26, 92, 96, 167, 199
Molière (Jean Baptiste Poquelin) 110
Molik, Zygmunt 36
Mollica, Fabio 103, 213
Moscow (Russia) 28, 100, 103, 108, 123, 126, 132–133, 136–139, 159, 175, 199–201, 203, 213–214
Munch, Edvard 166
Munk, Erika 251
Munk, Kai 170

N
Nag Hammadi (Egypt) 42, 47
Nakajima, Natsu 184
Namboodiri, Krishna 184
Nekrošius, Eimuntas 81
Nemirovich-Danchenko, Vladimir 110, 213
New York (USA) 10, 36–38, 41, 46–47, 52, 58, 101, 105, 107–108, 112, 119, 197, 199, 201–202, 207, 228, 239, 251
Norway 14, 81, 83, 86, 159, 165–167, 184, 233–234, 238

O
Ohno, Kazuo 184
Ollolai (Sardinia) 185
Olmedo, Alberto 195
Omolú, Augusto 169
Onassis, Aristotle 253
Opole (Poland) 36, 141–142, 147, 149, 159, 167, 235, 251
Osiński, Zbigniew 5, 18, 34, 38, 49, 69, 95, 139–142, 145–146, 151–152, 155–156, 192, 233–234, 263
Oslo (Norway) 81, 167, 171, 184, 189, 229–230, 234, 240, 245
Osorio, Raúl 87
Osterwa, Juliusz 80, 149–150, 152, 155–156, 158, 167
Ouspenskaya, Maria 200, 202